THE NOBILITY AND THE MAKING OF THE HUSSITE REVOLUTION

JOHN MARTIN KLASSEN

EAST EUROPEAN QUARTERLY, BOULDER
DISTRIBUTED BY COLUMBIA UNIVERSITY PRESS
NEW YORK

1978

EAST EUROPEAN MONOGRAPHS, NO. XLVII

John M. Klassen is Assistant Professor
of History at Trinity Western College

This book has been published with the help of a grant from the Social Science Federation of Canada, using funds provided by The Canada Council

To My Mother, Susan Heinrichs Klassen

IN ACKNOWLEDGEMENT

In writing this book I have received the assistance of individuals and institutions: to both I would like to express my gratitude. I am above all indebted to my former professor, Howard Kaminsky. He has been most generous with his extensive knowledge on the Hussite movement as well as with his personal library. It gives me great pleasure to thank him at this time. I would also like to thank Professors Gordon Griffiths and Imre Boba of the University of Washington and Jerald Zeman of Acadia Divinity School for their helpful suggestions.

I also owe a debt of gratitude to the Institute of Czech and World History in Prague. Its director, Dr. O. Říha, made the archives and library available to me. I particularly want to thank Dr. F. Šmahel, formerly of the Institute, for his useful comments and his time and efforts on my behalf. Similarly Charles University in Prague assisted my studies. Professor J. Polišenský and Dr. Z. Hledíková were especially helpful with their comments and facilitated my access to libraries and archives.

Finally I am grateful to Imre Bard and to Alice Umble Klassen for their suggestions and to my colleague Dick Mitchener for the careful drawing of the map.

Fort Langley
British Columbia   1978   John M. Klassen

ABBREVIATIONS*

AČ	Archiv Český
Čechy	Bartoš, F., Čechy v době Husově
ČČH	Český časopis historický
ČsČH	Československý časopis historický
DMP	Tomek, V.V., Dějepis města prahy
DNČ	Palacký, F., Dějiny národu českého
Documenta	Palacký, F., ed. Documenta Mag. Joannis Hus . . . illustrantia
Glossarium	Brandl, V., Glossarium illustrans bohemico-moravicae historiae fontes
HHR	Kaminsky, H., A History of the Hussite Revolution
HR	Bartoš, F., Husitská Revoluce
Hrady	Sedláček, A., Hrady, zámky a tvrze království českého
JSH	Jihočeský sborník historický
LC	Libri Confirmationum ad Beneficia ecclesiastica Pragensem
MJHN	Novotný, V., M. Jan Hus, život a dilo
MJHS	Sedlák, J., M. Jan Hus
Pozůstalostí	Sedláček, A., Pozůstalostí
RČSAV	Rozpravy Československé akademie věd
RT	Emler, J., ed. Reliquiae tabularum terrae regni Bohemiae a. MDXLI igne consumptarum
SA	Soudní akta konsistoře pražské
Šlechta	Novotný, V., Hus V Kostnici a česká šlechta
Strana	Kavka, F., Strana Zikmundová v husitské revoluci
Úvahy	Sedláček, A., Úvahy o osobách v stížných listech l. 1415 psaných
Žižka	Heymann, F., John Žižka and the Hussite Revolution

*Note on Spelling: I use the Czech spelling for names of individuals and places except for well-known cases like Nicholas for Mikulaš, Prague for Praha and Tabor for Tábor.

TABLE OF CONTENTS

Abbreviations

Introduction   1

1. Society and Economy in Pre-Hussite Bohemia   5

2. The Noble Patron and His Parish   27

3. The Owners of Church Patronage in Bohemia   35

4. The Nobility's Feud With King Wenceslas IV: 47
    1394-1405

5. Noble Politics: 1405-1415   61

6. The Role of Čeněk of Vartemberk   75
    in Noble and Hussite Politics

7. The Nobility and the Hussite Movement   85
    Until 1415

8. Hussite Patronage and Politics Until 1419   99

9. Catholic Nobles in Defence of the Faith   114

10. The Nobility During the Revolution   125

11. Conclusion: Noble Gains in the Hussite Revolution   138

    Appendixes: I   Commodity Prices   144
                  II Families Holding Offices in the   146
                      Land Government
                  III Noble Families and their Politics   148
                  IV Gentry Utraquist Compact of 1417   152

Bibliography   000

Index   181

INTRODUCTION

The dualistic government of the late middle ages, composed of king and estates, underwent cycles in which for a period the monarch was strong, only to weaken in the face of advances by the aristocracy. In Bohemia in the 1390s, the nobility stopped the trend towards an increase in royal power, beginning one which by 1471 had brought them into a commanding position in the realm. It was in the course of these years that the Hussite revolution, lasting from 1419 to 1434, swept through the country. The fact that the Hussites were able to prevent the legitimate heir, King Sigismund of Hungary, from taking the throne obviously helped the estates, especially the nobility in obtaining a position of superiority. The nobles' wars with the king in the 1390s, their contributions to the Hussite revolution and their gains during the reigns of Kings George and Vladislav suggest that their involvement with Hussitism was part of their overall drive for hegemony in the realm. However, an examination of the nobility in action reveals no unified approach to the issues of church reform and shows that the political achievements of the revolution fell to them by default.

There have been no studies devoted to the question of the role of the nobility in the Hussite revolution. F. Kavka's 1947 dissertation for Charles University at Prague, on the party of King Sigismund in the Hussite revolution, has come the closest, in that the king's party consisted mostly of nobles. However he identified Sigismund's with the Catholic party thus leaving out the Hussite nobles. In addition he concentrated on the period 1419 to 1434, that is the period of the revolution proper. J. Pekař's study of John Žižka and his times devoted substantial attention to the nobility but his interests also lay in the later period without an analysis of the relationship of the politics of the nobility between the two periods. The major histories of late medieval Bohemia, by Palacký, Tomek and Bartoš treated the Hussite period apart from the nobles' revolts, an approach which for their purposes was justified. However, the history of the late medieval Bohemian nobility and their striking achievements after the Hussite wars enjoins us to examine the aristocratic role in the making of the revolution. One important means by which the nobility affected the fate of the movement was its right of patronage, that is the power to choose the priests and control the economy of the parish.

Despite the significance which church patronage had for the Hussite movement, historians have almost entirely ignored the subject. No study has been undertaken to ascertain what percentage of parishes the church had succeeded in acquiring from the nobility nor has the use to which the nobility put its right been analyzed. The following study, in response to this deficiency, shows that over sixty percent of the parishes had noble patrons, and then proceeds to show that because of a split within the nobility over the religious issue, only a minority of nobles put their parishes at the disposal of Hussite priests, the remainder securing orthodox Catholic clergy in their offices.

When the nobility, in the 1390s, formed armed confederations aimed at limiting the king's power, they did so conscious of themselves as spokesmen of the land-community. The nobles interpreted the fact that King Wenceslas IV, the third king of the Luxemburg line, was restricting their independence on their realms as well as their property rights, as a threat to the welfare of the land. After defeating the king and regaining some of their autonomy, the nobility was wooed by the Hussite university masters seeking their aid. The masters asked the nobility to act in the name of the land to save their program of church reform and introduced them to an expanded concept of the land-community, one not represented by one estate, but by all Czech speaking people, faithful to Christ. Unfortunately for these reformers, they were only able to convince a minority of the nobles.

The failure of the Hussite leadership to bring the full force of the noble controlled government of the land behind the reform movement meant that the only concrete provision which the Hussite nobles could offer the reformers was access to the churches on their domains to which they owned patronage. Although they owned only ten percent of all the parishes in the Prague diocese, in reserving them for the Hussites the nobility provided the reform movement with ground on which to operate in a legitimate context. Throughout most of the rest of the country, after 1417, Hussites were prosecuted by all authorities, the pope, the archbishop, the king and by Catholic lords. Only Hussite nobles gave the movement the freedom to work above ground.

The church's refusal to accept the Hussites' proposals for reform, followed by its attempt to repress the movement had the effect of radicalizing large segments of the Bohemian population. When the nobles proved unable to provide leadership and protection for the movement throughout the realm, the initiative passed to the radicals. In 1419 these successfully rallied the masses of the people behind their banner trans-forming the reformation into revolution, directing their attack at all elements of the power structure: the church hierarchy, the king and the nobility.

It took the nobility, in alliance with the conservative town elements, fifteen years before they could isolate the radicals from the moderate Hussites so as to defeat them and reassert themselves as arbiters in the kingdom. The fruits of the revolution, won by the town masses, the peasants and the gentry, were taken over by the nobility. They were able to further exploit the uncertain status of the Hussite religion in Bohemia, and of Bohemia in the European community, so as to weaken the power of the king while at the same time undermining the influence of his traditional allies, the towns, to the point that the nobles determined the makeup of the Bohemian polity until the Habsburg victory in 1620.

The nobility and the Hussites each contributed to the other's advance-ment. This mutual assistance was however at least partially inadvertant since the nobility never intended the revolution to occur, and the revolutionaries fought to keep the nobility from reaping the results of the battles which they, the radicals, had won. The nobles who did support Hussitism had in mind a moderate reform program within the legitimate structure of European Christendom. The radicals for their part sought to exclude the nobles from the offices of government and gave up only when forced to by military defeat.

The nobility provided Hussitism with an environment in which ideas of reform and revolution in their early stages could be nourished. Their help was exemplified in the encouragement and impetus which they gave the reformers in two critical periods: during Hus' trial and death in Constance in 1414-1415 and during the church's concentrated attack on the move-ment beginning in January 1417. The nobles' letter of protest to the

Council of Constance on 2 September 1415 was significant for Hussitism in that it raised the morale of the Bohemians. By rebuking the Council for its treatment of John Hus, the nobles were an example to their fellow countrymen in that they stood up to and criticized a body representing all of European Christendom. The Hussites' later resistance to the crusading armies, their forays into neighbouring lands and their diplomacy at the Council of Basel in the 1430s were but a continuation of this self-confident attitude.

Just as the nobility's actions in 1415 built up the Hussites' confidence, so their patronage in 1417, of Hussite priests at the expense of Catholics, provided the movement with security and legality. The fact that nobles provided Hussite priests with parishes and protection, especially in the south and east made it possible for Hussites to present their religious program to an audience and to practice their rites. It was no coincidence that Tabor in south Bohemia was the first centre of popular Hussitism and the people who streamed there in 1419-1420 were at the forefront of the revolution.

For their part the revolutionaries provided the will and the military successes which protected the Hussite religion and kept King Sigismund from the throne. Sigismund's fourteen year long fruitless attempt to gain his throne by force placed him in a poor bargaining position when the Czech estates, led by the nobles, negotiated his accession after 1434. The nobility made use of the king's weakness and exacted rights and privileges for itself before it granted him the crown. This situation set the stage for relations between king and estates for the next two hundred years in Bohemia.

The credit which belongs to the nobility for thwarting the growth of a strong monarchy must not be overlooked. Although they had lacked the will to fight King Sigismund in 1420 they did not permit the church's efforts to exterminate heresy to be identified with the royal cause. Neither did the Catholic nobles use the idea of a crusade to attack the positions and castles of the nobles who favoured the Hussites. As a result they avoided the fate of the nobility in southern France, where two centuries earlier the nobles of the north had attacked those who were shielding the Cathar heretics. In France it was the king who seized the spoils of the struggle by following it up with his own crusade against a weakened nobility. In Bohemia, even though not agreed on the religious question, the nobility was basically unified in its class interest and thus escaped ruin and in fact came up on top in the struggle for control of the polity.

CHAPTER 1
SOCIETY AND ECONOMY IN PRE-HUSSITE BOHEMIA

When discussing periods of upheaval historians have tried to determine the roots of dissatisfaction and anger which moved people to attempt to overthrow the old order. Most of the polemic which accompanied the actions and violence of reformers and revolutionaries in traditional Europe, before the industrial and French revolutions, was couched in religious terms. This has led writers like Jacques Ellul[1] to assume that social issues played no role in arousing people to revolutionary deeds before the eighteenth century. Such a conclusion can only be reached because of a lack of information which with respect to the Hussite revolution stems from the fact that historians[2] have not provided western readers with the results of the research on the society and economy of pre-Hussite Bohemia which has appeared since the second world war in the Czech language. A careful study of Bohemian society in the late middle ages shows that people were dissatisfied, not only with the religious practices of the day, but also with the social and economic position in which they found themselves.

This does not mean that pre-revolutionary society was a mass of wretched poor people awaiting the opportunity to revolt against their wealthy tyrants. In fact in the countryside economic developments in many ways favoured the peasants. Many had been able to capitalize on new opportunities and had improved their economic status. The discontentment of these stemmed from the fact that they were expected to remain content with their low social status. Their less able neighbours however fell victim to economic changes and did not see any real possibilities for advancement. People like these fell into or remained in conditions of poverty where even old securities provided by family and village ties had disappeared. In the city a bleak future faced most people. The movement of the population from the country to the city, which had relieved the demographic pressure on the farms, drove prices up in the cities and held down wages. When the Hussite reformers preached their ideals, including a system of ethics based on living a simple, modest life and caring for the less fortunate, those whom society had left out of its spoils easily identified themselves as the good people, because they lived simply, and the wealthy as the evildoers because they lived opulently at the poors' expense.

Pre-Hussite Bohemian society had basically the same elements and characteristics as the rest of medieval Europe. Its economic base was largely agricultural, the sphere from which peasants and nobles made their livings. However by the end of the fourteenth century there also existed some one hundred walled towns inhabited by people earning their bread through trade, commerce, specialized crafts and ordinary labour.

THE COUNTRYSIDE

The noble class enjoyed the most privileged and powerful position in rural society. To be a member one's family had to have established a tradition of living in the style of a noble. This meant refraining from urban enterprises and living off the land in as much opulent splendour as one's resources could afford which included observing the chivalrous etiquette of the period. If material misfortune curtailed his style of life the noble could still pull out the family seal or coat of arms as evidence that his family was well-born. Because in Bohemia the king had the sole right to grant a coat of arms, people wishing to enter the noble class were wise to develop connections at the royal court as well as landed wealth.[3]

Within the nobility there were several ranks. In Bohemia the upper nobility, the barons, were identified by the title, *pán* (Czech), *nobiles, barones* and *magnates* (latin). The barons, especially after their successful feud against King Wenceslas, which will be discussed more fully below, were the most powerful element in society. Their power stemmed from their large estates each with a fortified castle dominating the surroundings. By the fourteenth century the older manorial estate, combining both large domain and smaller peasant holdings, had largely disappeared except for a few landowners, mostly monasteries, who continued to use it as a form of estate management. The lord's domain was closely supervised by his official and its fruits were used to fill his storehouse. It was worked by peasants performing labour services (*robota*) and by hired workers. The rest of the estate, divided into small tenancies was held by peasants who paid the lord their rent in either money, labour services or natural produce or a mixture of all three. However most of the baronial estates had only a small domain and the bulk of the land was rented out to peasant tenants. These baronial lords were only indirectly involved in agriculture, living off the rents they collected. Lastly, a few barons ran their estates in a fashion similar to that of the later latifundia. Here the lord himself took a direct interest in producing for the market with the help of paid labour and peasant services.[4]

Most of the lords entrusted the administration of their land to a hired official, the burgrave, who rendered his accounts to the lord or his treasurer. Lesser tasks on the estate were carried out by a whole hierarchy of servants and the lords' interest in their land was limited to perusing the accounts of their burgraves who collected the rents from the tenants. The lords therefore seldom met their peasants but dealt mainly with their officials.

The gentry or the lesser nobility were called *armiger, cliens* or *famosus vir* in latin. The term *strennuus miles* was used less frequently and then sometimes applied to the upper nobility as well. By the late middle ages the word for lord, *dominus,* had lost its precision and could refer to either priest or noble.[5] There were two groups within the gentry but the distinction between each was not always clear. Those in the upper ranks were referred to in Czech as *rytíř* (knight) or *vladyka* (squire). The lower ranks were described by the term *panoše* (squire, servant or page). Those who owned at least one whole village or estate, had been knighted, and were of longstanding noble birth belonged to the upper ranks of the gentry. The term *zeman,* referred to the economic status of an individual who might not have been knighted but was considered noble because he possessed at least one free estate with title in the land records. However all four Czech terms, *rytíř, vladyka, panoše* and *zeman* were at times used as a general appelative to describe members of one estate, that of the gentry.

In general the older manorial estate, divided between lord's domain and peasant tenancies, continued to dominate the agricultural economy of the gentry who retained considerable control over their operations. Most of them personally oversaw the day to day administration of the domain without the services of a burgrave. Their farms in fact did not differ greatly from those of the richer peasants except that the gentry did not owe payments or services to any lord. What additionally set the gentry apart from most rich peasants was the fact that they had their own dependent people, the peasants over whom they exercised authority and who owed them rents and services.[6]

Just below the gentry on the social ladder were the freeholders. There is very little known about this class since most of our information about the rural economy comes from the lord's records on which this class did not appear. All that is known is that there existed a group of peasants who held their land free of any rent and who had no lord except the king.[7]

The wealthiest of the dependent population in the villages were the officials in the lord's service. These men, drawn from the ranks of the gentry, freeholder or dependent peasants, had shown ability and initiative for which the lord had chosen them to administer his newly colonized estates. The most significant was the lord's representative in the village (advocat, vogt, schultheiss or rychtář) who combined both judicial and administrative tasks. He judged cases and imposed fines involving minor crimes, that is all except murder, sexual violence, forgery and arsen. In a newly established village this official had been the contractor who on the lord's behalf had founded it, obtained the settlers, got them started and divided the land. As such he got every sixth or tenth field plus a third of the fines collected by the village court. In addition he enjoyed certain privileges such as freedom from rent, the right to collect the rents of other peasants on the lord's behalf and the right to hunt and to brew his own beer. Many took advantage of their positions to become sufficiently wealthy to purchase or build fortified residences. Their zealous enforcement of the law and collection of rents elicited the ire of the peasants so that in one of the archbishop's towns the official requested the local priest's permission, in case of need, to take refuge from the people's wrath in the church tower.[8]

Another group in the village with privileges not enjoyed by the ordinary peasant was that of the millers, innkeepers and other artisans. The lord of the estate employed them and required the villagers to utilize their services when in need of a given product. There were ample opportunities for these merchandisers to accumulate money by overcharging or diluting the product with impurities such as sand or water. As a result they frequently reached a standard of living considerably above that of the peasants.

By the end of the fourteenth century there was a wide range of economic wealth and position even among the ordinary peasants. Since land was the main source of income the peasant's holdings can be considered a rough indication of wealth. Using this measurement, a survey taken in 1410 of the villages belonging to the monastery of Strahov, shows that out of a total of 550 tenants there were 163 who had less than a quarter of a field and some had only the ground on which their homes stood. At the other extreme were 136 wealthy tenants with either a full field or more. A little less than half, 251 were peasants with moderate size holdings.[9]

This group of rich dependent peasants was a new phenomenon in the late middle ages. The popular literature and sermons of the period describe their efforts to live and dress in the style of the nobility with disdain and disapproval. Some dependent peasants were rich enough to stand as creditors for substantial loans and were able to pay large amounts of ready cash when purchasing land. The episcopal visitation of 1379-80 of the Prague deaconry discovered 52 persons guilty of usury. Twenty-seven of these were peasants (*villani*). Letters bearing the seals of dependent peasants show that their wealth allowed them to ignore the custom that only the personally free had the right to affix their seals to documents.[10]

The cottagers assumed the lowest rung on the social-economic ladder. These people had been unable to cope with the economic changes and had consequently found themselves left out of the division of society's wealth. Even in this category there were some better off than others. A cottager had either very little or no land at all except that on which stood his dwelling. On one settlement forty-two cottagers shared two fields, each getting a little over one acre. Others in the same settlement had no land and made their living entirely as day labourers. Even peasants with land, when they fell behind in payments, worked as labourers for short periods. Hence the size of this group is hard to determine. However the fact that the wages of farm workers did not rise as dramatically as they did in the west suggests that there was a large number of hands looking for work so that employers could offer little money and still find men willing to work.

As is well known the law in the middle ages did not apply in the same way to all segments of the population. The nobles had their own legal system which we shall discuss in another context. Here we are concerned primarily with the law's relationship to the peasant population. In the course of the thirteenth and fourteenth centuries nobles had acquired from royal officials the right to judge all cases involving their dependents. There were some exceptions where especially vigorous towns had extended their jurisdiction over surrounding villages at the expense of the gentry. In such cases the peasant benefited since town law offered greater legal protection than did that of the noble. Where this had not occurred the landowner was for all practical purposes the absolute lord over his dependents and responsible for the maintenance of justice.

To deal with legal and criminal matters the owners of the larger estates had two courts. Most of the lighter cases involving peasants were heard in the lower court presided over by the noble's bailiff (*rychtář*). This official worked with the help of village counsellors so that the court represented not only the will of the lord but also that of the important elements of the village. The noble's higher court heard cases involving capital crimes and was presided over by the lord himself.

The most common penalties handed out by the authorities were fines and corporal punishment including the standard medieval tortures and multilations such as flogging, the stocks and others. One employer who suspected his worker of stealing, tied the man's hands behind his back, raised him off the ground and lit a fire beneath him in order to get a confession. From the standpoint of the lord's material welfare the most important penalties were the fines. Just as in the west these provided a substantial source of income and a rowdy Saturday night party could prove more remunerative than the harvest from several fields. The revenue on the Nový Hrad estate in 1391 for half the year was 12,000 groschen. Nearly twelve percent of that, about 1,400 groschen,came from the fines imposed by the village courts.[11] The lords recognized the potential of the courts to increase their incomes and reformers like Thomas of Štitný and John Hus criticized them for using the courts not so much for maintaining order as to enrich themselves.

As precarious as the medieval peasant's lot was there were several developments which improved his legal status with respect to his land holdings. The Bohemian peasant, as the European peasant in general, shared in the benefits which accrued to his class from the expansion of agriculture after the eleventh century. In order to draw peasants to uncleared lands, away from familiar villages and friends, lords had to offer a written contract with attractive conditions such as a period of reduced rents or rights of inheritance. The lords of established villages, in order to keep their peasants, had to reciprocate. The end result was beneficial to the the peasant. The change from paying the rent in money rather than in labour services or in produce, discussed more fully below, was part of this trend. At the same time, in terms of land tenure, the tenant acquired more and more guarantees permitting his family to keep the land from generation to generation and in some cases peasants got the right to bequeath it at will.

The so-called emphyteutic law, brought in by colonists, was one of the most significant developments giving peasants and their families a perpetual use of the land in exchange for the annual payment of a rent. According to it the tenant had the right to use and enjoy the advantages and profits which the land provided while the lord continued as the legal owner. Most tenures of this sort had the conditions, such as the amount of the rent which were then permanently established,   put into writing. In other words the lord could only with difficulty increase the rent. The peasant had hereditary tenure and could pass it on to his son. Only if there was no direct male heir did the land devolve to the lord.[12]

At the same time two other laws under which peasants held land continued in existence: the Czech law and the Old law. By the end of the fourteenth century the Czech and the emphyteutic law had merged to become almost the same. The most important difference was that emphyteutic peasants had a fixed rate at which they paid the royal tax whereas for those under the Czech law it was determined by the lord. Other than this there was no substantial difference. Holders of emphyteutic lands also had to pay their lord extraordinary obligations and aids. They had to provide board and room for his travelling justices, make contributions to his troops on a campaign and in some cases, even though it was not included in the original contract, they had to perform labour services. The peasants who lived under the Old law were entirely at the mercy of their lords, in other words little more than slaves.[13]

Some lords, influenced by developments in the towns increased further their peasants' rights to dispose of their land by granting them what was called "the rights of towns". According to these charters, peasants could bequeath their property to whomever they wished. This meant that a peasant, if he had no natural heir, could leave the future use of his land to a friend in exchange for cash. The peasant thus got some extra money with which to live out his old age and his neighbour got additional land when the tenant died. If however the peasant died without a will, according to the charter, his property went to the nearest relative, male or female. In other words with the granting of such charters lords gave up their right to devolution according to which a holding reverted to the lord when a tenant died without a male heir. Religious leaders like Archbishop John of Jenštejn (1380-1402) and John Hus in 1407 had urged lords to give up this right although the archbishop himself did not free his peasants on his domains from devolution.[14]

When they granted freedom from devolution the lords were hardly altruistic. In some charters they explicitly stated that the freedoms were sold for a fee, a common method of raising money in the middle ages. Other lords claimed to grant them out of pity because the plague or a fire had been particularly disastrous. It may be that they hoped to attract peasants to compensate for those they had lost. The Hussite lord, John of Hradec, in 1407 candidly stated that in granting his peasants the freedom to dispose of their land he hoped to attract settlers to his villages.[15]

Although only a minority of peasants received charters of town rights, these and other contracts of land tenure represent some improvement in the conditions of land tenure before the Hussite revolution. In the economic sphere however developments were not always beneficial for those that lived off the land. Increasing commercialization confronted them with new opportunities but also with unknown pitfalls. Those who were able to understand and take advantage of the changes improved their position and became wealthy. Others, not able, remained where they were or became impoverished.

The change which most affected the economic conditions of late medieval Bohemia was the commercialization of the agricultural economy in the thirteenth and fourteenth centuries. Trade with other countries and increased artisan productivity at home introduced consumers to more and more goods for which they needed money. As a result lords and priests required of their dependents and parishioners that they pay their rents and tithes in coin rather than in kind or labour services. For the peasants this meant taking part of their produce to town markets in order to raise the rent money. Both landowners and peasants recognized that the residents of the rising towns were prepared to pay money for farm produce. They responded by producing as much as possible for sale in order to earn money for their own wants. The more wealthy and aggressive peasants exploited the changes better than did the poor who often were overwhelmed by them. The rich could hold back his harvest from the market until the price was high whereas the poorer frequently sold his promptly at harvest because he needed the cash to make his rent payment which fell due on 16 October of each year.

Hence agricultural production for the market and the accompanying commercialization opened up society. Those who had the skills and initiative took advantage of the market by clearing more land, surreptitiously usurping slices of the village commons and investing their money wisely. On the other hand there were dangers. Overinvesting in new tools and machinery could lead to ruin if disaster or disease struck. Many landowners and peasants did not understand the forces of the market and were at the mercy of the rules made by the more experienced speculators and creditors from the towns. In the end some landowners became rich and others poor, contributing to the social tensions in the countryside. The rich peasant resented the fact that he had to put up with the inferior legal and social position of his class, the poor that his hard earned income could only with difficulty supply him with what he needed to live. People saw neighbours and former peers advancing themselves and sometimes exploiting people as poor as they themselves had formerly been. Those who were left behind felt the bitterness of failure and the frustrations of not knowing how to respond to the more fiscal agricultural economy.

The quality of a peasant's material life was basically determined by two factors in the economy. First, what were the dues and obligations which he owed the authorities; king, church and lord? And second, to what extent did the labour of his hands, whether on his own lands or working for others, remunerate him? The peasant's most regular obligation was the rent he paid his lord. Throughout the fourteenth century the rent remained static. Most contracts had set it at sixty groschen a field where it remained up to the revolution. Lords in practice were still able to raise the rent through various devices such as remeasuring the fields and making two where there had previously been one, or by granting peasants improved inheritance rights to the land in exchange for a higher rent. However in general the rent remained at the level stated in the original contract. Static rents, a century earlier in the west had resulted in a situation where some peasants, because of rising prices, paid as little as two percent of their income as rent.[16] The Bohemian peasant in the fourteenth century was not as fortunate. He paid on the average ten percent which would still have been tolerable had it not been part of more extensive material obligations. The peasant also had to give his lord certain products of lesser economic significance such as thirty eggs or five pounds of honey which were seen as tokens of his dependent status. Furthermore, during busy seasons such as harvest, ploughing time and haying, labour services, although not onerous, still claimed the time of peasants on some estates.

The rent was not the peasant's only expense. In addition he had to make a whole series of payments to authorities who in the middle ages laid claim to the fruits of his labor. The royal tax on the whole land (*berna generalis*) was rarely levied after 1310 when the nobles gained control over it. They restricted it as much as possible so as not to deplete the resources of the peasants which they preferred to exploit themselves.[17]

With this source no longer available the kings relied on the special tax (*berna specialis*) levied on royal lands, monasteries and royal towns, to supplement their incomes. During the reign of Charles IV it had become an annual tax and in 1403 it was exacted four times, twice by King Sigismund and twice by Wenceslas after his return from captivity. Because of the inefficient methods of collecting, the royal treasury received less than half of what the taxpayer paid which explains partially the frequency of the tax. According to the procedure the lord paid the king's collector a certain sum. The lord then took in the tax from the people in the name of the king. For example, from one of its villages the monastery of St. Thomas in Prague collected 420 groschen. Of these 120 went to the royal treasury, sixty went to the royal official and 240 remained with the monastery. The latter figure represented in fact one more obligation which the peasant paid his lord.[18]

The peasant also owed the Church several financial obligations. He had to pay the relatively light tax of one-half to one groschen levied on each hearth by the bishop. The peasant also had to pay a tithe to the parish priest. This was not, as the name implies, a tenth of his income because the amount had been set in times past and amounted to two or three measures of grain per field.[19] There were various other ways in which the priests got the peasants to give up their income. One of the more ingeneous exactions was that of the so-called iron cow, that is one that lasted for ever because a perpetual obligation was imposed on the peasant by this device. What happened was that the priest loaned a poor peasant a cow for his use for which he paid a regular fee. When the cow died the peasant had to replace it and continue to pay the fee. For all of these obligations the peasant had to have ready cash on hand.

There were basically two ways in which a peasant could pay his obligations to his lord or creditor. He could raise and sell a product or he could work for wages. The degree to which he succeeded depended on the price he got for his product or on the wages he received for his work. Despite the fact that the data are scarce there are enough to make it useful to look at what the peasant received in money for his products and his labour.

When charting the developments of wages and prices in the Middle Ages one needs to proceed with caution. The data are uneven and not available for each year, appearing in certain years and in different regions. Furthermore there are sharp changes in prices for grain within a given year at the same market place depending on whether it was during or just after the harvest or whether it was spring and grain was scarce. The price of rye for instance varied from one groschen to thirty per measure (strych or korec which equaled about 2.5 bushels) within one year in which there was a famine. Nevertheless the data (see page 145 for graphs) reflecting the price of two grains, wheat and barley, the two for which we have the most complete figures, show that over the twenty one year period from 1379-1401 in the town of Kolín, in east central Bohemia, the price of grain remained static with a sharp drop in 1395. Prices in Prague for wheat and barley rose slightly but it is not known whether the peasant benefited from this or whether it was the middlemen who increased their profits. The few references to livestock prices available suggest increases in the price of pigs and cattle. It is doubtful however if the poorer peasant profitted from any increase here since his investment in animals was minimal.

Static or even slightly rising prices for the peasant meant that in fact they declined since the silver content of the coins with which he was paid decreased during this time. According to a royal regulation of 1378 the Czech groschen was to have a standard of 3,237 grams of silver. Already during the reign of Charles IV (d. 1378) the coin had been devalued. Some groschen had a silver content of only 2,069 grams. Devaluation continued despite the regulation. During the reign of Wenceslas IV (1378-1419) the groschen with the highest silver content known had only 2,531 grams, the lowest had 1,118. Devaluation of the heller, the coin with which most day labourers were paid, was even more rapid. In 1405 it took thirteen heller to equal one groschen; in 1407 it took fourteen.[20] In other words the unsuspecting peasant accepted the groschen at its older value but when he wanted to use the same coin to purchase something from the merchant or master craftsman or if he wanted to pay a debt he was told the coin was not worth as much as he thought because it contained less silver. As a result he had to add a heller or two to his bill.

As we saw, at the bottom of the rural social ladder was a group of people who made their living working for others. These included the cottagers with a plot of land as well as men and women servants, ploughmen, threshers, day labourers and even artisans in the employ of peasants and lords. Their ability to meet their financial obligations as well as their material welfare depended on the wages they received.

In western Europe wages in the country rose steadily throughout the fourteenth century, a development directly related to the demographic collapse in which in some areas between 30 and 50 percent of the people died as a result of the Black Death and other calamities. The shortage of workers made it possible for a ploughman in England to ask and get four times the pre-plague wage. There are also references to plagues and famines in the literature of fourteenth century Bohemia but it seems nothing as devastating happened there as had farther west.[21] In Bohemia it was the movement of peasants into towns, especially Prague, which relieved the downward pressure on farm wages. The little information available shows that wages of day labourers in south Bohemia doubled in the last thirty-five years of the fourteenth century, rising from half a groschen a day in 1367 to one groschen a day at the beginning of the fifteenth century. We have more complete information on the wages of house servants. Those employed by the monastery in Trebon received no increase in their income from 1378 to 1408, the period for which figures are available.[22] Judging from the fact that peasants continued to move to the cities, conditions in the country cannot have been very attractive for the hired workers.

Rural society therefore, which provided the revolution many of its recruits, was not characterized by steadily decreasing standard of living for all. Nor was it a mass of seething misery. It was rather a society in flux. Some people became wealthy while their neighbours and friends remained poor. Some of those who had become moneyless saw others whom they regarded as social inferiors living better than they did. If a scapegoat for one's troubles was needed he could easily be located. The impoverished, whether noble, gentleman or peasant saw his oppressor in his wealthy creditor or lord who might be a noble, a priest, a towns-person or a peasant who had amassed tracts of land at the expense of his own poverty stricken family. The poorer peasant was often especially incensed because men from his own class, in the service of their lord, exercised authority over him. The lines of the antagonism were therefore not drawn so much between social classes but rather between those who had power and wealth and those who did not. The successful peasant, especially if he was a dependent, also had grounds for discontent. He wanted social and political acknowledgement of his economic power. It is normal that he should expect privileges, such as carrying weapons, owning a coat of arms and seal and freedom from the need to call another man his lord, privileges which people whom he surpassed in wealth enjoyed. It is understandable then that the call of the Hussite reformers to lords to exercise authority mildly and to treat the poor fairly, and of the revolutionaries to do away with one man's authority over another entirely, met with a sympathetic ear in the country.

In addition to the strains within rural Bohemian society there were also conflicts between town and country. The heart of the problem lay in the fact that town merchants and artisans controlled the conditions of the trade between themselves and the rural producers. From the beginning it had been the towns which acquired monopolies over the marketplaces. Towns had exclusive rights over their regions. Within one mile of its walls no one was allowed to establish a market or to undertake a craft which existed in the town. As a result the peasant had to come to the town to sell and buy according to the regulations and prices estab-lished by the merchants and artisans which they did in their own interests. Craft guilds, for example, set the price of their goods so that they received more for what they sold to the country than they paid for what they bought from it.[23] Merchants also exploited the rural population. Some of them bought crops cheaply right after harvest, or sometimes while it was still on the field, from the peasants who needed the money to pay the lord his rent. The burghers then waited until grain was scarce whereupon they sold it for a high price. Furthermore, according to medieval custom, the merchant had the right to confiscate the goods which the peasant of a delinquent debtor brought to the market to sell. Despite the condemnation of popular preachers and the church, merchants continued to collect from the peasant debts which his lord owed them.[24] The resentment and hostility which the peasant felt towards townspeople surfaced during the revolution when, coming to Prague in 1420 to help the city besieged by Europe's anti-Hussite crusade, the rural people stripped the Praguers of the fine clothes and ornaments which the brothers and sisters from the country regarded as symbols of mortal sin.

In addition to the conflicts between town and country, medieval urban life spawned its own tensions within itself. Whereas the society of rural Bohemia presents an ambivalent picture, with some getting richer and some poorer, life in the towns became increasingly difficult for most people except the clergy and the small group of patricians.

THE CITY

Prague, with it population of some 35,000, was by far the largest city in Bohemia.[25] Emperor Charles IV had made it his chief residence and had further elevated its status by having the pope make it the seat of an independent archbishop and then by establishing the first university in central Europe. In addition, in the second half of the fourteenth century many people came to the city from the country resulting in the establishment of a new section of the city with its own government, called New Town. Most of the residents were Czech whereas Old Town and Lesser Side, across the Vltava river, were largely German.

Charles' patronage of churches and of the university combined with the influx of new residents needing houses resulted in increased construction activities providing employment during much of the fourteenth century. However because Bohemia had no export trade to speak of and because her artisans produced mostly for local markets there was a definite ceiling on how far the economy could expand and provide work. In international trade Bohemian merchants limited themselves to handling the eastern spices and Italian and Flemish cloth which passed through Prague. The city had the surplus labour on which large scale industries thrive but the thinking of its rich and powerful was not open to new possibilities. Rather than launch a vigorous industry providing jobs and developing foreign markets, those with capital to invest, like the church, nobles and patricians, put their money into rural lands and houses in the city which they rented out and which as a result tended to drive up the cost of housing because land became more expensive.[26] We shall consider later evidence showing that the expansion of the economy under Charles IV had come to an end at the beginning of the fifteenth century and that lower classes found it increasingly difficult to find work with wages sufficient to pay daily expenses.

Medieval Prague society was typical of that of medieval towns in general. At the top was the small patrician class, consisting of the wealthy merchants, city landowners, prelates and some of the more successful artisans from among the butchers and bakers. This group, wealthy, politically powerful and self-employed assumed the uppermost place in the urban hierarchy and imposed its will on those below, extracting from them the fruits of their labour. As the population had grown and as more and more people sought to become self-employed masters, the wealthy guilds, both merchant and craft, began to exclude the newly trained aspirants to their ranks in order to protect their own incomes. The result was that a large body of skilled workers found the road to self-employment blocked. They then had to seek work as employees and dependents of the established masters.

There were numerous gradations in terms of quality of working conditions among those who were masters but employed by someone else. The master-builders were mostly not self-employed because it was simply impossible for anyone other than the king or an ecclesiastical body to undertake the construction of a large building such as a cathedral. The master-builders nevertheless enjoyed considerable independence in their jobs and were well paid because of highly prized skills. More numerous, and much less well off were those in the textile trade. Most masters of the cloth making craft were not able to come up with the capital to purchase the raw product and machinery such as looms, frames and fulling machines and therefore had to work for those who could supply them.[27] As a result there existed a large group of people, masters of their craft who were dependent for their employment on entrepreneurs who controlled the conditions under which they worked.

Just below the masters who were unable to set up shop for themselves were the journeymen of all crafts, persons who had passed their apprenticeship and were awaiting the opportunity to establish themselves independently. In the earlier centuries a journeyman spent about a year working to save enough capital to open his own shop. By the fourteenth century throughout Europe in general, many spent their whole life working at this stage because additional legal and economic obstructions introduced by entrenched masters made it impossible for younger artisans to set up their own shops. For one thing entrance fees into guilds were increased so that persons embarking on their careers could only with difficulty pay them. Furthermore, guilds prohibited master tailors and shoemakers from having more than two finished suits or shoes in their shops at one time. This removed the temptation to slash prices in order to move one's inventory. Fewer items sold meant that there was less work for artisans.[28] Hence a considerable number of discontented qualified workers lived their lives believing that their abilities and skills were not being rewarded to the extent that they might expect because legal and economic obstacles hindered their entrance into the master class.

Just as every medieval city, Prague too had its group of unskilled workers who laboured on a daily basis with all the uncertainties of not knowing whether tomorrow would bring employment. These people worked at menial tasks, often as aids to skilled workers. In the building industry they carried supplies or stones or they treaded the big wheel which ran the derrick and crane used to hoist stones in the construction of cathedrals. In general there were more workers than there was work which meant high levels of unemployment, and in the days before unions and collective bargaining, depressed wages. Some of the city workers were able to find work in the nearby countryside during harvest thus relieving somewhat the pressure in the city.[29]

There were also in the city groups of people not directly active in production. These were salaried servants, students, entertainers, prostitutes and beggers. Servants included domestics, bailiffs of the town council and agents of merchants and entrepreneurs. Servants were materially relatively well cared for by their employer but they had to submit personal affairs, even marriage plans, to his or her supervision. On the other hand many servants, such as bailiffs and agents with plenipotentiary powers from their employer, were accustomed to the use of authority in public and all the resulting advantages.

At the edge of medieval society and of its laws lived those whose success in making a living depended on the community's tolerance and generosity: the beggers, gamblers and prostitutes. The lot of the begger had become more difficult in the fourteenth century because the church's beggers, the mendicant monks, were competing for the alms of the faithful. Those without work also practised their hand at gambling

They spent their idle hours in taverns where they awaited the working man on his way home from work and won from him his earnings.[30]

The prostitutes of Prague have been given special attention by those who have told the story of the Hussite movement. As the object of concern from the preachers of reform they stand as a bright example of the reformers' attention to the material conditions of some of society's downtrodden. Women in the profession were fairly numerous in the fourteenth century and Prague had its own red light district, a section of the city called Krakov. The reformer, Matthew of Janov claimed that his predecessor, Milič had converted 200 of them. Their existence in itself reflects a sour economic climate because some of them entered the trade in an effort to meet their own or their family's financial crisis by borrowing money from rich creditors. Later they found that they were unable to pay it back. A common tactic was for creditors to require the debtors to work off the unpaid debt. We know of some creditors, madames, who required their female debtors to become prostitutes and to work for them in conditions hardly different from those of slavery. The nature of the bondage of the prostitute to her madame is reflected in the relation of one Dorthy of Strygl to her creditor Anna Harbatová. Dorthy promised Anna that under pain of death she would not leave her employ until the debt was paid. We know the names of four such madames who among them in 1396 and 1397 had some 50-60 women in their service and altogether the girls thus in debt numbered in the hundreds. It was virtually impossible for a woman to free herself from such an entanglement because to do so she had to pay off the debt at once. Since the average debt was 250 groschen, an amount equal to the cost of a small house in New Town, few if any women in debt could do so. The authorities did little to discourage prostitution. In fact in 1395 one town official loaned one of the madames fifty groschen enabling her to stay in business.[31] Hence when the reformers preached against prostitution they did so not only out of an inclination towards sexual chastity per se but because they were aware that the sexual trade bound some women into the servitude of others from which they had almost no hope of escaping.

There existed then in Prague, just as in the cities further west, a large body of poor people. This was not a homogeneous group but in it were represented people from all trades and professions. Judging from the number of people exempted from taxation because of poverty, twenty-five percent of the people in Stříbro, and fifty percent in Chrudim, České Budějovice and Prague were poor. The poor at that time, just as always were subject to various petty restrictions and indignations. One of the more incongruous vexations for them was the fact that they paid higher prices for their groceries. In 1378 the poor of Brno in Moravia complained to the town fathers that if a poor man's wife tried to buy meat the butcher charged her two times the normal price and then abused and insulted her if she offered to pay what others did.[32] Similarly there were numerous stories relating how doctors resisted treating the poor who could not pay. The fact that the officials were concerned about this inequality is reflected in the many orders to millers, bakers, brewers and others prohibiting them from treating the poor less fairly than the rich. The frequency of the decrees is also an indication of their failure.

At the beginning of the fifteenth century Prague experienced economic difficulties which caused material hardship for all classes but which, as always, hit the needy harder. The economic decline was partly the result of political upheavals. In 1400 King Wenceslas IV was deprived of his imperial crown. This ended the access to seats of influence in Germany which he and his father had used to bring business to Bohemia. Furthermore, in 1405, as we shall see later in more detail, the Bohemian barons forced the king to concede much of his authority over regional government to them. Their inclination to impose tolls on merchants travelling through their lands cut into the latter's profits and discouraged trade. The slowdown was assisted by the exodus of German scholars who found the university, controlled by the Czech reformers after 1409, not to their liking.

The recessions was well underway by the end of the fourteenth century and affected all levels of society as can be seen from the declining profits of traders of textiles. The Regensberger merchant, a certain Runtinger, a dealer in Italian cloth, experienced a drop in his profits from seventy percent in 1383 to a little over thirteen percent in 1401, a trend which caused him to end his activities in Prague.[33] For the rest of the urban society the recession meant static wages, rising unemployment and increased cost of living. As a result, people fell into debt, mortgaging their houses and pawning their personal belongings in order to have the money to meet the daily needs of living. The person looking for the source of his grief did not need to look far. The enemy was close at hand, namely the wealthy burgers and the clergy to whom he was in debt and whom the Hussite reformers lifted out as especially in need of reform.

In discussing long term wages we have unfortunately no exact figures to instruct us. There are however several indications that wages in Prague remained static and in fact declined in terms of buying power. The very presence of a large number of skilled and unskilled workers had driven down wages so that they were lower in Prague than in the nearby villages. Furthermore unskilled Prague workers went as far as Vienna and Regensburg in order to find work. The few wage figures which are available show little change. In 1378 a day labourer working on the construction of St. Vitus cathedral received between nine heller and one groschen a day. Twenty years later labourers involved in various tasks received either half a groschen a day plus food, or one groschen without food. Wages in the nearby village of Velká Ves were somewhat higher reflecting fewer hands available. Skilled workers in Prague fared somewhat better, a bricklayer getting from two to two and a half groschen daily. In comparison a holder of a benefice in St. Vitus cathedral got 18,000 groschen annually or almost fifty groschen for each day of the year.[34]

The significance of static wages can be cast in a better light if we remember the declining buying power of money because of the depreciation of the coins as well as the rising prices. We have discussed currency devaluation above and need now to look at some of the daily expenses of town dwellers. Contemporary reports suggest that a person needed anywhere from one to four groschen a day to live. The foundation of an altar normally included about 360 groschen annual income which, according to an anonymous priest writing at that time, was not enough to live on. The city of Brno spent about one groschen a day on food and drink for each of its thirty soldiers sent on an expedition. This did not include lodging and other supplies which it was customary to requisition from the local population. Those employers who supplied their workers with board assumed a cost of one-half a groschen a day and therefore lowered the daily wage by so much.[35] This of course represented the bare minimum of a person's food needs. The conclusion can only be that the worker who received between three to six groschen *weekly* struggled vainly to make ends meet.

The increasing cost of living just before the revolution can best be seen from an analysis of the two most essential elements in life: food and housing. Again in discussing price developments we need to proceed with caution because the data are meagre. Yet the figures collected by František Graus [36] indicate a trend upwards in prices for the people of Prague. The rise in the price of grain, beneficial for the peasant, meant higher costs for the urban dweller. We unfortunately do not have bread prices but most likely the rise there was even more sharp since bakers had a monopoly on their craft. From 1381 to 1407 the raw product rose by two groschen per measure (korec/strych). In the nearby village of Velká Ves the price of wheat remained stable suggesting either that the middlemen marked up more moderately or, what is more likely, the supply was greater. Here the price went from four and a half groschen in 1394 to four groschen nine heller in 1403. The tables on page 145 show that the price of almost all items, with the exception of beer rose in the period before the revolution. Insofar as the data for coal (*carbones*) are indicative, the price of fuel was rising sharply. This trend was apparently related to the shortage in the supply of wood to which Emperor Charles IV responded in 1348 by taking measures to conserve forests on royal lands.[37]

Much of the blame for the rise in grain prices rested with the middlemen and speculators who bought the crop from the peasants just outside the city gates or directly off the land and then sold the food at artifically high prices which they could determine because they held the bulk of the food stuffs. The practice was so extensive and damaging that the church took steps to curb it. In 1405 its synod stated that "whoever buys the year's produce or wine at harvest or vintage, cheaper so that they can sell for a higher price later, such persons shall have sinned mortally."[38]

The period before the revolution saw a general and steep rise in the cost of housing in Prague. For one thing the value of land increased three or fourfold.[39] We know only little about the cost of constructing a house in late medieval Prague. However as we have seen the costs of labour rose only slightly and judging from the fact that building lime remained stable in price (see graph p. 145), the cost of materials also did not contribute substantially to the rise in housing costs. It is possible to explain the rise in housing costs by the shortage of wood mentioned earlier. However one of the most important reasons for the high cost of providing shelter was the growing cost of perpetual rents or what we might today call the interest rate on mortgages.

A homeowner, in order to acquire an immediate sum of cash undertook to pay his creditor an annual and perpetual rent, normally one-tenth of the amount of cash received or of the principle. The rent was a permanent payment and the owner had little hope of paying off the principle. In the early fifteenth century some creditors allowed the rents to be redeemed by the home owner if he paid the principle plus one year's rent regardless of how much had been paid to date. The rent was not only an unwelcome burden but also put one's house in jeopardy. If an owner defaulted on payment two years in a row the creditor took over ownership of the house.[40]

Some of the rents were the result of pious bequests to clergy. In such cases the homeowner agreed to pay a priest or ecclesiastical institution an annual sum in return for which the priest was to perform regular masses or the church was to build an altar or give food and clothing to the poor. Most owners entered into the perpetual rent arrangement because they needed cash. Those who wanted to build a house submitted their dwellings to the rent right from the start. New residents to the city were required to begin construction of a house a month after taking possession of the land and to complete it within eighteen months. Those without capital went to the wealthy and agreed to pay the perpetual rent. Some bought their houses on the basis of perpetual rents rather than a one time cash payment because the seller preferred the continuous income.

A reflection of the growing economic pressure on the middle to poorer groups in society is the fact that the number of rents, their costs and defaults on payment increased just before the outbreak of the revolution. Between 1400 and 1419 530 out of 593 houses in Old Town were burdened by perpetual rents and fourty-four of these had an action for non-payment brought against them. Of the 273 houses in New Town (Počice) only thirteen were free of rents.[41]

Furthermore, the rate of interest increased. Or stated in terms of the fourteenth century, a person selling a perpetual rent received increasingly less cash for it. In the fourteenth century the normal rate was for the homeowner to get 600 groschen in cash for a rent yielding the creditor 60 groschen a year. At the beginning of the fifteenth century it was still possible to get this ratio but more and more homeowners found that for a rent costing them sixty groschen a year they received only 480 to 550 groschen in cash. In other words the rent had risen from ten percent of the principle to eleven or twelve. In contrast, in the same period the cost of rents in Switzerland fell from 7.35 percent to 6.27. In Austria it fell from 12.72 to 9.64 percent and in Munich from 11.06 to 7.03 percent.[42]

The population most affected by these developments were those people working for others including dependent journeymen, apprentices and day labourers. They found it increasingly expensive to raise cash for an emergency such as repairing houses or even building one. At the same time it became more and more difficult for them to pay the perpetual rents some of which had been undertaken by their ancestors and from which they themselves derived no immediate benefit. Many found themselves the objects of suits from wealthy clergy and townspeople claiming non-payment of the rent. The result was not only a continuous flow of wealth from the lower classes to the church and to the wealthy burghers of Old Town Prague, but in addition people saw what was often their family's only symbol of material security, their house, taken from them by the legal suits. It was therefore not difficult for them to see themselves as victims of the church.

The economic pressure on the population can also be seen in the increasing rate at which people pawned their personal possessions. Persons in need of smaller amounts of cash, for example, to pay fines, buy food or make a religious bequest, could borrow money using movable property as security. If one had real property such as land or a house it functioned as surety and the person could borrow money in "good faith" (*bona fide*) in which case the debt was registered with the city officials who helped collect it in case of default. In any case the value of the collateral generally greatly exceeded the amount of the loan. If the borrower could not pay it back he lost his surety or he had to work off his debt.

People made these loans for what they regarded as essential needs and not for frivolous wants. This can be seen from an analysis of the items which people used as collateral based on the records of New Town Prague. Since Jews, innkeepers and clergy were not required to register their loans with the city the following is only a partial breakdown of the people's debts. Of these, by far the majority, 87.9 percent, of the objects pawned were those required for making and maintaining one's living. This included things like waggons, snares and hunting traps, knives and half-completed pieces of leather. Within this group ordinary items of clothing such as shoes and caps made up the greatest percentage, 38.7 percent. In contrast, luxury items such as crucifixes, multicoloured or metal ornamented clothing represented only 12.1 percent.[43] The short term need to stay alive compelled people to jeopardize their long term chances of improving their lot by giving up items needed to do so. It is clear from this that townspeople were suffering economic hardship forcing them to surrender articles which they had been able to afford earlier in a more prosperous time.

Late medieval Bohemian society was one that had undergone changes many of which people were still trying to understand. People who had formerly enjoyed power and status in society by virtue of noble birth, or through loyal service to one of noble birth, found this long accepted principle undermined by that of wealth. Individuals with no noble connections who had prospered because of good fortune, hard work and skill often lived better than those whose families had owned land and noble crests for generations. In addition society had become sharply differentiated. Those who had not understood how to exploit the economic changes found themselves excluded from the wealth which the strong and the ambitious were accumulating. The wealthy and powerful were often in positions to determine the conditions of life for the rest and did so to their own advantage. As a result many found it increasingly difficult to make ends meet especially in a city like Prague and regarded themselves as victims of unjust circumstances. It was this injustice to which the Hussite reformers addressed themselves. Since to undo social injustice was to them an integral part of the Christian faith there was no dichotomy between social and spiritual religion. They saw, as theologians are beginning to see today,[44] that the gospel of Jesus of Nazareth had to be applied to the social, economic and spiritual aspects of people's lives at one and the same time.

The nobility by and large still represented the most powerful and wealthy group in society. Why were some of them then interested in a movement such as Hus' with its implications for social reform? Was their support for Hussitism simply a continuation of their feud with the king? Was it only the impoverished and disaffected nobles who supported the reformers? To what extent did the nobles aid the reformers and when did they draw back? These are the questions to which the following chapters will seek to provide answers.

CHAPTER TWO

THE NOBLE PATRON AND HIS PARISH

One of the most effective ways in which nobles advanced the cause of their religion at the beginning of the Hussite revolution was when they put their positions as lords of their domains behind the priest of their choice. This included using their rights as patrons as well as the threat of armed force to expel those who did not agree with them. Such interference in the tenure of a priest on the part of Hussite nobles was contrary to the church's law, not only because it gave support to heretics but because it violated canonical prescriptions which required episcopal supervision over priests entering office. It was this type of domination over clergy by laymen which the Gregorian reforms of the eleventh century were designed to eliminate. During the thirteenth and fourteenth centuries the church made great strides in applying its principles on the proper relationship of secular lords to their priests. However, much of the progress was superficial and although patrons adhered to the letter of the law, in reality they continued to dominate, sometimes violently seizing church property, their priests and expecting loyal service from them.

The right of the patron to present a priest to a parish went back to the time when a lord, having built a church on his land, placed one of his men into it as its priest. These churches were both legally and economically a part of the lord's property. The lords chose their priests from the ranks of their subjects. The priest was mostly untrained in spiritual tasks and frequently served his lord in a non-spiritual role acting as a notary, tax collector and administrator of justice. The lord remunerated him as he did his other subjects from the fruits of the manorial economy.[1]

The men who developed the Gregorian reforms in the eleventh century also intended to include lower benefices and parishes along with bishoprics and abbeys when they prohibited lay investiture of the clergy. It was not however until the twelfth century that the Roman Curia felt sufficiently strong to seriously attack the principle of lay ownership of parishes. The Lateran synods of 1123 and 1139 rejected the idea that a lay person was the owner or lord of a parish church and as such had the right to install its priest. Instead the church stated that a priest could be invested into lower benefices only by the bishop. The person on whose land the church was built no longer owned it. Nevertheless the church left to him or her the right to present or propose to the bishop a priest for installation. The church said it granted this right in recognition of the fact that the patron had contributed the ground and the building as well as an endowment from which the priest lived.

The medieval priest never became fully independent of the lord of the estate for his income. The priest generally was in control of his prebend, that is the income from fees collected for performing ritual services such as baptisms, confirmations and burials for which the residents within his parish boundary had to come to him. The nature and size of the endowment, on the other hand, was largely determined by the donor. The endowment, consisting of land and rent payments had two sources. First, there was the parish's original endowment also called the tithe although the amount was set at the beginning and could be changed or revoked entirely by the patron. The endowment was made by transferring to the priest either a piece of land or a specified rent or payment which certain peasants owed the lord. Henceforth both property and peasant came under the lordship of the priest. The lord granted the parish priest additional payments from new settlements as they became established as part of the parish. These were financially not significant but represented acknowledgement that the new villages belonged to the parish. The second source of income for the endowment was the land and rent payments transferred to the priest or to altarists in the parish by individuals, other than the patron. In exchange for these gifts the donors expected the clergy in question to perform a mass or other religious service in his or her family's memory. All of these incomes were for the priest's own use. If the church building required repair or renovation the parish community as a whole was responsible for coming up with the needed material.[2]

The church in Bohemia did not vigorously supervise the installation of priests until the beginning of the fourteenth century. John of Dražice, bishop of Prague from 1301 to 1343, began the process by insisting that a priest must have his approval before he could take office. His successor, Archbishop Ernest of Pardubice, continued in the same direction. At a clerical synod in 1349 he passed a series of measures designed to implement the church's regulations and to remove abuses against the clerical estate. The synod threatened to revoke the right of patronage of those who protected such priests who had not taken the oath to uphold ecclesiastical principles and of those who presented a candidate simply because he agreed to a lower salary or made some other material concessions. Furthermore the archbishop threatened patrons, who imprisoned uncooperative priests or summoned them before their courts, with excommunication. A synod of 1355 again passed statutes aimed at patrons' arbitrary installation of priests.[3] One result of the archbishop's work was the beginning of the *Libri Confirmationum,* the books in which were kept the records of all confirmations to the benefices of the Prague diocese. In this respect the archbishop was successful for by the end of the century over ninety percent of all installations went through his office. Furthermore, throughout the fourteenth century the archbishop's court established jurisdiction over cases involving disputed patronage, contracts and disputes between a cleric and a layperson and over all matrimonial discords.[4]

The process of getting episcopal confirmation could be quite complex. In medieval England, after a priest applied to be confirmed, the bishop routinely summoned the rural chapter and sometimes even a special jury. Its task was to determine whether the parish was in fact empty, what its income was and who was its patron.[5] In the Prague diocese, whose procedure was introduced by Archbishop Ernest in 1354 and based on that current in the archbishopric of Mainz, these questions were considered only if objections were raised after a priest had been publicly proclaimed to be a candidate. Upon receiving letters of presentation from the patron or collator, the archbishop's vicar general appointed a priest from a nearby parish as the executor who then proclaimed the presentation in the presence of the congregation. Anyone having objections either to the right of the patron or to the qualifications of the priest had a certain amount of time within which to raise them. If the archbishop's office decided the objections were valid the candidate had the opportunity to answer the charges or to show that he had a dispensation and need not comply with a given regulation. If there was no sustainable opposition the priest took an oath of obedience to his superior and swore to observe the statutes of the diocese and to fulfill the obligations of his office. He was then granted letters of confirmation for which he paid a fee ranging from twelve to sixty groschen. The actual installation was done by either the dean or archdeacon of his deanery.[6]

The vicar general's supervisory role over the clergy also extended into the area of discipline in that he was empowered to suspend priests from office for various infractions. Before 1417 most priests were deprived of office because they had not obeyed citations or for specific offenses. One priest, for example, was suspended because he "profaned the divines", another "because of his excesses", a third, because "his offenses required it", a fourth because he made no effort to acquire higher orders and a fifth because he had killed a craftsman.[7] In 1417, in the suspensions for religious reasons, which we shall discuss more fully below, the archbishop himself intervened to expel priests from office.

Despite the church's efforts at reform, the lay patron, in Europe and in Bohemia specifically, continued to exercise control over his parish. Patronage remained a part of the total rights of dominion which a lord had on his lands and was inherited, sold, traded, pawned or loaned out. The lord claimed the right to the income of the benefice during a vacancy and to administer the estate of the deceased clergy. Secular lords frequently ignored the ecclesiastical judiciary. In Bohemia, between 1390 and 1410, there were numerous complaints that patrons removed and installed their candidates without regard to law, that they postponed presentations in order to collect the interim income and that the clergy, in order to get a presentation were compelled to yield material rights and incomes to the nobility.[8]

Patrons continued to protect their priests against the ecclesiastical hierarchy whether or not they had obtained a confirmation. Thus a certain Clement Holub, having been presented to the Přepychy parish by an unknown patron in 1375 requested to be proclaimed its priest. The vicar general pronounced him unfit because the dispensation which he produced to excuse himself was insufficient and because he testified falsely in court. At the same time two others claimed to be lawful priests there. Each had been presented by a different local squire. We have no record of how the court resolved this dispute, but in 1413 the priest in Přepychy, Clement, who in 1375 had been declared unfit, appeared as a witness on a document, and in 1416 the priest there was executor for the presentation in a nearby parish and was recognized as such by the episcopal office.[9] The episcopal books of confirmations have no record of Clement's or of anyone else's confirmation to Přepychy. Evidently Clement was protected by his patron and functioned as a priest without confirmation despite the archbishop's earlier judgement against him.

Many nobles, when unable to get from the church or from priests what they wanted, through any other means, resorted to violence. The squire, Všebor of Chrast, the patron of the parish in Struhy in eastern Bohemia, seized the key from his priest and refused him entrance into his church. Similarly the church accused Lord William of Landštejn of wasting and burning the lands of St. Vitus Cathedral in Prague. It also denounced the squire, John of Újezd for inflicting "wild cruelties" on the priests subject to him, under the influence of some demonic instinct.[10] In the same vein the priest of St. Martin's in Žatec was despoiled of his church in 1410 and in 1416 the barons, Otto of Bergov and John Městecký of Opočno, with the help of several gentry, invaded the Benedictine monastery of Opatovice and drowned its abbot.[11] In all this the nobles were provided with the remarkable example of the king and his courtiers who appropriated and damaged the archbishop's property in the course of their quarrel in the 1380s when Archbishop John of Jenštejn attempted to free the church from exactly that kind of secular domination.[12]

In most cases the patron exercised control over his priest more subtly and without resort to violence. Just as in Germany the church in Bohemia accommodated itself to the fact that the patron in appointing his priest was more concerned about his own and his family's advantage than he was about the church and whether it received a canonically qualified priest.[13] Frequently the late medieval patron, just as his predecessor, the owner of the proprietory church, used his right to choose a candidate to church office as a means to provide an income for a servant or relative. The episcopal records only seldom inform us of the relationship between patron and priest. Yet there were in this period, 1354-1419, eleven known cases of patrons granting offices to relatives,[14] twenty-eight to local friends or favorites[15] and twelve to persons in the patron's service.[16] This suggests that many collators regarded the benefice and its income as their own to grant as a reward to someone for friendship or service.

There is also evidence that patrons continued to arbitrarily dismiss their priests and that the church implicitly accepted this practice because it confirmed his replacement. The patrons' strong willed expulsions are reflected in the number of resignations from church office for which no explanation was given. When the episcopal official confirmed a priest he always gave the reason for the vacancy in the benefice. Three different reasons were given: the death of the previous occupant, resignations and, very infrequently, expulsion by church authorities. Vacancies by reason of resignation were explained as the result of two priests exchanging offices. They also came about when a priest went to another parish, replacing one who had died or gone elsewhere. In addition a few priests resigned because they were ill or too old to satisfactorily carry on the duties of office.[17] That not many priests were eager to resign for the latter reason is understandable since it meant giving up their only source of income. Priests belonging to a religious order could afford to do so but for the remainder there was very little provision made to care for them in their old age.[18] Furthermore, since death was frequently given as a reason for a vacancy we can conclude that it was normal for priests to continue in office until they died. A fourth category of resignations has no explanation in the text and as the graph below illustrates, sometimes reached as high as twenty-five percent in accounting for the vacancies filled in a given year.

RESIGNATIONS WITHOUT EXPLANATIONS
EXPRESSED IN % OF ALL VACANCIES[19]

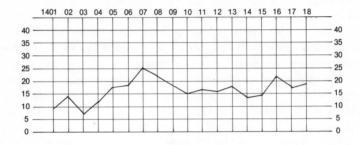

Most of these unexplained resignations were likely exacted by the patron and were the cause for the complaints of the church about the patrons' arbitrary treatment of their priests. Some of these stated resignations may have been merely a declaration that a benefice was officially vacant after its holder had left it voluntarily in order to pursue some other business. Perhaps the departure from their parish of some of the more radical Hussite priests who wanted to be free to preach wherever and when ever they felt so moved caused the increase in unexplained resignations in 1416.[20] The above graph shows that although some of the unaccounted for abdications may have included such priests, this phenomenon cannot be related to the religious quarrels. The years 1407 and 1408 show the highest rates and there is nothing in these years which would point to such an explanation. What happened was that patrons simply got rid of undesirable priests and, as the religious tensions increased, religion became one of the reasons why a priest was undesirable to his patron.

The lay patron's independence in general extended into the sphere of papal provisions. Most papal letters did not guarantee their holders benefices no matter what type of patron was involved. They merely claimed the office for the holder of the letter which was worded so as to cast the latter into the role of the plaintiff and the bishop, patron or cathedral chapter as the defendant. It was then up to the local ecclesiastical judicial machinery to decide on the providee's merits along with other claimants.[21]

Papal bulls conferring empty benefices began to enter Bohemia in the early fourteenth century.[22] Most provisions were given for honourary and sinecure benefices: those associated with cathedral chapters, provosts, deaneries, archdeaconries and canonries.[23] A chapter by law had the right to fill any vacancy by a vote of its members. In practice these elections were influenced by any number of parties; royal, noble or papal who sought a sinecure benefice for someone in their service. Such offices were therefore held by men who, perhaps of humble origin, had made their way into the administration of the king, the archbishop or perhaps a magnate via a university education and who intended to continue their career in government administration. They were normally the most remunerative and handy for a careerist. Since they did not involve the care of souls most of the upper prebends had no residency requirement, thus freeing the holder from the necessity of hiring a vicar when he wanted to be elsewhere. In contrast the parish priest had to be consecrated within one year after taking office; he had to be at least 24 years old and have relevant training. All were requirements irksome to the person wishing solely to draw his income while pursuing his personal interests.[24] Such people were not likely to seek a parish, the category of office where lay people dominated as patrons. For this reason papal provisions did not often involve an office where the patron was lay.

As it became more difficult for clerics to get positions in the fourteenth century even parishes came to be desirable and aspirants began to seek papal graces for them. Nevertheless the papal curia responded slowly to the requests. In 1443 the councillors of King Charles VII of France expressed satisfaction that the pope was not intervening in the filling of offices where the patron was lay and this held true for fifteenth century Germany as well.[25] Similarly in Bohemia, papal graces rarely got an office for a priest seeking parishes. According to J. Eršil's study of papal graces for Bohemia for 1350-1378 the only recorded case where a papal letter helped a priest get a parish with a lay patron was one where the priest had broken some canonical prescription. This was Greater Popovice, where in 1363 Pope Urban V intervened and deprived the priest of that parish because he had not taken holy orders within the prescribed period of time. The parish, whose patron was the squire John of Popovice,[26] was given to a certain Frenclin.

Other candidates with papal graces in hand were not as successful. For example, in 1396 two men who had been presented to the parish in Český Jablonec in north-eastern Bohemia sought confirmation. The nobles Jarek and John Vartemberk of Děčín presented Wenceslas Varvort. Matthew Ursus, whose patron was the abbot of the Cistercian monastery in Hradiště, within the proper time limit, opposed Varvort's confirmation and claimed it for himself on the basis of a papal grace.[27] Nevertheless the episcopal office confirmed the Vartemberk candidate. A similar case occurred in Domašín in eastern Bohemia, in 1408. Here three candidates were presented, two having papal graces. The third, Thomas, to whom the benefice was awarded, had been presented by the provost of the Premonstratensian convent in Louňovice and had no papal letter.[28]

Although the layman had come to acknowledge some of the church's prescriptions aimed at freeing it from its control, the position of the parish priest, where he was materially dependent on his patron and vulnerable to his armed might, made much of the church's striving futile. Hence noble activities in 1417 expelling and installing priests without regard for the episcopal office does not represent a radical break from previous behaviour. What was different was that in 1417 power was exercised on behalf of one's religious convictions. Since the Church had been unable to tame the lay patron it tried to replace him by urging noble families to donate their right of patronage to an ecclesiastical institution as an act contributing to the donor's salvation. Again the results for the church were mixed. Some nobles heeded its invitation but the great majority retained the right to determine who the local priest should be, in their own family.

Despite the availability of data no one has undertaken a study and analysis of the ownership of patronage to the parishes in the Prague archdiocese. Václav Tomek gave us the names and standing of the patrons for the city of Prague and Josef Kurka identified those in the archdeaconries of Kouřím, Boleslav and Hradec Kralove and for the bishopric of Litomyšl. Even in those areas he however limited himself to the parishes which were within the Bohemian crown lands when he wrote in the early twentieth century.[1]

One of the developments within the late medieval church was the centralization of power and influence in the papal curia as it began to appoint more and more clergy to office throughout Europe. This has led historians of the Bohemian situation to assume that patronage and the rights to appoint priests to office was generally in ecclesiastical hands. This was for example, the underlying assumption of F.M. Bartoš, one of the leading writers on the late medieval period. Stating that papal provisions did not apply to benefices of lay patrons, he nevertheless accused the Avignon popes of reserving for themselves the filling of the great majority of church offices, from the rich bishoprics to the insignificant rural parishes and altars.[2] With such opinions prevailing it seems fitting therefore that before we embark on an examination of how the nobility used its patronage on behalf of religious reform, we find out whether it owned any patronage and if so how much.

The scope of our investigation includes all of the parish churches in the diocese of Prague as well as those in the Bohemian deaneries of the Litomyšl bishopric. The Prague diocese was divided into ten archdeaconries which were subdivided into a total of fifty-three deaneries, the city of Prague making up one of these. The Litomyšl bishopric was divided into six deaneries, four of which were in Bohemia and two in Moravia.[3]

Part of the late medieval papacy's fiscal policy was to collect a tithe of the income from all church offices. To this end its collectors created lists of all churches in the diocese for which they were responsible. The one for Prague has survived and along with other sources[4] permits us to establish fairly reliably that in late medieval Bohemia there existed a total of 2084 parishes including fourty-four in Prague. We have had occasion elsewhere to refer to the *Libri Confirmationum,* the records kept by the archbishop supervising the installation of priests. In addition to other data they contain the names of the patrons of the parishes allowing us to identify their class status. These records were interrupted at the outbreak of the revolution in 1419. Hence in the Prague diocese the last person acting in this role was taken to be the patron.[5] For the Litomyšl diocese the results of Kurka's study were used.

Because of the care with which the archbishop kept the records of confirmation we have a fairly comprehensive sample of patronage ownership. Almost ninety percent of the priests in the Prague archdiocese received confirmation after 1375, showing that they and their patrons adhered to the Church's requirement that candidates be submitted for approval.[6] The patrons of an additional three percent were found in the earlier records going back to 1354 when the archbishop first began to keep records. The priests of about seven percent of the patrons did not apply for or receive confirmation.

There could be several reasons for a church not having a recorded confirmation. There are, for example gaps in the manuscripts.[7] Moreover, a church could have been exempted from the archbishop's jurisdiction as sometimes happened when monasteries incorporated a parish and it became part of the order's economic and administrative structure.[8] A third possibility is that the priest simply neglected to apply for letters of confirmation perhaps because of the required fee. A similar cause was the fact that patrons sometimes delayed presenting a priest in order to collect the income in the interim. Insofar as the last two were reasons, the archbishop and his priests set a poor example because they were less scrupulous in obeying ecclesiastical prescriptions than the average. Ten of the forty-six churches where the archbishop was a patron, or where he owned the land, did not record a confirmation between 1375 and 1419, that is, about twenty-five percent[9] compared to less than ten percent for the remainder of the collators.

The patrons were divided into six categories: royal, barons, gentry, townspeople, religious orders and secular clergy. Identifying the nobility sometimes caused problems. Normally barons were identified by the title, *nobiles* and the gentry by *famosus armiger, cliens* or *vir*. As we saw in Chapter 1 there were gradations within the gentry. For reasons given there and because the distinctions are almost impossible to follow in the episcopal records the gentry has been treated as one class. When simply the name of the patron was given, or the name modified by *dominus*, I consulted the works of such authorities on the Bohemian nobility as August Sedláček and František Kavka in order to ascertain whether the

THE OWNERS OF CHURCH PATRONAGE

TABLE 1
PATRONAGE DISTRIBUTION IN THE PRAGUE DIOCESE

Archdeaconry	R	B	G	T	RO	SC %Cl	Sh	NC	Total
Prague	52	27	92	18	80	46(40.0)	18	32	365
Kouřím	5	50	104	15	68	33(34.5)	12	25	312
Bechyně	21	83	102	0	39	15(20.8)	5	36	301
Žatec	12	48	84	12	52	4(26.4)	9	20	241
Litoměřice	3	29	37	1	12	15(28.7)	1	10	108
Bilina	5	18	28	1	16	5(28.9)	2	1	76
Boleslav	13	75	60	0	32	10(22.1)	8	10	208
Plzeň	4	12	50	1	23	4(27.6)	2	5	101
Týn Horšův	1	10	18	0	10	8(38.3)	2	3	52
Hradec Králové	8	103	129	2	39	8(16.3)	11	20	320
TOTAL	124	455	704	50	371	148(28.6)	70	162	2084
PERCENT	6.2	24.5	38.0	2.7	20.6	8.0	–	–	100.0
Litomyšl	16	23	27	1	29	35(48.9)	3	19	153
PERCENT	12.2	17.6	20.6	.07	22.2	26.7	–	–	100.0

Symbols: R=Royal; B=Barons; G=Gentry; T=Townspeople; RO=Religious Orders; SC=Secular clergy; %Cl=% of combined clergy; Sh=Parishes shared by different classes; NC=Parishes with no confirmations.

individual belonged to the upper or the lower nobility.[10] Townspeople owning estates and having left bourgeoise occupations for agriculture were entitled to the rights and privileges of the nobility and hence were included in that estate.[11] Individuals identified as *civis* were classed as townspeople.

The results of my study on ownership of church patronage which are given on table one show that the church owned only twenty-eight percent of the parishes in the Prague archdiocese.[12] In the city of Prague it owned more than it did in the rest of the country. In the first place the metropolitan chapters of St. Vitus in the castle of Hradčany and St. Peter's in Vyšehrad elected their own canons and chapter prelates. Of the remaining forty-four churches in the city only thirteen were in lay hands, three were shared by lay people and churchmen and the remaining twenty-eight, over sixty-three percent, belonged to the clergy and the religious orders had sixteen of these.[13] Women did not directly influence the choice of clergy to any large extent. Sixty-four women were sole patrons and another fifty-five shared patronage with males making a total of 119 parishes, or about six percent of the parishes for which there was a confirmation recorded, in which they had a voice in selecting the priest. The distribution of patronage owned by the various orders is shown on table 2.

In the Litomyšl diocese the clergy, both regular and secular, owned almost fifty percent of the churches, a number considerably higher than that for the Prague diocese. This is partially explained by the fact that the bishopric was created out of the lands of the Premonstratensian monastery which continued in the possession of its churches, and by the extensive landholdings of Bishop John, who owned twenty-nine churches, seventeen as lord of the Landšperk domain and twelve as bishop.

In the Prague diocese the nobility, both upper and lower, owned patronage to over sixty-two percent of the churches, in Litomyšl only thirty-eight. In the city of Prague it owned not quite ten percent. The data for the city and for Litomyšl correspond to that found for England and Germany. There the patricians of the towns as well as the monasteries had gained patronage at the expense of the nobility whose decline was caused by debts and the extinction of families.[14]

In Bohemia the gentry remained the strongest class as far as church patronage was concerned. It owned thirty-eight percent. It had the most patronage in the Plzeň archdeaconry, and area in the west where Hussitism was not able to gain a foothold. Even in south-Bohemia, where the extensive baronial domains of the Rožmberks lay, the gentry held

TABLE 1

PATRONAGE OF THE RELIGIOUS ORDERS

Archdeaconry	C	B	P	JJ	TK	AF	AC	CS	Ca	D	M
Prague	19	28	8	6	–	5	2	8	1	1	1
Kouřim	19	21	15	–	6	3	–	–	–	–	–
Bechyně	11	4	13	4	3	–	1	1	–	–	1
Žatec	9	10	15	11	5	–	1	2	–	–	–
Litměřice	2	2	5	–	1	2	–	–	–	–	1
Bílina	4	4	–	–	4	–	–	–	–	–	–
Boleslav	11	3	–	9	1	4	3	1	–	–	–
Plzeň	15	5	2	–	1	–	–	–	–	–	–
Týn Horšův	–	4	5	–	–	5	–	–	–	–	–
Hradec Králové	7	14	1	1	3	4	8	–	1	1	–
TOTALS	98	95	64	31	25	21	19	12	2	1	3

Symbols: C=Cistercians;   B=Benedictines;   P=Premonstratensians;   JJ=St.   John   of   Jerusalem;   TK=Teutonic   Knights; AF=Augustine   friars;   AC=Augustine   Crusaders   of   the   Red   Star;   Ca=Carthusians; D=Dominicans;   M=Miscellaneous, i.e. Altzell monastery, Order of Mary Magdalene and one unknown.

thirty-eight percent of the patronage. It must be kept in mind though that for individuals among the gentry these statistics would not have been consoling. Often several brothers shared patronage to one parish and at times an unrelated person had bought part of the estate so that the right to present was further fractionalized. As a result many gentlemen were without patronage.

Most baronial families owned at least several churches. Three families stand out above the rest. The Rožmberks owned sixty, including two in which they shared. The Vartemberks owned forty-nine and the Berkas of Dubá, forty-eight. An important difference was that the Rožmberk churches were all held by one man. Lord Henry (d.1412) was the only male of his generation and his son Ulrich of his. Henry's uncles had insured the family against having its domains broken up by gaining a privilege from Emperor Charles in 1362 whereby in the event of the death of one of them his property would automatically fall to the remaining.[15] The forty-eight churches of the Berkas of Dubá were shared among nine branches of the family. Of these Hynek Berka of Honštejn and Henry Berka of Houska each owned ten churches. The forty-nine Vartemberk churches were shared by ten branches of that family. Here Čeněk owned the most; the seven to which he presented, the two he acquired on the Lipnice domain via marriage and the five he inherited from his cousin Peter at his death in 1416.

The information gained from the above study of patronage ownership sheds light on the state of affairs which tended to bring the nobility and the reformers together and which to a certain extent influenced the timing of their meeting. From the beginning, the charge that they supported the Hussites out of material greed hung over the nobility. John Hus had laid the basis for these suspicions when he invited the nobility to reclaim the rights of patronage and endowments which their ancestors had surrendered to ecclesiastical institutions. In his tract, "On Simony", written in 1413 Hus wrote that one of the ways whereby simony could be eliminated was for the nobility "to forbid the trafficking and the irregular appointments of unworthy prelates over the people. They could best accomplish it if they would not allow the waste of their fathers' endowments by taking them into their own hands and custody so that in the future they would not be misapplied."[16]

Historians of various ideological persuasions, in discussing the motivations of the nobility on a theoretical level have generally agreed that they acted out of material greed. In this the cue was given them by Andrew of Brod, an enemy of the Hussites, who in 1421 explained that the nobility acted in an attempt to get possession of the wealth and property of the burghers and the clergy.[17] He was followed by Catholic scholars like Constantine Höfler in 1865 and Joseph Schlenz in 1928.[18] More recently the socialist-Marxist school has also attributed material greed to the nobility as a motivating factor in their support for the Hussites. Jan Slavík in 1934 claimed that the nobles' style of life, the parties they hosted and their desire for luxury goods brought them into debt to the townspeople so that they eagerly turned their attention towards the extensive estates of the church. The nobles, Slavík wrote, welcomed the call of the reformers to dispossess the church of its property as their Christian responsibility. The same theme was elaborated by Josef Macek in 1956.[19] Lately, Howard Kaminsky, whose work is more difficult to place into an ideological category, agreed that the nobility was attracted by Hussite doctrines denying the church lordship over property.[20]

The most notable defender of the nobility was František Palacký, who in 1868 explained that the transfer of church estates into noble hands was really an act of King Sigismund, who used ecclesiastical property to repay the nobility for helping him fight the rebel heretics.[21] The trouble with all the above approaches is that they remain on the theoretical level without analyzing the nobility's landholdings, family relationships or ownership of church patronage, anyone of which could offer concrete information helping to explain why a given nobleman was found in the Hussite camp.

One of the reasons why historians have discussed the problems of noble motivation only on a theoretical level is that the sources for medieval Bohemia are not very complete, not as are those for lands like England and France where we have access to the relatively extensive records of the central and noble chanceries. Neither the Bohemian government nor the baronial chanceries provide comparable sources. The transactions of the nobles who held land in fief from the king are recorded in the royal records (*dvorské desky*). Most of the nobles however held their land in free tenure. Their property titles as well as the proceedings of the Bohemian land diet and law court were recorded in the land records (*zemské desky*), most of which were unfortunately destroyed by fire in 1541.[22] There are however registers which can throw light on the material standing of the nobility, thus helping to explain their behaviour with respect to Hussitism. These are the episcopal records of which the *Libri Confirmationum* are part and upon which the data in the above tables are based. However even these sources have been neglected by historians who in their brief attention to the nobility have been content to conduct their discussion without recourse to available data.

We have seen above how the right of patronage, as part of the medieval lord's dominion, offered him material advantages. It also added to his prestige and influence in the community. As the patron he determined who the local priest would be and his status assured him and members of his family prominent seats during worship and, at death, honoured burial sites. In John Hus' teaching patronage gained additional significance. Howard Kaminsky has shown that according to Hus' definition, patronage included the obligation on the part of the patron to seek the spiritual welfare of the parish and its priest. In exchange for this the patron was entitled to material fruits from the property of the parish.[23] Implicit in such a definition is the fact that a given nobleman could have been motivated by material fruits while at the same time interested in the reformation of religious abuses. Stated in concrete terms the nobleman who heard Hus' message knew that unless he was a patron he could not aid the cause of reform in supplying the people with priests who were capable and willing to preach God's truth. Fortunately for him, part of the message was a call to him to appropriate from ecclesiastical institutions, rights which they had acquired from his own ancestors. Who can tell whether he anticipated the prospect because of the possible material gain or for the sake of what he regarded as the spiritual improvement of the people? Kaminsky's conclusion was that the complex of idealism and self-interest in men's minds is impenetrable. This is largely true, yet despite the complications we cannot excuse ourselves from an examination of the material realities of peoples' lives which undoubtedly contributed to the human decision making process.

To begin, we cannot simply assume that people necessarily will back a movement which appeals to their apparent self-interest. In England and Germany, where as we saw, the church owned a good majority of the patronage, the Wyclifite-Hussite program had little support from nobles.[24] The mere prospect of gaining rights was not enough to persuade them. Similarly in Bohemia, lack of patronage cannot explain the Hussite sympathies of all individuals. The Hussite barons, Ernest Pardubice of Richenburk, Čeněk of Vartemberk and Boček of Poděbrady respectively owned patronage rights to thirteen, fourteen and fifteen parishes which was a relatively large number. Conversely leading figures in the Catholic camp, like Nicholas Hazmburk of Budyně, John Jr. of Hradec and John Vartemberk of Ralsko each owned only one church and Ulrich Jr. of Ústí had none.

Despite that word of caution the data show that the Church had had greater success in acquiring patronage in the regions where the Hussite nobility made its home, suggesting that this was an issue with this group. The very fact that the Bohemian nobility as a whole owned most of the patronage was a constant reminder to those families who had lost theirs, of their deficiency in this respect. If one's neighbour has patronage one is aware of one's own lack more so than if neither has any. There were many nobles who saw that their fellows had the opportunity to influence the religious life of the land while they themselves could do little because they were not patrons. Men like Theodore of Studená, who in 1410 lost a dispute in which he contended for the right to determine the priest in Onšov, felt the lack of patronage especially intensely.[25]

Poverty of church patronage was a factor especially with the members of the lesser nobility, the gentry. Among the 320 nobles participating in the 2 September protest letter to Constance were 287 members of the gentry representing 240 families. Almost all of these made their homes in south eastern Bohemia, a region bordered on the north by Litomyšl and on the south by Moravia and the baronial domains of the Rožmberk and Hradec families. This region corresponds roughly to the Litomyšl diocese and the Kouřím archdeaconry in the Prague diocese. We saw that the church owned a much higher percentage of patronage in Litomyšl than it did in the Prague diocese, namely close to fifty percent compared to twenty-eight. A similar, though less accentuated pattern appears in the Kouřím archdeaconry, where the church owned 34.5 percent, six points above the average for the diocese.

Turning to individuals we find a corresponding pattern; a large number of Hussite nobles had not had a chance to exercise the right of patronage and undoubtedly hoped that in a Hussite reformed church they might be able to regain lost rights. This is illustrated by the following figures. Nine of the thirty-three Hussite barons had no church and eight had only one. In other words, over half were patron to one church or to none at all. With respect to the gentry, the 240 families represented on the September protest letter made up almost seventeen percent of the 1433 gentry families living in Bohemia at the beginning of the fifteenth century.[26] As table 1 above shows, the gentry as a whole owned patronage to 731 parishes. The Hussite gentry owned only forty-three of these, that is, not quite six percent, more than ten percentage points below what they would have held if they had owned patronage in proportion to their number.[27]

For the nobility of eastern Bohemia the abstract issue of the clergy's ownership of property became concrete in their relationship to Bishop John of Litomyšl. His twenty-nine churches placed him fourth among individuals, behind the king, the lord of Rožmberk and the archbishop of Prague, as the owner of patronage. Several of the Hussite barons were his immediate neighbours. We will refer to the quarrels that Čeněk and Boček had with him over material issues. In a similar vein, the Hussite squire, John of Popovice, had reason to resent the bishop's secular lordship and use of force. Sometime before 1410, in an altercation with the elder Popovice, Ješik, Bishop John forcefully seized several estates and villages including the family fortress, Pušice. Ješik, who had been in several other scraps, as the price for royal intervention and pardon lost Pušice to the king.[28] At Constance Bishop John had been one of the loudest voices from Bohemia calling for Hus' condemnation. When the news that Hus had been burned reached Bohemia, the gentry from the vicinity of Litomyšl gave free rein to their anger and pent up grievances by attacking and plundering the bishop's estates.[29] These men obviously welcomed the prospects of applying Hussite ideology, which denied the clergy the right of secular lordship, to the bishop of Litomyšl.

The church's ownership of patronage was not the only factor contributine to the eastern nobility's action on behalf of Hus. If this were so it would be difficult to explain the inactivity of the gentry in southwestern Bohemia, especially around Týn Horšův where the clergy also owned a higher percentage of patronage than the average. Perhaps because the west was more germanized the nobility there was repelled by the strong Czech tendencies of the reform movement. There is however an additional explanation. The sending of the letter of protest, although reflecting the religious sentiments of the participants, was also a political act. The main draft was drawn up in Prague where the barons attached their seals to it. Copies of the letter were then submitted to the gentry meeting in at least three regional assemblies where the local squires appended their seals to it.[30] Since the king was not involved in the protest, the calling of these diets required the gentry's own initiative. Those in the south-east, of all the gentry in Bohemia, were most used to acting independently. The reason for this was that there existed no really large noble landholdings as there were farther south and north and no large royal domains as in central and western Bohemia. There were only the modest baronial estates of Lipnice, Vlašim and Chlum. Larger baronial estates like Šternberk, Holice, Poděbrady and Bydžov were farther north or east and not in the immediate vicinity from which came the protesting gentry. Not feeling the dominating presence of barons or king the gentry throughout the years had become accustomed to independent political action. As a result they were prepared to act in defiance of the international community and church on behalf of a man like Hus who expressed their religious feelings including the prohibition against the Church owning patronage.

This reservoir of support among the nobility in addition to the fact that this estate owned patronage to the majority of parishes, suggests that the Hussite university masters had much to gain in pursuing their friendship. As we shall see, however, before 1412 noble activity on behalf of reform was limited to requests that the masters be allowed to read Wyclif's works and to freely preach, initiated by noble students at the university. Similarly until 1417 the nobility used its right of patronage on behalf of the Hussite movement only to a limited extent. The reason for this was that the Hussites had made little attempt to enlist their aid.

The results of the study of ownership of patronage explain the early lack of interest on the part of the Hussite masters in the nobility. They knew that, although the nobility as a whole controlled access to the majority of parishes, it did not own patronage to the ones they wanted, namely those in the city of Prague. The reformers had a strong bias in favour of the city and the king. Matthew of Janov, a fourteenth century reformer preferred to live and work in Prague rather than in his rural parish from which he drew an income.[31] The partiality of the Czech reformers for the Prague prebends and university offices was best expressed by Jerome of Prague, a graduate of the university from the 1390s. In 1416 when he explained to the audience at the Council of Constance some of the actions of his fellow countrymen he revealed that part of his colleagues' discontent stemmed from the fact that these city offices were beyond their reach. He said "In the University of Prague there were many Germans, in church prebends and in the colleges, to the point that the Czechs had nothing. Hence when a Czech graduated in arts, if he had no other source of income he had to earn his livelihood by being a school master in some town or village."[32] Since Prague was a royal city the Hussites were right to assume that the king could determine the filling of church livings there even if he were not their legitimate patron. When events forced him to it after 1414, he twice permitted such uncanonical transfer of offices in Prague in favour of Hussites.[33] Similarly it was the king, whose father Charles IV had founded the university, who could deliver control of its administration into the hands of the reformers as he did in 1409. In Prague the nobility owned patronage to only four of the forty-four parishes and to twenty-six of the 216 altars. Hence it was hardly worth the reformers' efforts to cultivate their support for reasons of patronage. It made more sense to concentrate on winning the king who in one person could provide them with both offices and secular power to protect them and their reform program.

However when they in 1412 lost the king's favour because of their opposition to the sale of indulgences, the nobility became more attractive as allies. Indeed the reformers received aid from some of the most influential barons in the land. But since even their powerful friends, like Čeněk of Vartemberk and Boček of Poděbrady, failed to win the nobility as an estate, they were not able to utilize the governmental institutions of the land. As a result the attempt of the Hussite leadership to provide the movement with legitimacy throughout the land had to be abandoned. This failure became clear in 1417, and henceforth all that Hussite nobles could do for the reformers was to protect them on their own domains and in their churches. These developments, beginning with the nobility's feud with King Wenceslas IV in the 1390s are examined next.

CHAPTER 4
THE NOBILITY'S FEUD
WITH KING WENCESLAS IV: 1394-1405

The late medieval system of government was characterized by a dualism between the estates (nobles, clergy and townspeople) and monarch. One aspect of this arrangement was an almost constant rivalry between nobles and king seeking control over the governmental apparatus of the land. The struggles were over political power to which economic well-being, then as now, was closely tied. The degree to which a ruler controlled the machinery of government, such as law courts and administrative offices, determined to a large extent his success in collecting his feudal dues and incomes. The noble dominated estates of course sought to restrain his powers in order to protect their lands from royal claims. The feuds in Bohemia of the late fourteenth century are one of the better illustrations of the economic roots of the political struggles between barons and king which marked so much of late medieval political life.

Wenceslas IV's ideas on royal government in many ways resembled what already existed in England. There the late medieval feudal system, according to J.M.W. Bean, was a fiscal arrangement whose most important feature was the body of legal rights which the lord enjoyed over the lands held from him. These rights entitled him to a share of the revenues from the lands which he received on the following occasions. He could collect a fee at his eldest son's knighting, at his eldest daughter's wedding and for ransom money in the event of his capture. In addition, and this was relatively rare, the land reverted to the lord if the tenant died without heirs or committed a felony. Furthermore, when the tenant died leaving an adult heir, the lord collected a relief payment before he accepted the new tenant's homage. Finally, if the tenant died leaving a minor heir, the lord received custody of the child's person and inheritance. The latter right, the right of wardship, was the most important in the later middle ages, because unlike the first three where the fees became fixed in the thirteenth century, wardship, in permitting the guardian to administer the incomes of the estate and marry off the ward, did not decrease in value because of inflation.[1]

Feudal tenure was almost unknown in Bohemia before the fourteenth century. It was brought there by the Luxemburg monarchs, first as a device used by King John (1310-1346) to raise cash by granting royal lands to be held from him for a fee.[2] His grandson, Wenceslas IV, resumed the effort but his tactics were radically different. He claimed the right to impose the body of legal rights, the feudal fiscal system enjoyed by monarchs further west, upon the lands the nobles regarded as their own held in free tenure. Using governmental machinery when possible and force when necessary, King Wenceslas on several occasions deprived baronial families of property. The barons, threatened at the base of their existence, namely with the loss of their estates, formed several armed leagues in an effort to put a stop to what they regarded as the king's abrogation of customary practices. In order to expose better the nature of the nobles' grievances it is necessary to look at the legal and administrative structure of medieval Bohemia.

The polity of Bohemia corresponded to that of the late medieval land to which Otto Brunner gave the classic description.[3] According to this, the land or land-community (*Landesgemeinde*) was a political structure consisting of all land owners and had a unified system of laws and customs defined by the land court. The king or prince was the wealthiest and most powerful landowner and as such the most dynamic force in determining the intent and expression of the land's law. But he could not define the law alone and if the land-community felt he had violated its rights and law, it had the right to resist the ruler with arms.[4]

In Bohemia the dualistic relationship between the duke as ruler and a group of powerful nobles (*potentes*) existed as early as the tenth century. The noble class was independently powerful. Its members owned their own great estates and did not in general owe their position to the king as was the case in parts of Germany.[5] Their economic independence gave them a great deal of political clout; as in most medieval lands they elected their king and then dominated his governing council. King Přemysl II (1253-1278) found out how dependent he was on them when he tried to govern without them. They subverted his foreign aims in Carinthia and Carniola leading to his defeat and death in battle against the Habsburgs.[6]

Until the thirteenth century one governmental apparatus had been sufficient to provide the administrative and judicial needs of the land-owners including the king. But as the interests and needs of the crown diverged more and more from those of the land, the kings developed a separate administration. The appearance of a new type of landowner, one who held land in fief from the king, hastened this division. By the fourteenth century two spheres in the Bohemian polity, the royal (*dvorský*) and the land (*zemský*) had become official each with its own offices and district.[7]

The royal government had jurisdiction over ecclesiastical lands, royal towns and royal estates including those held in fief. In this sphere the king was sovereign and absolute ruler. He did not need the approval of a diet when he levied a tax and the assemblies of his vassals which he did call were not deliberative sessions in which they had an effectual voice, but rather occasions where the king's will was pronounced. In disputes and other matters concerning property held in fief from the king, his vassals were responsible to the king's court (*dvorský soud*) and had no recourse to the land court.[8]

In the land government, on the other hand, the king was only first among equals. The highest power was the land court (*zemský soud*), to which even the king could be cited, and a four member committee of officials. These played important roles in the court during its sessions and exercised authority in the intervening period. The land court met four times a year in Prague and its meetings merged with the land diet especially during the reign of Wenceslas IV who called no special diet.[9]

All free landholders, knights and nobles were under the jurisdiction of the land court and of the justices in the rural districts. Members of the upper nobility were responsible only to this court unless they held lands in fief from the king. The cases of the gentry were heard in the land court proper only if the issue exceeded a value of 600 groschen. Their other cases were heard in the lower court which was administered by lesser but also noble officials.[10]

At the head of the land government, between sessions of the court, was the committee of four chief officials. Their functions and duties during the land court's sitting made it possible for them to affect if not determine its decisions. The office of the chief burgrave (*nejvyšší purkrabí pražský*) was in some ways the most powerful. It was up to him to summon the armies necessary to keep peace in the land. In addition, he presided over the land court in the king's absence.[11] The fact that the nobles were able to persuade the chief burgrave, Lord Otto of Bergov, to join their cause was crucial for their success. In 1394 Otto used the armed forces which he had called up to subdue a disturbance in the west, to instead take the king captive. He was alone among the four officials to defect from the royal cause. The others all remained friends of King Wenceslas and it was their friendship which up to 1394 facilitated the king's efforts to use the normal governmental machinery of both land and royal spheres, in pursuit of his goals. The second official, the chief chamberlain (*nejvyšší komorník*), was responsible for issuing citations, arranging the investigations, conducting the case and pronouncing the verdict.[12] The third official was the chief judge (*nejvyšší sudí*). It was up to him to see to it that during the court's proceedings all ancient legal formalities were observed and that both sides were treated fairly. He named the members of the jury who met for consultation and then gave their advice as to what the verdict should be.[13] Finally, the chief notary (*nejvyšší písař*), with his secretaries, was responsible for the correct recording and reading of all court actions.[14]

Present at the sessions of the court were the king, the princes of the royal house, the archbishop and his suffragans, the four chief officials of the land and all the members of the noble estates who took the trouble to travel to Prague. The actual judicial and legal work of the court was done by members of the leading families, that is, those who held the office of justice in the provinces or districts into which the kingdom was divided. From their ranks the chief judge chose a jury on whose counsel the verdict was based.[15] In addition to playing the prominent role in the land court, the district justices (*popravci* or *justiciarii provinciarum*) were also responsible for the administration of the law in rural Bohemia. The king appointed the justices, although in many cases he was obligated to choose them from certain ancient and venerable baronial families who had a hereditary claim to the offices. The justices were assisted in their administrative work by court-councillors (*konšelé zemští*) who were chosen from among the gentry.[16]

During the interregnum, after the death of Přemysl II in 1278, royal power suffered severely as a committee of barons in effect ruled the land. The decline of royal power continued under the reign of the first Luxemburger, John, who at his accession granted the nobles political concessions and alienated royal property into their hands.[17] His son Charles IV and grandson Wenceslas IV tried to reverse this trend and undermine the nobles' political power. Charles succeeded in gaining back some of the royal property and Wenceslas, with the cooperation of friendly nobles and townspeople was well on his way to bringing the land government under his control before the remaining nobles forcefully stopped him.

Charles began his drive to restore royal power by buying back castles and estates which had either been pawned or sold to magnates by his predecessors. He raised the money through taxes and feudal dues, applied especially to church institutions and by pawning other less strategic property. He had completed the task to his satisfaction by 1353. At the same time he tried to establish the crown as the peacekeeper in the land by using force even against nobles to quell violence. He also increased his control over the provincial justices, regulating their sphere of jurisdiction and, where he could, appointing men from the non-noble classes who were loyal to him. Where these offices remained in noble hands he weakened the power of individuals by adding to the number of men responsible for a district including among them nobles friendly to him.[18]

Charles also attempted to undermine the nobles' position by drafting a statement of Bohemia's land law, the *Majestas Carolina*. In addition to interpreting the law from a standpoint favourable to the king, a written law threatened to undermine the nobility as a law interpreting body in the land court. With no definitive body of law to resort to the nobles' claim to be the final interpreters of the land's custom was hard to challenge. However, once the law was in writing it would have given rise to an educated class of lawyers and judges competent to define its meaning by virtue of their superior knowledge and training. These would have replaced the noble landowners who as representatives of the land-community had traditionally defined its law. It comes as no surprise that the nobility declined to ratify the *Majestas* at a diet in 1355 and persuaded Charles to remove it in favour of observing the "old and customary law."[19]

At his accession in 1378 King Wenceslas resumed the attack on the nobility's power. His approach was more systematic than his father's and at first more successful. On 27 July 1381 he watered down the power of the nobles holding the offices of provincial justice by increasing the number of offices from twelve to nineteen. The officials of royal towns were placed in charge of all seven of these new offices and an eighth one, that of Plzeň, which traditionally had been held by the noble Švamberk family, was also granted to the officials of that royal city. The existing justices and officials were instructed to assist them in the exercise of their office and not to impede them.[20] In several cases the king's action struck especially close to the nobles' power in that a city such as Budě-jovice, in the south which received one of the offices was near the domains of the baronial Rožmberk family.

There are two other sources which reflect the king's efforts to weaken the power of the noble estate. One is a satirical poem, the *Nova Rada*, written by a nobleman, Smil of Pardubice in 1384[21] and the other is Wenceslas' response in 1394 to the twenty-one demands submitted to him by the nobility.[22] The general tenor of the nobility's complaints shows that the king had subverted the institutions of land government so that instead of serving the nobility's interests they served his. He had not made any basic institutional changes but had manipulated his friends into important offices. These men helped him gain favourable verdicts in the land court or if this failed made it possible for him to ignore it. For over fifteen years King Wenceslas in this way kept the nobility off balance and on the defensive.

Smil of Pardubice isolated three complaints against the king. According to him Wenceslas had opened his council to foreigners. He had permitted men to buy positions in the land court, men who were amenable to bribery and did not carry out justice. Finally, he complained that the king, acting as feudal lord, claimed his right of reversion, requisitioning property when its owners died apparently without heirs. With lands thus gained the king rewarded his favourites without respecting the wishes of the former owner and those of his family and friends.[23]

The nobles' demands submitted to the king repeated Smil's complaints but added others. They charged that the king had restrained the land court's freedom to judge and execute its decisions. Furthermore, he and his officials had interfered with the rights of heirs at the deaths of landowners and seized outright property of widows and orphans or claimed wardship when there were legal guardians or kinfolk (Nos. 4, 19). The king had ignored custom and placed men, not entitled to them, into offices administering both the royal and the land records (*dvorské* and *zemské desky*), that is, the books in which were recorded property titles held in fief and those in free tenure (Nos. 5, 6, 7).[24] As a result the nobles could not have faith that the records showed the true status of a given piece of property, whether it was held freely or in fief. In general, Wenceslas had strengthened royal government to the point that in disputes concerning property and inheritances the king's claims to rights and feudal incidents enjoyed by monarchs in England and France, received support from the legal and judicial apparatus. But the king's success proved his undoing; when he used his political position to attack the nobility's economic base, it rose up against him.

Between 1394 and 1403 the nobility concluded a series of armed leagues among themselves with which they brought the king around to their views on how the realm should be governed. The nobles were joined by two members of the royal house, King Sigismund of Hungary, the king's half-brother, and Margrave Jošt of Moravia, his cousin. The latter's brother Procop and Wenceslas' other brother, John, were loyal to the royal cause. Both nobles and king had support from among the gentry. Some seventeen lesser noblemen signed the truce with the king on 15 June 1399 as members of the noble league and ten others did so on behalf of the royal party.[25] One of the leaguing gentry, Wenceslas of Radím, also enjoyed rights of citizenship in Kutna Hora, a royal city.

The primary concern of the nobles was to regain control of governmental offices. Six of the twenty-one articles submitted to the king in 1394 concerned the filling of important positions. Point fifteen reads,

"The office of the burgrave of Prague is to be held by a native lord of the land, as of old, . . . And the same goes for the other offices that the lords have held from of old—in all such offices a native born lord is to be named."[26] In addition they required that the officials keeping both the land and the royal records, as well as the chief notary be chosen by a council of lords. The demands of the nobles also focused on the administration of justice in the land. They required that the king cease trying to circumvent the land court, that its traditional procedure be restored and that its decisions be carried out.[27] With respect to the intervention of royal officials in the work of the noble justices in the districts, the nobles demanded that "only the duly approved justices, as ordained of old" were to execute the legal punishments and that the ancient system of court councillors was to be reinstituted. The justices were to apply the law according to the old custom without any hindrance.[28]

In taking their action against the king the nobility regarded itself as acting on behalf of the land-community of Bohemia. The text of their league of 5 May 1394 stated "that all will and intend to be united and seek the good of the land, and to promote and effect true justice in the land and always to stand by it together, so as zealously to keep as our goal the entire welfare of the land."[29] Although the barons acted above all in pursuit of goals for their own class, they also sought to guarantee certain rights for the clergy and gentry as well as for the general population. On behalf of the gentry they specifically required that "the new practice of making the gentry pay duties and sales taxes in royal towns be discontinued, inasmuch as it had not existed formerly."[30] For the benefit of Archbishop John of Jenštejn, a friend of two of the leaguers, Henry of Rožmberk and John of Michalovice, who at this time was pursuing his own quarrel with the king over the issue of ecclesiastical independence, the nobles called for an end to unlawful secular intervention against the clergy. The remaining articles took up specific points such as customs and tolls, debts to Jews, property rights, violence on the highways and rights of orphans.

While aimed at the growing royal government, the nobles' attack was also directed against the increasing power of the towns which in the late middle ages threatened the dominance of nobles and princes throughout Europe.[31] Thus in 1397, in a statement addressed to the king, the nobility expressed its dislike for townspeople in royal government by contrasting Wenceslas unfavourably with his father Charles, who, they claimed, "did not summon a cohort of burghers and labourers to serve in his high council."[32]

With respect to royal-noble relations in late medieval Europe, the question has been asked whether certain kings had a deliberate policy designed to undermine the status of a class of nobles. Answering in the affirmative, K.B. McFarlane showed that Edward I of England (1272-1307) used violence and other illegal means to deprive comital families of land and inheritances necessary for maintaining an earldom.[33] Similarly, C.A.J. Armstrong concluded that the Burgundian princes from 1363 to 1477 pursued a policy eliminating any challenge to their authority from the nobility.[34]

King Wenceslas too launched a systematic attack on the landholdings of the nobility. Historians[35] who have dealt with noble-king relations in Bohemia have paid scant attention to the economic consequences for the nobility of the king's political gains. The fact that the records of the land court were largely destroyed by fire in 1541 renders difficult such a study. Nevertheless the late August Sedláček, who devoted most of his life to a study of the Bohemian nobility, combing both foreign and domestic archives for any information pertaining to it, has given us a comprehensive survey of the histories of the Bohemian landowning families.[36] His work is a chronological history of the owners of castles, fortresses and estates. Its main weakness is the lack of analysis and synthesis of the data which he left in its raw form so that general themes of development remain hidden and need to be unearthed. One such theme is the economic difficulties faced by the nobility as a result of King Wenceslas' subversion of the Bohemian land polity which we have described above. The effects of the king's action are best illustrated by looking at the lives of several of the individuals who participated in the feuds with the king from 1394 to 1405.

The nineteenth point of the nobles' demands speaks almost word for word to the grievances of Lord John of Michalovice who joined the noble league at its beginning on 5 May 1394. It stipulated that no one was to take over orphans by force nor to marry them off forcibly before they had come of age. Guardianship was to be left to the nearest of kin or to those who had a right to it.[37] Lord John had had previous disagreements with the king over property. His father, Peter, had found it necessary in 1361 to offer the free estate of Úštěk to Emperor Charles to be held by himself in feudal tenure as a *fief de reprise*. This was a requirement of Charles before he granted Peter joint tenancy over Velešín, with a distant female relative, the last living member of her line. Peter's intention was to keep Velešín from devolving to the king and thus losing it entirely. Another domain of the Michalovice family, Boleslav, was originally royal, but in 1317 King John yielded his rights. His successors, Charles and Wenceslas, however did not recognize his action. When John Michalovice, earlier in the fourteenth century, wanted to mortgage Boleslav he had to have the king's permission just as his grandson John did in 1391 when he wanted to get the right to hold markets for the town.[38] After Peter's death, while his son John was still a minor, the estates of Velešín and Úštěk were administered by the royal courtier Těma of Koldice who exploited them for his own gain so that when John came of age in 1379 he was faced with financial difficulties to the point that he had to sell Velešín. In addition he was forced to mortgage Úštěk, which he did to a friend of the king, Henry Škopek of Dubá in whose family it remained. Furthermore Těma had evidently married either John to one of his kin or one of John's sisters to his kinsman, Albert of Koldice.[39] Because the land court was hardly functioning, John could not get his case heard and had to accept the king's verdict that Boleslav was a royal fief. The quarrel between John and the king had erupted once in 1384 at which time a royal army attacked the former's castle. The king backed off only when several leading nobles threatened to cut off the head of the captain of the royal army should they catch him.[40]

The family of William of Landštejn, who also joined the baronial pact in 1394, had likewise had a dispute with the king over property. In 1341 William's grandfather offered to hold Landštejn from King John in fief for the time of his own life. After his death Emperor Charles confirmed the original freedoms and rights of the Landštejn family there. However, in 1381 King Wenceslas claimed Landštejn by reason of devolution, even though the family had not died out, and gave it to the Styrian Lord of Krajek.[41] King Wenceslas evidently ignored his father's confirmation of the Landštejn freedoms and the land court was helpless or unwilling to protect a baron's free domain. William, until 1390 a provost in the Vyšehrad chapter, and a minor, left the clerical estate in order to take over his family's other allodial property, the Lipnice domain. Since his father's death in 1380 it had been administered by the king's friend, Henry Škopek.[42]

Smil Flaška of Pardubice (and of Richenburk), the author of the allegorical work charging royal officials with using their offices for their material gain, was educated at the University of Prague and abroad.[43] He joined the noble league on 10 January 1395. His writing reflected his own experience, having personally suffered at the hands of the king's men. In 1387 his family had lost part of its domain to the crown which had claimed it, again by reason of devolution. The king's claim was based on the title which Vznata of Skuhrov had to the property of Smil's father, William. Vznata's title was based either on a loan made to William or on the fact that he married one of his daughters. In any case when Vznata died in 1384 without leaving any heirs, the crown claimed two free family estates, Pardubice and Stará.[44] William contested this in the court but failing to find satisfaction pursued his case by means of a violent feud with the king. In the end, in 1390, he had to give up to the king one-sixth of his domain, namely Pardubice and some surrounding villages. This was given to the royal courtier, John of Milheim, a German burgher of Prague. In this case the land court was able to intervene on his behalf and keep the king from taking all.

William died at about the time the dispute came to an end. Because of the expenses incurred Smil had to sell Stará in 1393, keeping Richenburk as his family residence. In order to avoid a similar situation for his heirs in the case of his death, he placed his estate in public trust for 60,000 groschen to two later members of the baronial league, Boček of Poděbrady and Otto of Bergov. According to the agreement they were to get the estate if he died without natural heir.[45]

Peter Vartemberk of Kost, although formerly a member of the royal council, joined the baronial league on 5 June 1394. While for some the fate of his brother Marquart illustrated the king's intention to keep peace in the land, for the nobility it boded only ill. In 1390, after refusing the king's suggested settlement, all three of his castles, Zbiroh, Rohozec and Žleby were taken from him forcibly by the king. He died two years later, propertyless and a broken man. The first two estates had been free. In 1356 Žleby had been sold to the king by Anežka the daughter of Hynek of Lichtenburk, the previous owner, on the condition that she could continue to enjoy its incomes until her death, which came just after 1370.[46] In 1377 Marquart was the lord of Žleby. It is not known by what title, and most likely his feud with the king was related to the uncertain status of the domain.[47] The spectacular defeat of Marquart, even though the king's claim may have had some justification, clearly left its impression on the rest of the nobility, not least of which on his brother Peter.

Herman of Lopata, who joined the rebels on 18 January 1400, also did so after he had lost property to the king. Sometime before 1377 he built the Lopata castle on a small free estate which he had just purchased. Although he was not a member of the earlier leagues his sympathies most likely lay with the barons for he soon found himself under attack from the king's troops. On 3 December 1397 Margrave Procop, as captain of the royal armies, laid siege to Lopata. After capturing it Procop placed his garrison on it. Lord Herman was apparently the victim of a trade off because Lopata was left to the king in the final settlement and Herman did not regain possession of it.[48]

Several other members of the baronial league also experienced financial difficulties although these were not always the responsibility of the king. The two brothers Boreš Jr. and Sr. of Osek (Riesenburk) were perhaps the first to revolt. They held no land in free tenure and because of debts they were forced to give up the estate which the family had held in fief from the king since 1339. Both brothers, along with the lords of Švamberk and some local squires, in April 1394 attacked the fortress in Toužím, belonging to the Premonstratensian monastery in Milevsko, robbing it and taking the abbot captive.[49] The armies called up by the chief Prague burgrave, Otto of Bergov, allegedly to punish this act, were instead turned against the king who was taken captive by the noble league.[50] Similarly, the Častolovice family felt the financial pinch so that near the end of his life, Půta Sr., in 1391 had to give up the Náchod estate which he held in fief from the king. His son Půta Jr. joined the noble leaguers on 5 June 1394.[51] John Vartemberk of Děčín joined the pact of January 1400. His relationship with King Sigismund may have brought him into the nobles' camp as much as anticipated material advantages. He had served Sigismund in Brandenburg in 1395 and to pay for expenses incurred there he had to pawn part of his allodial domain to his brothers. Later in 1400 he mortgaged Střekov castle which he held in fief from the king and which he was unable to redeem within the year agreed upon.[52]

While some baronial families of long standing had suffered as a result of King Wenceslas' policy, others had gained. The example of Henry Škopek of Dubá is illustrative of how a baron might enrich himself in the service of the king. Henry's father Albert shared the small but free estate of Libešice with his five brothers. The inheritance could obviously not maintain the brothers on a very high standard of living. Despite its small landholding the family had sufficient prestige so that two of the brothers, Albert and Zbyněk, had a place on the land court, a right reserved to those of the baronial class. In 1350 the family divided into two branches, those of Libešice and the Škopeks. The latter evidently sought their fortune in royal service. In 1376 Henry Škopek was the master of the royal court, a largely ceremonial office, receiving thereafter also the more substantive position, the captaincy of the royal city Wroclaw in Silesia. In addition the King favoured him by naming him the guardian of several estates which he had claimed by right of devolution. By 1387 royal service had provided Henry with enough capital to underwrite the mortgage of the large Úštěk domain which hereafter passed into his family's possession. The next year he bought the large Kostomlaty estate from the lord of Žirotin who held it in fief from the king.[53] Henry died in 1395 but his sons, Henry and Albert, were able to retain the wealth and status gained with the help of the king even though for Wenceslas himself the outcome of the baronial wars was not at all favourable.

The nobles were in general successful in improving their status and role within the polity of the realm. Periodically in the course of the struggle they forced the king to a truce in which a council of nobles was created to help govern the kingdom.[54] This was also the case in the last truce of 12 August 1401. According to it Archbishop Olbram, Henry of Rožmberk, Otto of Bergov and John Krušina of Lichtenburk were named to the council.[55] Its responsibilities were to fill those government positions whose holders were drawn from the gentry[56] and to dismiss any officials with whom they were not satisfied. It was also to have the deciding word in the disbursement of moneys for the needs of the kingdom, including those spent by the king. Royal officials and towns were to swear obedience to the council.[57]

Further aspects of the settlement had to await the end of the last violence committed against King Wenceslas. In the spring of 1402 King Sigismund, his brother, carried Wenceslas off captive to Vienna with the cooperation of Henry of Rožmberk and Bishop John of Litomyšl, two allies in the noble unity. Other members of the earlier leagues, Boček of Poděbrady and John Krušina of Lichtenburk, opposed the action and fought for the king's release which they accomplished in November 1403. The character of the episode, as Bartoš illustrated, appears to have been more a step taken by Sigismund for his own aims than one in which the nobility were involved seeking ends for their estate.[58]

The second part of the settlement was reached early in 1405. At this time the demand which the nobles had made in 1396, that the royal cities give up the right to execute justice independently of the nobility in the districts, was carried into effect. In December the land court had shown that it was no longer a tool of the king. With the nobility in control it ruled against the king depriving him of the disputed castle, Žirotín, and delivered the verdict that henceforth officials of the royal cities were to act only in counsel with the district justices who were in the future to be noblemen.[59]

The settlement restricted the king's authority to his own lands. The four chief officials of the land government, drawn from the old noble families of the land, dominated the royal council. Even the chief judge of the royal court, Břeněk of Skála, was a noble who had participated in the revolts. On the other hand, in questions of foreign relations the king retained his prerogative. These he entrusted to his own chosen members

of the council, men for whom he did not need the barons' consent.[60]
Later, in 1415 when they felt the Council of Constance had insulted the
Czech crown, the Hussite nobles extended the sphere of their activity as
they presumed to speak even on behalf of the Czech kingdom and people
to the international community.

According to F.M. Bartoš, the control which the nobles gained over
the district justices further reflected the victory of the nobles over the
king because "by far the majority of the justices were former members
of the noble league" and hence personal enemies of the king.[61] Although
the noble revolts resulted in a clear victory for that estate, appointment as a
district justice cannot be construed as a personal victory for the participants.

A study of the chart of office holders (See Appendix II) shows that
only eight of the twenty-one men appointed to the office of justice on
5 January 1405 were known members of the league. Four, including the
royal burgraves, had been loyal to the king. The remaining nine played no
known role in the revolts and were most likely neutral. Only in two
districts were all the justices former rebels: in the southern district of
Bechyně and in the east, in Upper Mýto. The latter was held by John
Krušina of Lichtenburk, and the king's enmity was certainly mellowed as
a result of the aid which John offered him in his escape from captivity in
1403. At least three districts were filled exclusively by the king's friends.

The same chart offers further evidence that the nobles' pro- or anti-
royal attitude during the wars was not a significant factor in their appointment to office. Only five or six of the thirty families who traditionally
held the district offices were not appointed in 1405. One was the Lacembok-Chlum family, the others were the lords of Osek, these of Skálá-
Švihov and those of Švamberk. The Lacembok-Chlum family had
fought for the king hence one cannot explain their absence as a result of
his hostility.[62] The other three families traditionally held the districts
of Žatec and Plzeň in western Bohemia, but in their places were named
men who had been loyal to the king. The lords of Osek continued to
fight with the king until 1418 and the lords of Svamberk and Skálá-
Švihov until 1414.[63] The fact that no one of these families was named as
justice reflects the fact that their differences with the king had not yet
been resolved.

The principle which governed who was appointed district justice was
that of tradition. Those who had held the office for years, by virtue of
substantial landholdings in the region, acquired it again in 1405   regardless of whether they had fought for or against the king. In regions where
the king's lands and castles dominated, his castle burgraves administered

justice along with the nobility if it too owned property in the area. The question at issue in the revolts was the control of the institutions of land government. The Luxemburger monarchs, especially Wenceslas IV, in the fourteenth century had extended their authority into the land sphere, which the nobility regarded as its own by tradition. For the nobility there was however more at stake than the right to execute the law on their domains. They were spurred to action by the threat of losing their hereditary possessions on which their livelihoods depended. Their success in curtailing the king's power marked the beginning of a trend which culminated in the nobility gaining complete mastery of the Bohemian polity after 1471. This trend was, however, interrupted by the Hussite revolution, whose forces the nobility helped unleash. In order to better understand the relationship between the politics of the baronial revolts in the 1390s and those associated with the Hussite reform movement in 1414-1415 it will be helpful to turn our attention to the activities of the nobles in the years 1405-1415.

After the nobles had taken control of the land government they were in a strong position to influence public policies and actions. As the religious issues raised by the Hussites began to dominate discussions in the kingdom, resulting sometime in strife and violence, it was logical to expect the nobility to intervene in the interest of the land. In dealing with the religious disputes one of the factors influencing the behaviour of the nobility, especially its leadership, was how to maintain and extend its position as arbiter, a role in which nobles determined what was good for Bohemia. The question was, which side to support: the Hussites or the church? There were advantages to each. Hussite ideology offered them, as the secular power, authority over the church and religious matters. The church on the other hand represented a stabilizing support to a social and economic structure which had and continued to reward the nobility relatively generously. Nobles answered the question individually. Those nobles who emerged from the feuds with the king in a weak position were found in both camps. Some supported the Hussites, others the traditional church and society. The same can be said for those nobles who experienced a direct increase in their power as a result of the revolts. Similarly the lines defining the two parties among the nobility, those for and those against the king, had little meaning during the years of Hussite agitation and revolution.

After reports of the death of John Hus reached Bohemia in 1415 the nobility of that country formed two separate leagues: the Hussite of 6 September and the Catholic of 1 October. The sequence of developments from 1390 to 1471 in which the nobles' political gains after the Hussite revolution corresponded to the goals for which they fought King Wenceslas has led historians to relate the pacts of 1415 to the earlier noble confederations. Some saw the nobility's involvement in the Hussite revolution as simply an extension of their previous feuds and as part of the perennial struggle for power between the two parties, nobles and king.[1]

Other historians, in a somewhat loose fashion, have suggested that the members of the Catholic league of 1415 were the same as those belonging to the anti-royal leagues of the 1390s. According to this scenario King Wenceslas grew bitter and resentful when in 1415 the Catholic nobles appeared before him and he recognized in them his old enemies, men still faithful to his half-brother King Sigismund, their ally in the earlier wars. As a result he lost his earlier inclination to support the Catholics.[2] Similarly František Kavka tried to establish a connection between the personalities involved in the wars against the king and those of the Catholic league by pointing out that four of its members had also participated in the baronial leagues of the 1390s.[3]

If we look at the issues and personalities which dominated the struggles of the two periods we find that the nobles were not a united group which continued smoothly in pursuit of its goals whose outlines had been charted in the 1390s. The lines of loyalty to monarch or to noble estate broke down and the individuals and families who aided the Hussites were not the same as those who opposed King Wenceslas. Furthermore, the goals and concepts for which the nobles fought differed significantly in each struggle.

That King Wenceslas had little reason to look upon either Hussite or Catholic leaque as representing the old baronial opposition becomes clear from a study of the individuals involved. The table in Appendix III contains the names of the nobles who participated in the feuds of the 1390s, those who joined the Hussite league, those of the Catholic league and those who, after King Wenceslas' death, sent letters of challenge to Hussite Prague in 1419-20 in an effort to pressure the city into deserting her revolutionary allies. The information shows that, first, at least nineteen of the thirty-one rebels had died by 1414. Secondly, the family of Čeněk of Vartemberk, the man who eventually picked up the trend towards increased noble power established by the leaders of the feuds, had not participated in the revolts. Thirdly, although there were indeed four members of the Catholic league who had also participated in the revolts against the king[4] so had three members of the Hussite pact.[5] In addition, five men who joined the Hussite league were the sons of men who had opposed the king in the 1390s whereas only one Catholic's father had done so. In other words the families of eight Hussites had been against the king compared to those of five Catholics. At least three families were split over the religious issue, of which only one, the Hradecs, had fought against the king.[6] Lastly, at least three members of the Catholic league came from families which had been loyal to the king.[7] As a result it is unlikely that the king thought of either league as being friendly or unfriendly to him on the basis of whether their members had been his friends or enemies in 1394. The lines and connections of the 1390s were washed away as nobles faced decisions on new issues which had been raised subsequently by the masters at the University of Prague, the home of Hussitism.

The reform movement in Bohemia consisted of three features which coalesced about the year 1400. They were the devotional pietism of people like Milič of Kroměříž (d. 1374) and Matthew of Janov, (d 1393) an emerging Czech self-consciousness and Wyclifite political ideology. The place where the ideas of the movement were worked out was the University, among the students and masters. The Hussites there had connections with the nobility, which, when the need arose, were turned into relatively extensive and crucial support for the reformers.

Fourteenth century Bohemian pietism was a search after a pure religious life patterned on the New Testament Church. Its adherents took various approaches in pursuit of their goal. They had before them the examples of medieval saints and mystics who through intense asceticism and mysticism claimed to have had union with God. Leaders of the religious renewal such as Thomas of Štitný, a squire who gave up the family estate and retired to Prague to write, translated and paraphrased the writings of people like St. Augustine, Hugh of St. Victor, St. Bernard of Clairveaux and Bridget of Sweden. Thus spiritual insights of Europe's leading religious thinkers became available to the people in Bohemia. Another Czech reformer, Matthew of Janov, also of gentry stock, wrote a mammoth interpretation of the New Testament outlining how Christians should live. In addition the reformers placed great emphasis on reading the Bible, both at home and in more formal fellowships, although it was not wholly translated into Czech until the fifteenth century.[8]

The faithful in Bohemia also received inspiration from the popular preachers including Milič of Kroměříz, John Hus (d. 1415), Jerome of Prague (d. 1416) and John Želivský (d. 1422) who presented many of the same ideas as the above writers. Milič was one of the more interesting persons. He gave up a good job in the imperial chancery for the priesthood and then renounced a lucrative sinecure benefice. He adopted a severely ascetic style of personal life giving up all his material possessions except for the clothes on his back. He attracted large audiences to his sermons in which he denounced the proud, those who accumulated wealth, who oppressed the poor and he criticized the loose sexual morals among both lay people and clergy. He identified the forces of sin with those of the anti-Christ who according to his interpretation of the Scriptures was to come just before the end of the world. Because he saw so much sin in his society Milič preached that the end was near. Milič not only preached but also acted so as to improve people's lives. With the help of a former prostitute, Keruše Hofart, who contributed two buildings, former brothels, he founded a community for prostitutes seeking a new life. With their source of income exhausted, these women needed material assistance which Milič with the help of Emperor Charles IV provided. Although these buildings, at his death were given to the clergy who opposed his ministry, Milič's community remained alive and eventually found a new building and new leaders in Bethlehem chapel and its preachers. It was here that John Hus began his ministry in 1402.[9]

Through his sermons Hus sought to prod the church to renewal in which Christians, clergy and lay people lived ethically and morally as had the Apostolic Church. It was clear to him and to his listeners that such a reform of religious life entailed a radical change in society as well. As his opponent at the Council of Constance, John Gerson, the chancellor of the University of Paris pointed out, Wyclifite and Hussite ideas on reform questioned not only existing ecclesiastical structures but the secular as well in that they led the untutored masses and the peasants to revolt and to rise up.[10] The adherents of Bohemian pietism then sought salvation through fellowship, meditation and reading of Scriptures and devotional literature, through listening to the Word of God being preached, through frequent communion and through acting in society bringing about real changes in people's lives.

The reformers fought for their vision of a reformed church at the university as well as in chapels and parishes. Most of the reformers at the university were Czech speaking students, a group which had increased in numbers more and more in the latter part of the fourteenth century. As they experienced that the opposition to their reform ideas came above all from non-Czechs they developed an increasing self-consciousness of themselves as a group which spoke the same language and sought the same goals. Hus himself frequently expressed his love for his country although not to the extent of setting it above what he understood to be God's cause. This is not to say that all Czechs at the University were Hussites. There was however a group, the most outspoken of whom was Jerome of Prague, which resented the domination of the university by foreigners, mostly German. Part of this group's discontent stemmed from the fact that aliens held most of the important and financially secure church sinecures and academic positions. When these foreigners used their positions to frustrate the Hussites' efforts at church reform they aggravated the anger felt by the Czechs. In this situation Jerome of Prague developed a concept of a community which combined nationality and right religion as prerequisites for membership. Those who were of Czech origin on both paternal and maternal sides and those who had an immaculate faith, that is who were supporters of the Wyclifite-Hussite reforms, were eligible for membership in what he called the sacrosanct Czech community. Not all Hussites went this far but a strong feeling for the Czech language and people came to be an important element in the Hussite reform movement in the early part of the fifteenth century.[11] The early preachers of reform such as Milič and Matthew of Janov had placed their hopes for improvement in individuals voluntarily changing their lives. By the end of the fourteenth century many of the reformers had come to realize that this approach was futile. They were therefore open to Wyclifite ideas on church reform which reached Bohemia at about the turn of the century. The teachings of the English academic, John Wyclif, provided the reformers with a political ideology according to which the secular power would be utilized to bring about reform. According to him the clerical estate and hierarchy were sinful just as were other people and the priestly office as such did not change this fact. Having invalidated the claim upon which the church based its expectation of obedience from the people, the Wyclifites proceeded to argue that ecclesiastics had no right to administer any sort of dominion over people and property. The clergy's role in society, they said, was to serve as examples of how one ought to lead a Christian life. To this end the Wyclifites in Bohemia, led by Hus, invited the monarch and the nobles to bring about reform by taking back the property endowments which their fathers had made to the church at the same time depriving it of any secular authority.[12] According to the reformers the church was to disappear as a separate administrative unit in the realm and the clergy was to be subject to the lay ruler. In England, where Wyclifism was born, the church was to be part of a realm at whose head governed a strong monarch. In Bohemia the Wyclifites also looked to the king for an alliance, and with considerably more success than in England. However when attempts to woo King Wenceslas proved futile, the Czechs could turn to the nobility, who after 1405 dominated the land government, and ask it to play the role relinquished by the king.

After Hus' death in 1415 there were several developments within Hussite ideology. Most important was the acceptance of utraquism, or the chalice as the symbol of the whole agenda of reform. While Hus was still alive a fellow reformer, Jakoubek of Stříbro, had begun serving wine to lay communicants along with the bread on the grounds that this had been the procedure of the Apostolic Church. The practice caught on and in March 1417 was declared by the University of Prague to be the correct one. Thereafter the chalice became the symbol, emblazoned on the weaponry of the revolutionaries wherever they went.[13] The Hussite program became more specific when in 1419, in response to an external threat the Hussites formulated the four articles of Prague which were a clarification of the minimum program. The articles stated the acceptance of communion in both bread and wine for the laity, that the Hussites stood for the free preaching of the word of God, that the clergy should give up pomp and lordship over temporal goods and that they stood for the purgation from the land of all "public mortal sins": This was the program around which the great majority of Hussites could unite for the purpose of fighting off the rest of Europe especially in the first two crusades in 1420 and 1421. In reality the Hussites were not nearly so united. On the one hand there were the conservatives such as the university master, John of Příbram, who agitated for reunion with the Roman Church wishing to retain only the practice of utraquism. His counterpart among the Prague radicals was John Želivský. Želivský made no significant doctrinal contribution. His great talent was to be able to lead the people to insist that the Hussites in fact implement the principles of the Apostolic Church for which they fought. The church should give up its property, priests should preach the gospel, believers should abandon the cult of saints and all the other practices and rites accumulated by the church of Rome throughout its history. He was a radical because he insisted in carrying Hussite principles into practice.[14]

In the countryside some of the most creative and brilliant minds were at work trying to conceptualize the nature of God's people on earth. One of the most important was the Taborite bishop, Nicholas of Pelhřimov who assumed the difficult task of defining the nature and spirit of the Apostolic Church. While Želivský could fulminate against his fellows because they did not abandon the rites and traditions of the Medieval Church, Nicholas undertook to organize a group of believers, who made their home in the fortress of Tabor, and formulate for them a theology consonant with their New Testament ideals while also taking into consideration the needs, social, political and economic, which they faced. His main insistence against the moderate and conservative Hussites was that their retention of the Roman rite of the mass was harmful to the worshippers; that lengthy prayers in a language not understood by the faithful left them bored and kept the priests from preaching. Instead the Taborite priests administered the Eucharist without elaborate dress and ceremony. Taborite religious services were marked by much preaching, congregational singing and readings of and discussions around the scriptures.[15] In choosing a ritual for worship the Taborites insisted that the Bible and not subsequent traditions of papal rulings be the guide.

Nevertheless Nicholas, in contrast to the Apostolic Church, sanctioned the use of force to back up the social, economic and political structure of the Taborite community. In addition there were men, more extreme and with smaller followings, like Peter of Chelčice and Martin Húska. Peter among other things questioned Tabor's reliance on military power to defend itself pointing out that the use of military and police force contradicted Nicholas' self proclaimed imitation of the New Testament Church. Martin similarly removed his community of believers from the establishment. According to him, religious life and ceremonies were not to be institutionalized and separated from everyday life. Hence the Eucharist was best observed when believers met for a normal meal at which time they talked about Jesus' acts of love and performed similar acts for one another. This activity transferred the participants into an elect of sinless men and women.[16] The nobility had this range of beliefs from which to choose. Most of them were allied with the moderate-conservative wing of Hussitism although one member of the gentry, Sigismund of Řepany followed Martin Húska. These developments however came later. During Hus' time the challenge from the reformers that the nobility use political power to reform the religious life of the land held unknown opportunities and pitfalls for that estate.

The Hussite message calling the people to be faithful to the Church of the New Testament had serious implications for the social and economic status enjoyed by the nobility. That this call was taken seriously by some nobles is reflected in the request some of them made to Hus for advice on certain social questions such as peasant property rights about which more will be said later.[17] The Hussites also called the nobility to new ways of conceptualizing the political community, concepts which were more inclusive than those which underlay the nobility's confederations of the 1390s.

As we noted above the noble pact of 1394 identified the nobles' interests with those of the land-community. The more comprehensive Hussite concept was best expressed by the university master, Jerome of Prague, who as part of the Hussite program elaborated a theory of the polity which included all classes. In 1409, at a disputation given at the university's anniversary, he declared that all "from the king to the knight, from the knight to the squire, from the squire to the peasant, from the archbishop to the canon, from the canon to the lowliest priest, from the mayor of this town to the counsellor and burgher, from the burgher to the lowliest worker, . . . " were members of what he called the sacrosanct

Czech community. Jerome left in tact the medieval social hierarchy but divested the upper estates of their exclusive right to represent the land. According to him the land was presented by people from all classes who spoke Czech and who had the proper faith, that is who supported church reform along Hussite lines.[18]

This broader concept of the polity was reflected in the letter of protest which the nobility sent to Constance in 1415 after Hus' condemnation and death. Despite Hus' common origins the nobles proudly claimed him as their "most beloved neighbour and fellowman."[19] Hus' enemies, the men responsible for his death, were also the enemies of the Bohemian kingdom and the nobles interpreted the Council's condemnation of this Czech peasant's son as an insult to "the most Christian Czech kingdom." All of this was not mere rhetoric, for in assuming the cause of John Hus the nobles laid themselves open to the charge of heresy. Both the Council of Constance and later Pope Martin V invited any defender of the faith in the role of a crusader to help himself to the property of the heretics, an invitation which, it was well known in Bohemia, many of Europe's nobility were all too eager to accept.[20]

In addition to the ideas raised by the reformers there were other events, issues and quarrels which replaced the hostilities of the 1390s and in which former enemies found themselves allied against common opponents. Most of the nobility maintained peaceful relations with the king. Those noble families whose grievances were not satisfied in the settlement of 1405 and who continued to feud with the king until just before the revolution were in general opposed to the Hussites. For them opposition to royal power was not identified with Hussitism. For further insight into the nature of the break between the two periods it will be helpful to look at the activities of some of the families involved.

Henry of Rožmberk, who is generally considered to have been the leader of the noble leagues,[21] did not occupy any office in the land government after 1405 except the position of the justice for the district of Bechyně, in the heart of his extensive domains in south Bohemia. A settlement in which the king allegedly made far reaching concessions to Henry has been shown to be a forgery with which later Rožmberks tried to establish certain claims.[22] Nevertheless the two men did live in peace and their cooperation extended to the suppression of those circles among the gentry who had supported the royal cause during the revolts. Many of these like John Žižka, the future commander of Hussite armies, continued their struggle against the power of the barons even though the help they hoped for from the king was not forthcoming.[23] In fact by 1412 the king was actively opposing rebellious gentry in cooperation with the barons. At that time he approached Lord Henry with a view to eradicating acts of violence in the kingdom. On 24 March the king wrote Henry for his counsel on how they might together work "against all those who rebel in the land and take and steal on the highways. . . ; for His Grace, (the king) with the help of God and the nobles. . . intends to avenge and stop these acts."[24] Some of the men responsible for the violence claimed to be acting on behalf of the king. With respect to them the king wrote that he wished to make short work of them and that "with divine and noble help he will really act in this affair and show such people that evil and impure people are not dear to him."[25] The king clearly did not wish to have anything to do with his allies among the discontented gentry and intended to keep his peace with the powerful baron.

There is some suggestion that Lord Henry favoured the Hussite reform movement. He died in July 1412 just after the quarrel over indulgences had broken out but before the nobles' action on behalf of the movement had gotten underway. Nevertheless, the fact that he used his right of patronage to provide several university masters and students with church livings suggests that he sympathized with the reformers. His wife, Eliška, a member of the Kravaře family of Moravia, of whom Lord Lacek was a strong supporter of Hus, was evidently inclined towards Hussitism. In 1418 she was the object of a warning from the Catholic theologian, Maurice Rvačka that she avoid the chalice as she would poison, a reference to the Hussite practice in which laymen and women took wine at communion.[26]

Bishop John of Litomyšl, another of the leading rebels, reached a settlement with the king at the same time as Rožmberk. Perhaps the best evidence for the reconciliation between the bishop and his king was the support King Wenceslas showed to John and his brother-in-law, Henry of Dubá, in 1413. The king ordered his troops to help Bishop John in his feud with Peter Malovec, a protégé of Čeněk of Vartemberk, declaring his willingness to attack Čeněk himself if need be. The king's accommodation with his former foe was not however unlimited. In 1418, albeit vainly, he opposed John's appointment to the coveted bishopric of Olomouc seeking to get papal confirmation for his friend, Aleš of Březí.[27]

John of Litomyšl was notorious in his opposition to the Hussite movement. If he was the same as the John of Šternberk, a canon of St. Vitus cathedral, he was an enemy of Hus from early times. About 1404 he had a lengthy dispute with John of Milheim, a benefactor of Bethlehem Chapel, who in 1402 presented John Hus there as a preacher.[28]

Bartoš described him as above all loyal to King Sigismund. He was the latter's candidate for the archbishopric of Prague but always lost it to King Wenceslas' men. Not all noble families lived in peace with the king. For these the issues which had led them to join the noble league in the first place, namely their precarious material standing, had not yet been favourably resolved by 1405. However since the more powerful barons had obtained satisfaction, those who had not had to continue their dispute with the king alone. These were the families of Osek, Švamberk, Skálá-Švihov and to a lesser extent Otto of Bergov. The first three families were all from the west where the king owned many strong castles allowing him to dominate the region to an extent unknown in the rest of Bohemia. An indication that the families of Osek and Švamberk had not reached agreement with the king in 1405 is the fact that none of them was named to the office of the justice for the Plzeň region although by tradition it belonged to them. It was given rather to the king's friend, Ulrich Zajíc of Hazmburk. The Skálas, the third family sharing a longstanding claim to the Plzeň office were also not named. Lord Břeněk of Skála, however was appointed chief justice of the royal court (*dvorský soud*), a position with considerable influence within the royal government.[29]

The financial difficulties of the brothers of Osek, Boreš Sr. and Jr. aggravated their relations with the king. Because of money troubles, in 1407, they exchanged Bečov castle which they held in fief from the king, with Ulrich of Hazmburk who transferred to them the smaller royal estate of Přimda which he held in pawn. From early 1415 to 1418 the lords of Osek with some local gentry and Lord Henry of Plavno fought off and on against the king over an issue unknown to us. They stopped only after Lord Henry lost his castle to royal troops. The king, exercising his royal right of pre-emption, authorized his friend Nicholas of Lobkovice to pay the Osek brothers their money on Přimda and to take over its administration.[30]

The dispute between the lords of Švamberk and the king related to an earlier unresolved issue, the nature of which is not clear. Of the four brothers only Bušek and Bohuslav joined the revolts of the 1390s. Bohuslav died in 1401 leaving minor sons, Janek, Bohuslav and Hynek Krusina but nothing is known of Bušek after 1395. Until 1412 the three sons were under the wardship of John Hanovec of Švamberk and Půta of Skála. In 1409 their uncle John, continuing a feud with the king which his brothers had left unsettled, was beheaded. As far as we know this did not evoke a protest from the other nobles who were content with their own gains and did not wish to disturb their peace with the king. Since the dispute involved land clearly held in fief from the king they did not regard it as business for the land government. In 1412 the younger Švamberk brothers took up the feud, and in June 1414 it was submitted to a council of royal and land officials for resolution.[31] On the 3rd of July the king pardoned them and dropped all charges. The brothers accepted the settlement in September and promised to give up certain documents which the king had given their father and uncle and upon which they most likely had based their claims leading up to the dispute. To seal their reconciliation, on 5 February 1417, after the Hussite populace had reduced the Premonstratensian monastery in Chotěšov to poverty with its attacks on it, the king gave the lords the right to 15,000 groschen income from the monastery for which they were to defend it.[32]

The one-time guardian of the lords of Švamberk, Půta of Skala, whose father Břeněk (d. 1407) and uncle Půta Sr. (d. 1401) had both been members of the baronial leagues of the 1390s, in 1409 quarreled with the king over some property. The feud may have been part of the one carried on by the lords of Švamberk. Půta had received half of Březnice, a free castle, as surety for a loan made to a royal favourite, Andrew Huler of Orlik. Andrew then sold it to King Wenceslas who wanted to redeem it by paying off the loan. Půta refused to give it up and was cited to the land court. When he failed to appear, the court on 10 May 1410 gave the castle to the king. After two years of further litigation the king ordered his troops to lay siege to the castle. This, however, proved unnecessary because at about this time Půta was mysteriously murdered while on a visit to Prague.[33] All of these nobles who had not resolved their differences with the king by 1405 did so before the king's death and the outbreak of the revolution in 1419. Not one saw the revolution as a potential ally which might aid them in recovering some of the property which they felt the king had wrongly taken from them. On the contrary, all fought for the Catholic cause and for King Sigismund.[34]

For the lords of Bergov the feuds against King Wenceslas bore mixed results. At their outbreak Otto Sr. held the office of the chief Prague burgrave, but at their end neither he nor his son, Otto Jr., held any government office. They were however somewhat materially compensated when just before 1394 they gained the king's castle, Trosky. Lord Otto Jr.'s basic discontent was expressed through wrangling with his neighbours. In 1414 he quarreled with Nicholas Zajíc of Hazmburk. Then in October 1416 he, with his nephew, John Městec of Opočno, in the hope of finding some great treasure, raided the Opatovice monastery. However even these two allies in the foray on the monastery were not united in their religious policies. John was a member of the Hussite league whereas Otto joined the Catholic pact. Otto was joined in his camp by his enemy of 1414, Nicholas Zajíc of Hazmburk.[35]

When the revolutionary temper began to quicken after 1415 these nobles, including John Městec in 1417, sided with the king and the church despite their discontentment. They were not foolish men. They recognized that the crown still had extensive property and official resources which the king could use to reward loyal service. To them supporting the established authorities and social structure seemed a more sure investment than aiding a reform movement. Even while represented by intellectuals at the university it had hardly seemed significant. When it became more and more the affair of the masses who saw in it possibilities for their own advancement it appeared positively dangerous.

Although events between the end of the revolts and the burning of John Hus washed away the lines dividing the baronial rebels from the royalist camp, the wars did leave a legacy which lasted into the Hussite period. Around 1402 a split appeared within the noble unity when several barons opposed the action of Henry of Rožmberk, Bishop John and King Sigismund who took King Wenceslas captive a second time carrying him off to Vienna. This incident represents the birth of the anti-Sigismund party because the families of the two barons resisting the second captivity, Lord Boček of Poděbrady and Lord John Krušina of Lichtenburk, later stood in the forefront of the baronial resistance to Sigismund and his efforts to acquire the Bohemian throne and restore Catholicism. In 1402 they saw that the principles of limited royal power had been achieved and wished no further action against the person of King Wenceslas, actions which King Sigismund might only turn to his own advantage. However they saw possibilities in cooperating with the reformers against the church. If the university masters required their help these barons were willing to use their new political power in the land to force the clergy into a reform of religious life as outlined by Hus and his friends.

The party of nobles who had been loyal to King Wenceslas was in several respects related to the patriotic-national tendencies in Bohemia which likely helped make the Czech oriented reform movement at the university attractive to them. For one thing, that group in the royal council in 1397 who were members by virtue of their friendship with the king favoured a domestic orientation to royal policy, one in which the king concentrated on Bohemia rather than on imperial affairs. For example the Škopek of Dubá family, one of the most royalist of nobles was also one of Hus' staunchest supporters. This group was opposed by

the anti-royal group, several of whom, including John of Michalovice and
Boreš of Osek, killed four nobles friendly to King Wenceslas because they
were trying to prevent the king from visiting Germany on imperial
business.[36] Secondly, John Hus favoured the royal cause and identified
it with that of the Bohemian land. In 1402 he severely criticized the
noble rebels for attacking Prague with the help of the foreigner, the Margrave of Meissen, saying that unless Czechs defend their kingdom they
were worse than dogs and vipers who at least have the sense to guard
their lairs.[37] Thirdly, F.M. Bartoš identified the group around Margrave
Procop of Moravia, who consistently fought for King Wenceslas, as the
Slavic party, primarily on the basis of its Polish alliance. Although money
helped induce Lords Boček and John Krušina to join the king's cause they
were likely also motivated by rudimentary patriotic considerations,
feeling that the king's second abduction served primarily the interests of
foreigners and as such affronted the Czech crown and realm. Boček's
sympathy for the Czech language is illustrated in that his was the first
noble chancery to use it.[38]

In any case the king's gifts of money helped break up the noble
coalition against him. On 14 November 1401, four months before his
capture, King Wenceslas gave Boček about 15,000 groschen income from
the monastery of St. George in Prague. Almost a year later, in September,
Boček, John Krušina and two royal favorites, Conrad Vechta, the future
archbishop and Sigismund Huler announced their intention to fight for
the king's freedom. Later, on 13 July 1403 the king, still in captivity,
gave Krušina, whose only action against the king was his participation in
the siege of Prague, 12,000 groschen income from the queen's Albrechtice domain.[39]

Breaking with the anti-Wenceslas noble group cost these men dearly.
King Sigismund took his revenge against Boček in 1403 by wasting the
Poděbrady estates while his troops were laying siege to the nearby royal
city of Kutná Hora. He similarly exacted material requisition from
Krušina when he in 1414 intervened on behalf of the queen who at that
time was involved in a dispute with Krušina's son Hynek over the
Albrechtice property.[40]

The Poděbrady family and Sigismund's circle continued their dispute
when in 1407 Boček and the bishop of Litomyšl quarreled. The known
details are few but sometime earlier Boček's cousin invaded the bishop's
town and rode off with two wagons loaded with booty. When an arbitration board found in Boček's favour, the bishop tried to retaliate by
persuading a friendly abbot in Vienna to excommunicate Poděbrady.

This did not bring the parties together and the dispute was finally settled through the mediation of Lord Lacek of Kravaře.[41]

After his release in 1403, King Wenceslas rewarded his rescuers. Boček became the chief notary of the realm and Krušina the chief burgrave where he replaced Henry of Rožmberk. Both the Poděbrady and Lichtenburk families were represented in the Hussite league in 1415 and theirs were the only baronial families who fought with Hussite Prague in 1420 against Sigismund's troops at the battle of Vyšehrad.[42] The elder John Krušina died in 1407 and Boček Sr. in 1417.

Although not a member of this group, Hynek Berka of Honštejn's enmity with the king had also ameliorated somewhat by September 1402. At this time he stood guarantor for Boček of Poděbrady in the instrument with which he stated his intention to fight for the king's freedom. By 23 February 1404 he was among those nobles accepting high office under King Wenceslas although Henry of Rožmberk, John of Litomyšl and King Sigismund, his old allies, had not yet made peace with the king. Hynek Berka a leader of the Catholic league in 1415 did not follow Boček in his support for Hus. As chief judge on the land court, an office which he held until his death in 1419, he was however party to the court's favourable responses to Hus from 1412-1414. His surviving sons, John, Hynek Berka Jr., Hynek Berka, Hynek Sr., and his nephew Hynek Hlaváč, all fought for the Catholic faith.[43]

In sum, the king had no reason to have special animosity or cordiality towards either the noble leagues of 1415. Nor did all the quarrels the nobility had among themselves point to the future split along religious lines. The rupture that emerged among the nobility over the question of King Wenceslas' second captivity was more permanent. Here the anti-Sigismund party, which took up support for the Hussite movement, was joined by a nobleman who had not participated in the earlier feuds, and who by 1415 had risen to be the single most powerful noble in the realm, Čeněk of Vartemberk. His rise and relationship to the other nobles is the subject of the following chapter.

CHAPTER 6
THE ROLE OF ČENĚK OF VARTEMBERK
IN NOBLE AND HUSSITE POLITICS

The victory of the nobles in the struggle with the king gave them a renewed self-assurance and a consciousness of being the representatives of the land. They had made real their claim to rule the affairs of the country including the administration of justice on their estates, the determination of the custom and law of the land in the land court and had assured themselves a voice in the king's highest council. Nothing important could happen in the land without their consent. Almost as soon as they had consolidated their victory they were introduced to still other opportunities. The Wyclifite masters at the University of Prague invited them to participate in the renewal of the church in Bohemia. The nobles, just as all other elements in society were called to strive to live a life free of sin. In addition, especially after 1412 when they lost the king's support, the Hussites looked to the nobility to play a more active and instrumental role in reforming the church; they expected it to use its secular power to enforce the principles of reform.

The nobleman who best exemplified the sentiment of his estate, both in its self-confident approach to political affairs and in its sympathy for the reformers, was Čeněk of Vartemberk. Čeněk's father had left him an inheritance of estates ridden with debts but by 1414 Čenek through skill and good fortune had built up his property holdings to the point where he was one of the richest men in the realm. The fact that his immediate family had remained neutral in the wars against King Wenceslas placed him in a unique position. Hus, who had resented the baronial actions, could regard him in a more favourable light and be open to the possibilities of cooperating with him. Čeněk's earlier neutrality also enabled him to play the role of honest broker between anti-royal barons like Henry of Rožmberk and the king and thus help two powerful parties in the realm baronage and crown, to cooperate in the task of governing. Čeněk used his talents and influence well and by 1414 he was chosen to be the chief Prague burgrave, one of, if not the, most powerful positions in the kingdom, which he placed at the disposal of the Hussite cause. In the course of his rise, in addition to acquiring the friendship of Rožmberk, he also aroused the enmity of Bishop John of Litomyšl. Both relationships were important in determining his role in the struggles over the religious issues of his day.

Although Čeněk himself did not participate in the noble leagues, he had family ties with those who did. His wife Catherine was the daughter of William of Landštejn, one of the early members of the league.[1] His mother was Kačna of Richenburk, the daughter of William and the sister of Smil Flaška whose quarrels with the king are described above.[2] Three of the Vartemberk lords who feuded with the king were distant relatives and a fourth, Henry, was a cousin.[3] Čeněk, a minor when the noble feuds began, came of age between 1396 and 1400 so that by the time of his death in 1425 he was about 40 years old.[4]

There is much evidence of the older Čeněk's financial difficulties. Sometime between 1388 and 1399 he sold or pawned his castle Trosky. He must have given up this castle with reluctance since he had built it himself as his family residence. This was however not the end of his misfortune as he soon thereafter lost the dowry property of his wife Kačna.[5] In 1393 the king and the noble Smil Flaška took over Bydžov castle and the domain, foreclosing on a debt which Čeněk Sr. had been unable to repay. Also a lady Johanka of Prague claimed a credit on the castle in 1396.[6]

These financial entanglements brought the younger Čeněk into contact with a future rival. Bishop John of Litomyšl, as creditor and guardian of Smil's orphans, laid claim to some Vartemberk estates. When Smil died in 1403 his share of Bydžov went to the bishop. Similarly, in 1405 the bishop shared the dominion over Veliš with Peter of Vartemberk, Čeněk's cousin. Bishop John was either creditor or guardian to the children of Peter's deceased brother, Wenceslas. Sometime before 1408 Bishop John took over Skála Hrubá castle from Peter and donated it to his cathedral church in Litomyšl.[7] As more and more Vartemberk property was being lost to the church, the threat to his family's domains from the bishop must surely have contributed to Čeněk's friendship with Hus. The reformer explicitly denied clergymen the right to such poverty.

In a few years, with a little luck and sound management, the younger Čeněk turned his insolvent inheritance into one which made him renowned for his wealth. The king, perhaps because the family had not joined the leagues against him, returned his share of Bydžov to Čeněk and his brother John at their father's death in 1396. Furthermore, just as needy home-owners in Prague, so Čeněk raised money by selling the right to collect an annual revenue from part of his estates for one large sum of cash. The lords of Žirotín and the abbess of the convent in Týnec loaned him money through such arrangements.[8] In 1407 Čeněk raised additional money by granting his peasants a charter of freedom for which they made him a one-time payment of cash. It may be that he also raised money from other communities whose charters have not survived. In granting such charters Čeněk was part of the trend discussed in chapter 1 in which peasants received what were called rights of towns, a trend supported by reformers such as Archbishop John of Jenštejn and John Hus. In the same year that Čeněk granted his charter, Hus, responding to an unnamed noble's request for advice, addressed himself to the question of peasant rights. Hus criticized the lord's customary claim to a peasant's land when he died without a male heir. This claim to devolution Hus said was motivated by greed and therefore sinful. He claimed that the peasant had a right to the property because he had worked for it and therefore it belonged to him, it was his property not merely something which the lord permitted him to use. The peasant should be allowed to do with the land what he wished, that is sell it, give it to his friends or distribute it to the poor.[9]

It was not only Hussite barons like Čeněk and John of Hradec who granted their peasants freedom from devolution. Nobles who were later in the Catholic camp did likewise. Čeněk did however go further. The other nobles granting charters gave their peasants the freedom to bequeath property at will allowing it to fall to the nearest male relative if there was no will. Čeněk's charters were similar but he also gave his peasants the liberty to sell their possessions at any time and move from his village to another one or to the city. We do not know whether he had a surplus of labour on his estates in which case his action would not have cost him anything. We know that for the kingdom as a whole there was a general migration to the cities and that some lords offered attractive conditions to peasants in order to hold them. Was Čeněk's action a moral response to Hus' call to the lords to treat their peasants with dignity? More information on the demographic conditions existing on Čeněk's lands is needed before we can better answer the question.

To a large extent Čeněk's material prosperity resulted from his ability to realize claims he made to property of deceased relatives. Thus in 1407, at the death of his brother he inherited his share of the Bydžov estate and became its sole owner. The circumstances under which he took over Veliš were less clear. Perhaps he ejected the orphans of his cousin Wenceslas from their share[10] or perhaps he claimed it only after they died in 1412. In any case he was soon embroiled in a dispute over the estate with Wenceslas' brothers, Peter and Henry. On 6 February 1413 they reached a temporary agreement according to which Henry was to get Veliš. Čeněk was not satisfied with this arrangement and the dispute was finally resolved by the queen on 4 October 1414 who determined that Čeněk should pay Henry, who by now was in her employ as the burgrave of Hradec Králové, 90,000 groschen and give him half the fish from a certain fish pond. Čeněk got Veliš which by this time included Jičín and Brada. When Peter died childless around 1416, Čeněk got all his property including Vysoké Veselí. By this time he had also taken over Lipnice when the owner, his wife's brother Vitek died childless sometime between 1405 and 1408.[11] In addition in 1412 Čeněk became the guardian of the Rožmberk children which made him the administrator until 1418 of lands which were second in size only to the king's. Čeněk undoubtedly was an able person and administrator, recognized as such by his peers, but the fact that his relatives died what were for him timely deaths contributed materially to his fortune.

Lord Čeněk's rise from indebtedness to prosperity is all the more remarkable when we consider the financial difficulties of the many families noted in the preceding chapters. Not only did he recover the inheritance which his father had lost, but at the same time he cultivated political ties so that by 1414 he had enough friends among the barons who then elected him to the office of the chief Prague burgrave. The degree to which Čeněk could flex his political muscle became apparent in 1413 when he backed a squire who lived within the Rožmberk sphere of influence, Peter Malovec of Pacov, against Henry of Dubá, the brother-in-law of Bishop John of Litomyšl. In this dispute the rivalry between the bishop and Hussite baron broke into the open.[12]

The quarrel originated when both Malovec and Dubá had been in the court of Margrave Jošt of Moravia, where the two had become friends and Malovec had entered Dubá's service. When they left the margrave's court at his death in January 1411, Malovec had apparently filched some items from Dubá and kept one of his pages. The latter may have been a hostage guaranteeing the truce the two reached in the squabble over the appropriated goods although Dubá claimed that Malovec held the page unjustly. Dubá at this time was also involved in a dispute with the vassal of the abbot of the Premonstratensian monastery in Želivo. According to Dubá, the abbot had incited Malovec against him when he found he was losing his case before the king.[13] The quarrel soon involved their more powerful friends, Lord Čeněk of Vartemberk and Bishop John of Litomyšl. Henry of Rožmberk, as Malovec's powerful neighbour, had referred it to Čeněk for resolution. Čeněk, at Henry's death in July 1412, became the guardian of his estates and on 17 September Dubá wrote Čeněk that although he was at peace with him, before he would make up with Malovec he expected recompense for the items taken.[14] Thereafter Bishop John took up Dubá's cause both in correspondence with Čeněk and with military assistance. The king considered the matter in his council and perhaps the land court also heard it.[15] In any case on 20 February 1413 the king gave instructions that royal troops along with those of some nobles and of the bishop should attack and lay siege to Malovec's fortress, Pacov.[16]

Čeněk held out in his support for the squire from Pacov despite the bishop's offer for a peaceful settlement and despite the fact that even before the king had arrayed his military force against him, leading barons had advised him to acquiesce. In early February Bishop John wrote him demanding that Malovec return the captives and property which he had taken and that Čeněk help settle the issue because the bishop "would not like it if it came to further destruction and war between them." He suggested that he might have to go elsewhere for a solution, a veiled threat which he soon fulfilled when he brought the matter to the king.[17]

On 15 February Lord Erhart of Kunštat wrote Čeněk urging him to make Malovec return what he had taken, and that he should not permit such treatment towards his good friends. He exhorted him to value his relationship with the bishop higher than that with Malovec, ". . . for you know well that in him you have a good friend and that he is much more suitable for more important affairs than is that Malovec."[18] In November the previous year the nobility, in its session of the land court, had faced the question of whether to support John Hus. The Hussite faction had won only a partial victory.[19] Lord Erhart, a Hussite, obviously did not wish Čeněk to make enemies over a few chattels when they needed all the support they could get for the more important religious issue. Similarly the Hussite lord, Boček of Poděbrady chided Čeněk, saying he could not understand why he had not constrained Malovec to meet the bishop's demands. Furthermore, both Archbishop Conrad and John Jr. of Hradec, at that time chief Prague burgrave and co-guardian of the Rožmberk orphans, urged Čeněk not to rebel against the king.[20]

Yet Čeněk did not yield. We do not have Malovec's side of the story so we do not know if there was anything in the case itself which drew Čeněk's support. Perhaps it was simply his response to Rožmberk interests which he thought dictated that he come to the defense of a Rožmberk client even though Malovec took his action without Čeněk's knowledge.[21] From the information we do have it does seem rather imprudent of him to increase the bishop's hostility over a few articles of property when his efforts could have been directed towards creating solidarity among the nobility.

Nevertheless Čeněk bore himself well perhaps at this time gaining the renown for eloquence attributed to him at a later date.[22] He protested the king's action both to the noble officials and to the king himself. The former he wrote that he had been represented before the king with letters and delegations through which he had asked the king to permit Malovec to stand before the land court and that he was even now ready to have him appear. He reminded them that neither he nor the Rožmberk orphans had ever been at war with the king and denied outright that he had sent the king a letter of challenge as he was accused of doing.[23] To the king he added that the rumours emanating from the royal council, that he was not willing to be of service to the king were untrue. He wanted "gladly to serve if His Grace will be pleased to accept it."[24]

Čeněk survived the affair with his prestige and power enhanced. Apparently in early March 1413 Čeněk offered a truce. On 11 March the bishop rejected it because his conditions had not been met.[25] What actually happened thereafter is not clear. The suggestion of A. Sedláček, who frequently attributed to the monarch more authority than in truth he held, that Malovec found himself in narrow straits and after appealing got a royal grace, is doubtful.[26] All we know is that he did not lose the fortress Pacov, which royal forces had placed under siege. It is however more likely that it was Čeněk's protection which saved him. Čeněk, early the next year, assumed the second highest office in the land when he became the chief Prague burgrave. It is a testimony to his political skill that he achieved the office, which required the consent of the leading barons, even though several of them had disagreed with his course of action in the Malovec affair.

The dispute brought Čeněk into open opposition with a man who since the days of the wars against the king had been a friend of King Sigismund of Hungary, the heir-apparent to the Bohemian throne. Bishop John of Litomyšl had thrown his lot in with Sigismund a long time ago and expected rewards when the time came for him to assume the Bohemian throne. It was only natural that competition between bishop and baron should arise since Čeněk had his own ambitions as well as a solid base of power from which to play a leading role in the polity of the realm.

In addition to personal rivalry the two men differed in ideology. The bishop's success in secular and military affairs had earned him the nickname, the man of Iron (Jan Železný). The Hussites, Čeněk's mentors in religious affairs, were diametrically opposed to such worldly activity as well as to ownership of property on the part of churchmen.

Although Čeněk took no known stand on behalf of Hus until 1412 it is safe to conclude that his encounters with Bishop John and other clergy in the preceding years in the role of property owners influenced him towards church reform. We can understand that the Wyclifite tenets forbidding the clergy to hold secular dominion evoked a favourable response from Čeněk after the bishop in the role of guardian, in 1408, gave an estate which had belonged to the Vartemberk family, to the Cathedral Chruch in Litomyšl. His drawn out quarrel with the priest in Lomnice in 1406 over a debt likely produced a similar effect. Čeněk was doubtlessly also attracted by Hus' call for the nobles to reassert their rights of patronage over the churches on their estates. We have seen how the question of patronage ownership influenced some nobles to support Hus. Although not as crucial a factor with Čeněk, he was personally also not immune to it. The church had not made as great strides in acquiring patronage over parishes in the deaneries of Jičín and Bydžov (fifteen percent) where Čeněk's estates lay, as it had in the Prague diocese as a whole (twenty-eight percent). However the fact that the patronage to the church in Bydžov, one of Čeněk's main residences, and its filial, New Bydžov, was owned by the canonry of St. Appollinary in Prague must have been an unpleasant reminder of patronage lost to the church through the generosity of his ancestors.[27]

Equally important for Čeněk as well as for the other nobles was the Wyclifite program to reform the church of the Bohemian realm. Already during the revolts of the 1390s the nobility had been allied with the archbishop, John of Jenštejn, who had tried to reform the church. Jenštejn sought to remove the clergy from secular dominion whereas the Wyclifites wanted to make the church legally subject to the secular ruler. Both however, strove to improve the moral lives of the clergy.[28] Since the archbishop had failed and the king by 1412 had proved unwilling to play the reforming role assigned to him by the Wyclifites, the nobility, as the dominant force in the land government, could logically step in. For the Hussite nobility this meant extending their jurisdiction into two new spheres. First they entered the realm of foreign relations when they, in the name of the Czech crown and language, wrote to the Council of Constance protesting the condemnation of John Hus on charges of heresy, an act which they alleged slandered the Czech crown and people.[29] Secondly, and this applied to the Catholics in their sphere to a lesser extent, the nobility assumed authority over the church and religious affairs as the secular ruler.

In 1416, after the death of Lord Lacek of Kravaře, a Moravian magnate and one of the prime movers on behalf of Hus, the full burden of leadership fell on Čenĕk. His goal was to gain the church's acceptance of at least three of the Four Articles of Prague: utraquistic communion, freedom to preach the word of God and an end to the clergy's lordship over temporal goods. After 1415 the whole program was generally symbolized in the first point, that lay people be served wine from the chalice at communion.[30] Čenĕk hoped to get this program accepted through negotiations with King Sigismund, who he expected would be the next king. Thereafter Čenĕk tried to chart the difficult if not impossible course of keeping the more radical Hussites satisfied with concessions while at the same time negotiating the minimum program with the authorities in the hopes of gaining for the Hussites legitimate status.

In general Czech historians have exempted Čenĕk from the harsher criticisms which they have directed at the nobility whom they charged with following a vacillating policy during the Hussite wars motivated by greed. The exception is the Marxist school led by Josef Macek who called Čenĕk a Catholic and saw in him the personification of that mentality of these "exploiters, who were quick to join this or that party depending on where they had most to gain."[31] V.V. Tomek, on the other hand, contrasted Čenĕk and his steadfast adherence to Hus' cause to the other nobles who had formerly agreed with Hus but by April 1420 had become enemies of his party for the sake of their own gain. He attributed Čenĕk's resolve to a deeper religious conviction.[32] Václav Novotný praised Čenĕk's political astuteness and maturity which he showed by exploiting Sigismund's arbitration verdict against the Polish king, by opening negotiations with the Pole regarding his accession to the Czech throne.[33] Josef Pekař praised Čenĕk for his return to Sigismund's camp a few weeks later in May 1420 because thus Čenĕk avoided an alliance with the revolutionary burners of churches and monasteries while at the same time working towards the goal of an acceptance of the moderate Hussite program.[34]

From 1420 to his death in 1425 Čenĕk changed sides eight times,[35] not exactly a record of steadfast adherence to a cause. His multiple reversals reflect the agonies of a man who had placed his considerable prestige and power at the disposal of the reform movement only to find his leadership rejected on all sides. The reformers left him because, according to them he did not act decisively enough on behalf of their religious beliefs. The nobles, whose estate he continued to regard as the leading power in a broadened Czech land-community, did not trust his ability to convince the heir, King Sigismund. Čenĕk's several maneuvers were efforts to regain his influential position.

Nevertheless the lord of Vartemberk had made a basically sound assessment of the religious and political situation in Bohemia. He himself recognized the need for change in the religious life of the people as it was described by the reform minded masters at the university. He also recognized that there was a strong popular sentiment, expressed by the more radical priests, for more far reaching changes in church life such as discarding ceremonial-liturgical worship practices adopted in the Middle Ages. These people were in fact prepared to cut all ties with the Roman Church, the only recognized religious body in Europe. Such a step entailed grave consequences for Bohemia including isolation and defiance of the heir-apparent King Sigismund. While Čeněk had to step carefully to keep in check the revolutionary forces he also needed to bring King Sigismund, notorious for his hatred of Hus, to the point where he could accept a moderate reform program. The best means to this end was to establish a strong united front among the nobility. His actions such as giving parishes to radical priests in 1417[36] followed by an apparent turnabout when he paid homage to King Sigismund in his camp in 1420 were aimed at reducing the resistance of both extremist groups to his moderate solution to the religious dissensions which were disturbing his land. With the official acceptance of the Four Articles he hoped to assuage the reformers and bring about Sigismund's coronation.

In addition Čeněk had realized that Lacek of Kravaře's inclination to seek an alliance and possibly a candidate for the throne in Poland was unrealistic.[37] He understood the strong support Sigismund had among the Bohemian nobility and he hoped that he could convince them of the need for a moderate program of reform in order to control the forces of revolution.[38] He failed however to hold together the nobility. Some may have been jealous of him but most of them simply were unwilling to take on Sigismund, who was both king of nearby Hungary and of the Germans, that is the lord of men willing to accept Bohemian lands as rewards for loyal service against heretics. Where the nobles hesitated, the radical plebians acted. Hence Čeněk's solution had to wait until 1436 after his death to be adopted but after that it worked passably well, allowing Catholic and non-Catholic to live side by side until the Habsburg restoration of Catholicism in the early seventeenth century.

It was a tragic failure for both Čeněk and the Bohemian people, that he was not able to convince his fellow nobles to accept his program. With the approaching accession of King Sigismund, Čeněk's allies among the nobility deserted him in droves.[39] At the death of King Wenceslas in 1419 there was no unified estate which could, together with Prague, present the new king with a set of religious demands as they did after they had defeated the forces of the revolution in 1434. Had they done so, Sigismund would have had little choice but to accept them and the nobility and Prague, controlled by the patrician magistrates, acting with the king would easily have subdued the revolutionary masses of rural Bohemia. Under such circumstances the country would have been spared the fifteen years of warfare and bloodletting which in the end accomplished very little that was materially beneficial to the populace. It is to Čeněk's credit that he anticipated this and sought to avoid extreme actions.

As Čeněk's leadership came to an end so for a time did the nobility's momentum towards an increase in power and jurisdiction in the polity. Nevertheless Čeněk's activities as the head of the Hussite league were not without effect. It will therefore be useful to trace the growth of noble support for Hussitism from its beginnings.

CHAPTER 7
THE NOBILITY AND THE HUSSITE MOVEMENT
UNTIL 1415

On several occasions medieval heretics found protection among members of the nobility. In the early thirteenth century those of southern France sheltered the Cathars until a drive by an expanding monarchy, cooperating with northern nobles put an end to both heresy and southern independence. In England, the Wyclifites or Lollards obtained support and patronage from the nobility, particularly from a small group of knights, members of Richard II's court. They were able to protect the Lollards from the full extent of ecclesiastical umbrage until the noble, John of Oldcastle, in revolting against King Henry V in 1413, combined heresy with disloyalty to the crown thus putting an end to royal sufferance.[1] The Wyclifites in Bohemia similarly found support among the noble courtiers of the king. However in contrast to the Lollards they also succeeded in gaining the support of landed noblemen, so that when the courtiers lost their power because of a change in royal policy, that part of the independently landed nobility which had found Wyclifism attractive was able to continue to provide the movement its patronage and protection.

During the first years of his ministry, beginning in 1402, Hus and his friends had little need for support from the secular power. The new archbishop, Zbyněk, a member of the baronial Hazmburk family, favoured reform so that the opposition from the prelates who were threatened by the reformers' call to a simplified life, was largely ineffective. Hus and Zbyněk cooperated in prohibiting pilgrimages to the site of a burned-down church where allegedly the wafers were turning into the colour of blood. Furthermore the archbishop invited the reformers to address the periodic church synods where they could lay out their program of reform before the gathered clergy.[2]

Under growing pressure from the canons of St. Vitus cathedral in Prague castle and from some masters at the university, Zbyněk parted ways with the Wyclifites. The split came into the open in June 1408 when Hus accused the archbishop of holding unorthodox views on the Eucharist. In July Zbyněk retaliated by forbidding reformist preachers to vilify the prelates, clergy and the Roman Church. Shorty thereafter he prohibited the use of Wyclif's works. The split became final when, during the preparations for the Council of Pisa, Zbyník remained loyal to Pope Gregory XII whereas Hus and Jerome of Prague favoured the renounciation of obedience to the pope.[3]

The issue of papal loyalty provided the reformers with an opportunity to get the king's support for their cause. The king too wished to unseat Pope Gregory in the hope that a new pope would recognize him as King of the Romans instead of Rupert of the Rhenish Palatinate. In order to achieve his ends he needed a delegation of professional theologians to send to Pisa where a council intended to carry through the papal deposition. The archbishop refused to send one as did the university where the German students, holding three votes to the Czechs' one, were loyal to Gregory and to Prince Rupert. Cooperating with Hus, King Wenceslas altered the university's constitution and gave the Czechs three votes putting its administration in Hussite hands. The reformers reciprocated and voted an official delegation which was to represent Bohemia at the council in Pisa.[4]

The king's cooperation with the reformers over the question of the university's administration did not mean that he agreed with their reform ideals. This became clear when the issue of indulgences acquired importance. In September 1411 Pope John XXIII declared a crusade against the deposed pope, Gregory XII and his protector King Ladislas of Naples. To underwrite the cost of the war he offered indulgences for sale which in the Prague diocese were sold with the king's approval because he expected a portion of the profits. The reformers who saw indulgences as unchristian tried to stop the sale, taking to the streets when all other efforts failed. As part of the popular demonstrations, some of which led to violence, one of the royal courtiers who sympathized with the Hussites, arranged for a student dressed as a prostitute to march through the streets with a copy of the bull, authorizing indulgences, around his neck.[5]

In his efforts to make peace the king dealt harshly with the reform party. In July 1412 his officials executed three youths who had loudly interrupted a preacher of indulgences. With respect to the three young men, the king told the city officials that "should there be 1000 such, let the same be done to them, and if you do not have enough executors and hangmen in this realm I will have them brought from other lands."[6] In October, Hus, with a papal anethema over him and interdict over any town in which he stayed, and under pressure from the king, left Prague seeking refuge in a castle of a noble friend. Hus' plight symbolized that of his movement which had first lost the sympathy of the archbishop and then the cooperation of the king so that as a result the reformers had to begin seriously to cultivate the support of their friends among the nobility.

Although not at the top of the reformers' list of priorities, support among the nobility for religious renewal existed prior to 1412. Members of the nobility bought houses in Prague and settled in the community of pious believers which had existed since the days of Milič and which since 1391 had as its centre Bethlehem Chapel. Materially the nobility contributed to the movement by endowing buildings, altars and scholarships for priests and students. Furthermore several noble students at the university allied themselves with the movement. From these fragmented origins sympathy among the nobility grew to the point where several of them made an attempt in noble assemblies to put the full weight of the land's authority behind reform.

Some of the reformers themselves, for example Matthew of Janov, came from the gentry class.[7] Similarly Thomas of Štítný, a member of the impoverished branch of the lords of Bechyně, rented out his manor in 1373 and moved to Prague with his daughter Anežka where he spent the remaining years of life translating and writing devotional literature.[8] Anežka joined the community of devout women living around Bethlehem Chapel, which had been especially endowed for the preaching of the gospel. These noble women bought several houses nearby and took up a religious style of life similar to the Beguines and centered their lives on daily listening to preachers of the gospel.[9]

One of them, Lady Catherine of Vraba, the widow of Conrad Kapléř of Sulevice, supported the reform movement with an endowment. In 1402 she provided a living for a preacher in St. Vitus cathedral. Her endowment reflected the values of the reformers stating that the preaching of the word was among the foremost of the matters necessary for salvation. Her empathy for the Czech language was reflected in that the preacher was to preach in Czech on each holy day and three times weekly during Advent and Lent. At about the same time she endowed a group of twelve virgins and widows "who had given up the vanity of this world and committed themselves to the service of God."[10]

By the fall of 1409 the Hussites had evoked support among the nobility to the extent that Archbishop Zbyněk, writing to the pope about the reformers' views on subordination of the clergy to the secular power, complained "they have attracted many of the magnates to their erroneous opinions."[11] Already in 1408 members of the nobility had begun to speak up on behalf of the freedom to study Wyclif's writings and to preach the word of God, a course which led finally to their action on behalf of John Hus himself as he embarked for Constance. The support began at the university among some of the noblemen, students there who found Wyclifite teachings attractive. On 17 July 1408 Archbishop Zbyněk ordered Wyclif's writings to be submitted to him for examination, intending to burn such as contained errors. Among five students who refused to give up their books were two nobles, Hroch of Podveky[12] and John of Landštejn.[13] Subsequently the archbishop ordered Wyclif's writings to be burned, at the same time prohibiting the free preaching in chapels, a measure aimed primarily at Bethlehem Chapel. He decreed that those disobeying were to be deprived of benefice and hereticized. On 25 June 1410 the nobles, John of Landštejn and Sdeslas of Zvířetice along with John Hus and five other students, with the support of the squire Gallus of Knín, appealed the archbishop's action to the pope.[14] The appeal was fruitless and in September several other nobles added their efforts on behalf of the Hussites. At that time the Moravian brothers, Lords Lacek and Peter of Kravaře along with Nicholas Potštejn of Žampach and John of Michalovice sent letters to the pope urging that the prohibition against Wyclifite literature and preaching in chapels be lifted.[15] All except Michalovice in 1415 joined the protest of the nobility against the Council's action declaring Hus and his movement heretical.

When the split between Hus and the king broke open over the issue of indulgences in 1412 Hus needed above all a protector to whose castle he could go for safety. He found him in Henry Škopek of Dubá the owner of a castle near Prague where he stayed from October until March 1413 and from which he returned occasionally to participate in the political maneuvering going on in Prague. It was most likely Lord Henry who urged Hus to appeal to the land court.[16] This appeal of Hus' began the process in which the nobility sought to bring the official support of the government behind Hus' cause.

The action unleashed by Hus' appeal was momentous both for his movement and for the nobility. For the reformist university masters it meant that the path of cooperation with the archbishop and king, which they had originally chosen for the pursuit of their goals, had to be abandoned. The church hierarchy had refused their efforts and the king had declined to force it to cooperate. Nevertheless the masters continued to seek a legitimate status within the realm and for this they turned to the nobility whose gains during the feuds of the 1390s had given it control over the land government. Recourse to the nobility carried uncertain prospects because the estate was fractionalized and each member independent, making it necessary to woo them separately.

The Hussite nobility's action on behalf of Hus, even though it represented only a minority, stands out as unique among the acts of the medieval aristocracy. It was in sharp contrast to the way the French nobles and king deserted Joan of Arc a scarce fifteen years later.[17] In the years 1412-1415 when the nobles undertook their support of the Hussites they had no way of knowing that the ensuing wars would bring their estate increased power. In fact their actions were frought with risks from the beginning which explains why they received only limited support on the land court or diet, a body which itself never took an official stand on behalf of the reformers. It heard Hus' case, tried to have it solved at home by the archbishop, but, although Hussite nobles were prepared to force a religious solution, the court itself did not rule on the merits of the religious issue.

Hus appealed to the court at the end of November 1412, as well as to the king and queen, asking for their protection and aid in bringing an end to the disputes in the realm. He pointed out to the nobility that the recent prohibition of preaching in chapels affected them as well, since many of them enjoyed the use of chapels in their castles for worship purposes.[18] The court, departing from its custom of hearing only the cases of nobles, granted his request. It along with the king and queen ordered Conrad, the administrator of the diocese and its future archbishop, to settle the dispute at home in a clerical synod.[19] Although the court did not grapple with the religious issues themselves and impose its solution its action nevertheless benefitted Hus in that it required the clergy to solve the problem at home and not force Hus to go to hostile Rome. Its decision reflected the fact that a majority of nobles on it wished to see the movement continue to exist without harassment.

We do not have a record of who was present at the November 1412 session of the land court. There was however enough continuity of membership between its various sessions[20] to allow us to construct the following. Those who were present at the court's last known meetings just preceding, that is, in June 1411[21] and February 1412[22] and in the next known one in October 1414[23] most likely participated in the deliberations in November 1412. These were the four leading officials of the realm; the chief burgrave, John Jr. of Hradec,[24] the chief judge, Hynek Berka of Honštejn, the chief chamberlain, Aleš Škopek of Dubá and the chief notary, Nicholas the Rich of Prague. In addition William and John of Švihov, Úlrich of Ustí, John of Michalovice, Ulrich of Hazmburk, Čeněk of Vartemberk, Boček of Poděbrady, William of Zviřetice, John Sr. of Hradec and Smil Šternberk of Holice were present. Also some of the individuals who attended only one of the three sessions were there in November 1412 but exactly who these were we cannot say with certainty. In any case only the last five named above, plus Nicholas the Rich, judging from later behaviour, were friendly to Hus, in themselves not a majority.[25] Hence we must assume the existence of a moderate group among the nobility, men who supported the reformers' goals and who wanted them to be able to work for them but only within the legitimate structure of the church. After the movement had been declared illegitimate by the Council of Constance in the summer of 1415, these moderates refused to challenge the church. We cannot say for certain who these men were, but most likely the group included John of Michalovice, who in 1410 wrote the pope on behalf of saving Wyclif's writings from fire, and perhaps Aleš Škopek of Dubá who may at this time have gone along with his brother Henry, a close friend of Hus.

Efforts to settle the dispute broke down because Hus would not accept the proposals of the commission set up by the king and archbishop. In the spring of 1413 he again sought refuge in the country. This time he was given shelter in Kozí castle, most likely by Stibor of Kozí who undertook the responsibility at the instigation of Čeněk of Vartemberk, the guardian of the nearby Rožmberk estates.[26] At the end of June 1414 Hus spent some time in the city of Ústí, protected apparently by Lady Anna of Mochov. Her influence and power were not great enough and because some of the other lords of Ústí opposed his presence, Hus had to leave the region. From there he went to Krakovec, the castle in west-central Bohemia belonging to Henry Lefl of Lažan.[27]

Henry's protection of Hus, though likely precipitated by expediency, resulted in friendship between the two men. He took Hus in so as to keep him secure and out of the way while a solution to the religious dissension was worked out. Henry came from Silesia and had bought Krakovec in 1410 and later acquired Bechyně in south-central Bohemia as well. At his request, Wenceslas, the titular patriarch of Antioch, bestowed indulgences to all pilgrims who came to the chapel in Krakovec to pray.[28] It is interesting to speculate on the dynamics of the situation when such pilgrims arrived there expecting their sins to be remitted and were instead greeted by a preacher from Prague inveighing against the very object of their pilgrimage.

Henry Lefl was the member of the royal council charged with solving the Hussite dispute. Because it had proved impossible to reach a settlement at home, another way had to be found, perhaps before the whole church meeting at Constance. It was known that King Sigismund desired Hus to go there. In April 1414 he sent a knight in his service, John Kepka of Chlum and Lord Wenceslas of Dubá to Hus with an invitation and a promise of safe passage to Constance where he was to vindicate himself and clear his country of the charge of heresy.[29] Perhaps an agreement was reached between Lefl and King Sigismund of Hungary, whereby King Wenceslas gave his consent to Sigismund being crowned King of the Romans, in return for which Sigismund promised Hus a safe-conduct complete with armed escort to travel to Constance and back. This offer was brought in August by Mikeš of Jemnište who at the same time warned Hus that he most surely would be condemned at Constance.[30]

If the judicial result was a foregone conclusion, it is difficult to see why the Hussite party thought going to Constance would resolve the dispute. Presumably Sigismund's safe conduct would prevent the council from administering the customary penalty and thus Hus might be expected to return home. If it did not he would die there. Neither eventuality would remove the religious dissensions in Bohemia between prelates and reformers and the problem would be no nearer solution; this must have been clear to most leaders in Prague. Hus' enemies hoped that his condemnation and punishment would deter others, but anyone favouring the reform movement could only expect that Hus went to Constance in the hope that, through a fair public hearing, he would, persuade Europe to, if not adopt his reform program, at least permit it to exist legally in Bohemia. Otherwise, unless he consciously sought martyrdom, it made no sense to go.

The request for an open forum along with attestations of Hus' excellent character was the message which his friends among the nobility sent to Constance. Before he left Hus got statements from the king, the queen and several royal courtiers, bearing witness that he had tried to answer charges before the local ecclesiastical authorities, but that no one had officially charged him with any error.[31] Similarly the Prague inquisitor, Bishop Nicholas of Nezero, issued a statement certifying Hus' innocence. It was witnessed by several nobles, some of whom in 1415 added their seals to the protest letter.[32]

Before he left for Constance, Hus and his friends made one more attempt to settle the matter at home. In October 1414, John of Jesenice tried to enter the clerical synod where he wanted to ask the prelates to place charges. Having failed, he advised Hus to appeal again to the court for assistance. Again the court honoured the request. In the light of the fact that the archbishop had not brought any formal charges, the court asked him for a statement on the orthodoxy of Hus' faith. Archbishop Conrad complied and in the presence of the gathered nobles he solemnly declared Hus to be free of heresy as far as he was concerned.

On 7 October three leading barons, Čeněk of Vartemberk, Boček of Poděbrady and William of Zvířetice sent a letter to King Sigismund attesting to this. Along with this they asked the king to see to it that Hus got a public hearing and that he not be falsely charged since such would cause the Czech tongue and realm to be dishonoured.[33] To what extent the three wrote in an official capacity is unknown. There is no record of the court itself taking any stand so we cannot assume that they wrote in the name of the noble estate or of the land. The letter acquired its significance from the fact that Čeněk was the land's first official, the chief Prague burgrave and that at least he and Boček were two of the most powerful and wealthy landed barons.

The makeup of the court of October 1414 suggests that the Hussite leadership had not been idle but had made an effort to build up the representation of its party. The names of twenty-four barons are recorded as present. Ten of these were new and nine of these were Hussites who participated in the letter protesting Hus' death a year later. Again, however, the Hussite party was not a majority and in order to have the court take up Hus' request they needed the help of others, men more moderate, who were not willing to support the movement after Hus' death.[34] The makeup of the court suggests that Čeněk had succeeded in getting those who were strongly sympathetic to attend and the court's action reflects the fact that he had convinced a majority to make at least a minimal intervention on Hus' behalf.

On 11 October 1414 Hus, accompanied by the nobles, Wenceslas of Dubá, Henry Lacembok of Chlum and John Kepka of Chlum and their entourages, left for Constance. He arrived there on 3 November without King Sigismund's safe conduct in his possession, but by the 10th, Dubá had fetched it from the king who was still underway.[35] However on 28 November, the cardinals ordered that Hus be confined and he was promptly imprisoned in a Dominican monastery. In the light of his predicament his friends among the nobility at home and in Constance did what they could for him.

In Constance John Kepka protested, first to the cardinals for their behaviour and when Hus was not freed, he publicized their unlawful action. He showed the safe conduct to all people of importance whose attention he was able to get, including counts, knights, lords, bishops and the notable citizens of Constance, as he wrote his friends in Bohemia.[36] Next on 15 December he went from church to church attaching to their doors a similar protest in German and Latin. Nine days later he repeated this. In it he stated that Hus had had a safe conduct and that in not honouring it the cardinals were not taking cognizance of legal forms operative in the rest of society.[37] He also informed his homeland of the situation in general, sending a copy of the protestation which he had affixed to the church doors.[38]

It was at this stage that the alliance which had been developing between university masters and the nobility received the expression for which it is best known; the letters sent to Constance on Hus' behalf. The barons regarded the treatment accorded Hus as a slur on themselves. To them Hus was a good man who wanted to bring the church back to a more simple, less worldly and materialistic life. Furthermore, Hus was a Czech; he spoke their language and had grown up and studied in their country, a land almost on the borders of western Christendom. They resented the attitudes among some circles in Europe; fostered by the Order of Teutonic Knights, which assumed that the Poles, whom several of the Hussite nobles had aided in their war with the Order, were pagans.[39] They were also angered by the fact that the church leaders did not recognize Hus' christian qualities. When neither their king nor his brother and heir apparent, King Sigismund the convocator of the Council, took any action on behalf of their realm and one of its subjects, the nobility decided to act. But they themselves were not able to express their sentiments cogently and effectively. Here the university masters stepped in and offered their services. They resented the Council's treatment of their colleague even more keenly and were skilled in drafting just such letters as the nobility sent to Constance.[40]

The Bohemian and Moravian nobility sent four letters to Constance on Hus' behalf between January and May 1415. The first, sent from Greater Meziříčí in Moravia, reminded King Sigismund that Hus, a just and blameless man, went to Constance voluntarily to answer false charges against himself and against the Czech crown. It continued that Sigismund had sent him a safe conduct, and still hoping that Hus would be able to vindicate himself and his movement, they asked that Sigismund release him and get for him a public hearing. They agreed that if Hus were convicted, that what was fitting in such cases should happen, as long as the safe conduct had been observed.[41]

Before the next letter was sent, Hus' supporters had experienced telling proof that King Sigismund was not doing his utmost to save their friend and leader. On 21 March Pope John XXIII fled from Constance taking with him his servants including Hus' jailors. The latter left the keys to the prison with King Sigismund thus giving him the opportunity to free Hus without creating a stir. The king instead delivered him over to

Otto, the bishop of Constance, who imprisoned him in his castle, Gottlieb.[42] Sigismund's behaviour indicated to the Czechs that they could expect little if any help from him.

The Bohemian nobility reacted more sharply to these events than did the Moravian. This reflects perhaps a stronger pro-Hus feeling in Prague and consequently a more intense dissillusionment with the authorities entrusted with his case, namely the Council and King Sigismund, who since October 1414 was also the emperor of the Romans.

The sentiments of the Moravian nobility are reflected in a letter sent from Brno on 8 May.[43] The contents were basically the same as the one from January but with respect to the pope's flight, without blaming Sigismund for Hus' renewed imprisonment, they included the neutral rebuke that Hus "was taken from prison, God knows best by whose authority, and given to the bishop of Constance, who placed him into more cruel confinement."[44] Furthermore as an expression of continued faith in the ultimate fairness of the Council towards Hus they concluded with the request that he be freed and given a public hearing.[45]

In Prague the feeling against the emperor was more intense. The May 12 letter sent from there and signed by 250 Czech and Moravian nobles, knights and squires[46] laid the blame for Hus' continued captivity directly on the emperor. For the time being those forces eager to rebuke Sigismund had their way. Commenting on his behaviour after the pope's flight, the letter pointed out that:

> . . . the pope then having left Master John Hus, went away and left him in your power; in order that Master John Hus, not being guilty and having already suffered enough, might be released and freed, and not, forcibly and contrary to the law, be imprisoned anymore to the shame and dishonour of the whole Czech tongue, seeing as Your Grace cited him and granted him a safe conduct.[47]

In an other place the letter made a similar point when it stated that Hus "being already in your dominion and in your city as we hear, was captured having your promises and letters of safe conduct."[48]

A separate letter was sent the same day to the Czech members of Sigismund's court urging them to induce the king to take action on Hus' behalf. Its tone and the fact that only one of the signers,[49] John of Vlašim, appeared on the protest letter of 2 September, suggests that it represented a moderate faction, men whose landholdings were modest who may have wanted to establish their independence of the richer barons. They too were concerned about Hus' welfare but did not want to affront the heir-apparent, King Sigismund, nor were they willing to later protest the Council's condemnation. With respect to Sigismund's behaviour after Pope John's escape they included only the second, the less pointed of the above phrases.[50]

Both 12 May letters reflected a loss of confidence in the Council's fairness. They described how they understood the invitation to come to the Council; how papal letters assured safety and freedom from persecution to all, both good Christian and heretic, so that all might come to Constance to negotiate on matters of faith. They pointed out how adherents of Popes Gregory and Benedict, who had been declared heretic, were permitted peace and security while their own John Hus was cast into prison. The call to the king was however altered. The October 1414 letter from Prague, the January letter from Greater Meziříčí and the 8 May letter from Brno all asked that Hus be granted an open hearing. By 12 May the nobility had lost faith in the Council's process. Neither letter of that date requested an open hearing.[51] The letter with 250 signatures, pointed out that there had been much talk recently casting doubt on the king's guarantees. It then stated, "And Your Grace can easily stop all this and procure for Master John Hus, that just as he went freely in accordance with your will, so let him again freely return to us in Bohemia. . . ."[52] The letter of the more moderate group similarly asked for Hus' safe return with no word about a hearing.[53]

Though dropped as part of the demands of the nobles, the Council granted Hus a hearing on 5 June. It was not the kind of hearing Hus had requested: one in which he presented his program of reform before the rest of Christendom as an equal. Rather he was brought before the Council and told to respond to specific charges of heresy. One month later he was ceremoniously condemned as a heretic and executed. This action as well as the Council's denunciation of utraquism on 16 June was a landmark in that it set the stage for making official the cleavage within both the ecclesiastical and secular parts of the Bohemian realm.[54]

The moderate faction disappeared for the time being as its members decided either for orthodoxy or joined those condemning the Council's actions. The latter group, which came to represent the secular power of the Hussite church, reacted to the condemnation and execution by sending another letter, this time directed at the Council itself. Dated 2 September, it rebuked the church fathers for their action, reiterated its praise for the man John Hus and reminded them of the long loyalty of the Czech people to the Roman Church. They proceeded to give notice that anyone who accused their kingdom or its subjects of heresy would be regarded as a traitor and as a son of the devil, a warning presumably directed at their countrymen at the Council.[55] They added that they would appeal to a future pope to resolve the issues and would be obedient to him insofar as he ruled in accordance with reason and the law of God. Nevertheless they intended, they wrote, "to defend and protect, without fear, the law of our Lord Jesus Christ and his devoted, humble and constant preachers up to the point of shedding blood and in disregard of human statutes . . ."[56]

By September the nobles decided to be more circumspect towards King Sigismund than they had been in May. They knew that he disliked John Hus and that he had assured the prelates at the Council that they could proceed against him without fear.[57] Nevertheless they excepted him from blame for Hus' fate. Having recited all the evil done to Hus the letter reads: "Only the person of the Most Serene Prince and Lord, Lord Sigismund, in the above we believe and hope to be innocent."[58] This discretion towards the king was intended to get as wide support as possible among the nobility for their action while at the same time keeping open the door for future negotiations with the king, though to many his innocence was not at all worthy of faith.

The letter to Constance bore the names of 320 nobles from Bohemia. August Sedláček has identified them according to region and family and shown that they were overwhelmingly from eastern Bohemia.[59] Using this material F.M. Bartoš drew a line following the rivers Jizera, Vltava, Otava and Volyňka which runs southwestward from the headwaters of the Jizera on the northeast border to those of the Otava on the southwest. He showed that all of the gentry came from east of that line and only five barons came from regions further west.[60]

The fact that no gentry west of that line participated in the protest led Bartoš to conclude that the line had a military significance which permitted only those lesser noblemen who had the protection of the neighbouring Hussite barons to throw down the gauntlet to the Roman Church. It is true that the presence of a Hussite magnate made it easier for the gentry to oppose the church but one should not conclude from this that the gentry simply followed the example of the upper nobility.[61] William of Hermanice who came from the fortress near Litomyšl, under Bishop John's authority provides a case in point of one who did not.[62] One might mention in this connection the examples of the squires Nicholas and Beneš of Vlačice who held that estate from the Benedictine monastery in Želivo.[63]

The gentry's freedom of action is illustrated when we examine those in eastern Bohemia who did not join the protest. The map on the following page shows that most of the protesting gentry were grouped

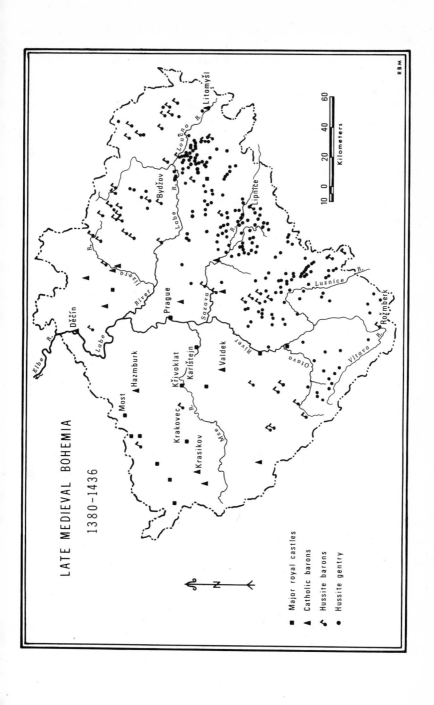

LATE MEDIEVAL BOHEMIA

1380–1436

Major royal castles
Catholic barons
Hussite barons
Hussite gentry

Kilometers
10   0   20   40   60

Elbe R.
Děčín
Labe
Most
Hazmburk
Krakovec
Krasíkov
Mže R.
Bydžov
LouČna R.
Litomyšl
Lipnice
Prague
Křivoklát
Karlštejn
Valdek
Sázava
Jizera R.
Berounka River
Otava R.
Luznice R.
Vltava R.
Rožmberk
River

into three areas: one near Chrudim between the Loučná and Chrudimka rivers, the second along the Želivka and Szava rivers south of Čáslav, and the third, beginning just north of Borotín and running south-east past Ústí upto Hradec Jindřichův. The owners of all castles, fortresses and estates in these territories are identified in Sedláček's *Hrady*, volumes I, XII and IV.

His information, which he left unanalyzed, enables us to compare the number of Hussite gentry living in the regions with that of non-Hussites and shows that a large number of gentry did not participate in the protest.[64]

In the Chrudim region (*Hrady*, I) there were thirty-five estates whose gentry owners did not affix their seals to the letter, compared to fifty who did. In Čáslav (*Hrady*, XII) the ratio was 108 abstainers to seventy-four who joined, and in Ústí (*Hrady*, IV—later the Tábor region) it was thirty-four to thirty-eight. A glance at the map also shows that many Hussite gentry did not live in the three cited regions and they all had neighbours who did not join their protest. We need to make allowances for the fact that fifteenth century political machinery and net of communications lacked a certain degree of efficiency which made it difficult for the Hussite leadership to sweep all members of the nobility into its net. Some perhaps did not join because they could not be reached. Nevertheless, the fact that this many members of the gentry, living in regions where Hussite barons dominated, were free to exercise their right not to participate in the protest speaks also for the convictions of those who did. The squires who affixed their seals to the letter presumably had the same freedom and chose to protest.

Although only a minority of nobles supported the Hussite cause to the point of protesting his death to the Council, the number of adherents was not the only factor which determined what sort of action the nobility would take on behalf of the Hussite Chruch. This action depended to a large extent on the intentions of men like Lord Čeněk, who were used to playing leading and forceful roles, and were willing to do so on behalf of the Hussite movement. Undoubtedly the most significant action was their use of the right of patronage on behalf of Hussite priests in 1417 at a time when the reformers were under attack from most other authorities.

CHAPTER 8
HUSSITE PATRONAGE AND POLITICS
UNTIL 1419

The death of John Hus and the Council's condemnation of his movement divided Bohemia into two religious camps. The fact that many nobles remained loyal to Rome meant that the appeal of the Hussite masters to the land court to defend them and grant them legality had failed just as their earlier attempts to woo the archbishop and king had. Hussite nobles and masters however continued in pursuit of their goal to establish a reformed church in their land recognized by European christendom. This too however was frustrated by Archbishop Conrad's attack on them which began in 1417. In response to this test of loyalty, the nobility, under Čeněk's leadership disregarded ecclesiastical prescriptions controlling the filling of office and expelled priests from their churches giving them to Hussite reformers and revolutionaries.

The 2 September 1415 protest letter sent to the Council of Constance was part of a larger program of action undertaken by the nobility in its role as the protector of the Hussite reform movement. On 6 September the Hussite lords formed a league which, in addition to communicating its reproach to the Council, was to provide guidelines for joint action and enforcement of their religious principles. As captains it named three of the leading barons, Čeněk of Vartemberk, and Boček of Poděbrady of Bohemia and Lacek of Kravaře of Moravia, under whose direction the rest were to act. The most significant feature was that the nobles promised each other aid in protecting their priests in case the church should afflict them with citations and excommunications. Several weeks later, and probably in response to the Hussite league, the Catholic nobles, led by Bishop John of Litomyšl, met in the archbishop's town of Český Brod to map out their own strategy.[1] As a result of the split within the nobility there could be no general establishment of the Hussite Church throughout the kingdom. Having failed to bring the noble controlled land government behind the reformers, the Hussite nobles had to act alone. One aspect of their aid was to place their priests into the 211 parishes to which they owned patronage, as well as into those on their estates held by ecclesiastical institutions but which the nobility now took under their control. The movement as a result was much reduced in scope. Whereas originally it was intended to replace the existing one and become the church of the realm, after 1416 it could count on an existence only on the domains where secular lords exercised their rights in favour of Hussites. The result was the establishment of the principle made famous one hundred years later in Germany when each prince was allowed to determine the religion of his region.

Immediately after Hus' death the situation in Bohemia was turbulent and uncertain. There are several reports from the period referring to violence done to Catholic priests by the nobility. In a letter of 27 March 1416 the Council of Constance, writing to the Catholic nobility, complained that, "Priests, both regular and secular, are being despoiled, driven away from their benefices, injured, killed and horribly treated, against the liberty of the Church."[2] Similarly two chronicles refer to difficulties suffered by the Catholic clergy at the hands of the nobles. The Hussite chronicler, Laurence of Březova wrote: "After the death of John Hus the preverse clergy. . . , were by just judgement of God afflicted every day, by having their property taken away by laymen, by being ejected from their places and offices, . . ."[3] The writer of the chronicle of the University of Prague made a similar point.

These reports have lead major historians of the period like F. Palacký, F.M. Bartoš and H. Kaminsky to believe that shortly after its formation the Hussite league went on the offensive against the ecclesiastical hierarchy.[4] No doubt such reports reflect at least partially events in Bohemia in that they point to activities, as a result of which Hussite priests took over offices at the expense of their occupants. The archbishop's enforcement of the interdict in the fall of 1415, when all Romanist clergy ceased performing worship services only to be replaced by eager Hussites, probably contributed to such a state of affairs.

It was not however the Hussite league which was to blame for this, and reports to that effect cannot be taken at face value. In the first place the writers of the Council's letter in March 1416 were far from the scene and they might easily exaggerate reports of violence coming from Bohemia and incorrectly associate them with the formation of the noble league. Perhaps they confused the turnover of November 1415 with the stated intention of the league to defend its clergy. Similarly, Laurence of Březova, who wrote in the 1420s, was imprecise, not saying when and by whose hand God punished his enemies. If he had in mind the Hussite nobility he must have referred to their action in 1417 and after. Lastly, the writer of the university chronicle referred only to the city of Prague, claiming that Catholics were expelled from office sometime between 1415 and 1419. The Hussite nobles were not responsible for events in Prague, a royal city, where they themselves owned no patronage.[5]

The records of the confirmations to church offices, the *Libri Confirmationum,* are a more reliable source for studying the nobility's action than are letters from the council and chronicles. The episcopal records throw a great deal of light on the relationship between the nobility and the reformers. They show, first, that nobles as a class before 1417 did not use their rights of patronage to any great extent on behalf of Hussites and, second, that the campaign, begun in 1417, to turn Catholic priests out of office in favour of Hussites was a defensive reaction. The nobles' move was not an attack against the old religion but a measure of last resort in response to the archbishop's offense directed at their clergy which began in January 1417. The action of the Hussite nobles was decisive for the success of the revolution even though this was not their intention. What they did was provide the Hussite priests with authoritative support and a degree of legitimacy during a period of crisis for the movement: from 1417 to 1419.

As sympathy for the Hussites grew among the nobility in the years before Hus' death, it would be logical to expect that one measure of support would have been for nobles to use their rights of patronage to fill their churches with Hussites. The available evidence suggests that this was not the case. A study of this problem is made difficult by the fact that only a small number of confirmed priests can be identified as Hussites. However, since the home of the reform movement was the University of Prague, we can get some idea of how extensively the nobility had offered its patronage to the reformers by examining the frequency with which members of the university population appeared in the confirmation records.

Between 1400 and 1415 the noble estate did not make use of its patronage on behalf of university students any more than did other classes; in fact since it owned two-thirds of the patronage, proportionately less. The following table shows the number of times the right of patronage was exercised on behalf of university students by the various estates. Altogether about forty baronial and gentry families patronized students. During this time a total of some sixty Masters, ten Bachelors of Arts and ten non-matriculated students found patrons among all classes.[6] Some students, mostly, Masters, appear in the confirmation records more than once and had more than one patron because they held several offices either simultaneously or consecutively, only a few of these, however, were Hussites.

A comparison of the names of the masters present at the 1411 *Quodlibet,* a disputation held on the university's anniversary, with those

PATRONAGE ON BEHALF OF UNIVERSITY OF PRAGUE STUDENTS
1400–1415

PATRONS	1400-1405			1405-1410			1410-1415			
	NM	B	M	NM	B	M	NM	B	M	Total
Royal	0	0	3	0	0	2	0	0	5	10
Noble	2	2	5	3½	5	12	0	1	7	37½
Townspeople	0	0	5	0	1	10	1	0	3	20
Secular clergy	0	0	6½	1½	0	3½	0	1	7	19½
Religious Orders	0	0	3½	1	0	7½	1	1	3	17
TOTAL	2	2	23	6	6	35	2	3	25	104

Notes: 1. ½ indicates that patronage was shared between members of different classes.   2. NM=non-matriculated; B=Bachelor of Arts; M=Master of Arts.

masters appearing in the archbishop's confirmation records shows to what extent those associated with Hus had found patrons. The 1411 *Quodlibet* was basically a Hussite affair. Sixty-one of the sixty-six masters present were native Bohemians, the group in which the Hussites found most of their support. Hus, the major speaker, was under papal anathema and had been cited to Rome to answer charges of heresy. Under these circumstances, except for perhaps a few observers from the Catholic party, most of those attending were undoubtedly friendly to his cause.[7] By 1415, two-thirds of the sixty-six masters present had not been confirmed to any church office. The developing alliance between nobility and Hussite university students had begun to result in church offices for some of the latter. There was, however, no general effort on the part of those nobles who later appeared in the Hussite camp to act as patrons on behalf of Hussite students.

The tenuous relationship between university students and Hussite nobles is reflected in the fact that of those forty nobles who were patrons of students before 1415 only five protested Hus' condemnation and death to the Council of Constance.[8] Three of the five priests whom they gave office were known Wyclifites; Master John Kardinál, Jacob of Soběslav[9] and Nicholas of Pelhřimov, later the bishop of the Taborite church. Two other students received offices through the patronage of persons associated with Hussitism. In 1407, the squire Mikeš of Ulibice, who eventually fought alongside Čeněk of Vartemberk in the Hussite wars, presented a university student to the parish in Nemojčeves[10] and Margaret of Peruce, a noble lady living in the community of pious women near the reformers' Bethlehem Chapel, was one of the patrons who presented Egidius, Bachalor of Arts, to the parish in Chlumčany in 1400.[11] Lord Henry of Rožmberk's patronage of university students suggests that he also favoured them. He supplied offices to seven members of the university community, one of whom, Thomas of Lysá was a leading Wyclifite and friend of Hus.[12] We know that Henry's wife sympathized with the reformers and possibly the Rožmberks brought their young friend and later one of the most powerful men in the realm, Čeněk of Vartemberk, into contact with the Hussite university masters.

An exhaustive survey of patronage bestowed by the nobility on either Hussites or university students cannot be conducted because of a lack of information. As a result only those who can be identified as either student or Hussite have been included. There were undoubtedly many priests who had perhaps attended the university for a year, adopted Wyclifite ideas, dropped out and then were presented and confirmed to a parish.

Only if a priest later became notorious, as did Peter Hromádka, is it possible to identify him and his patron.[13] Despite the limitations it is evident that, although until 1415 the nobility had not extensively put its patronage at the disposal of the university students, there existed a select group of eight nobles who had early recognized the possibilities inherent in their positions for assisting Hussite priests to find jobs and to spread their ideas.

The Hussite league of 6 September 1415 had taken pains to show that it considered its action lawful and that for their part its members were prepared to maintain a legitimate relationship with the ecclesiastical structure. In their pact the nobles had specified that their priests were subordinate to the Romanist bishops and would answer to them if charged with any error. They added that they would accept a decision on a priest's guilt or innocence only if it were based on the Word of God.[14] There is no suggestion that they intended to deny the patronage rights of ecclesiastical institutions on their estates and to obstruct the established procedures of presenting priests for confirmation to the archbishop's office. In the year immediately following the formation of the league, the Hussite nobility did not find it necessary to oppose the episcopal office and each continued to recognize the other's jurisdiction.

This can be seen from the fact that until 1417 the archbishop's office took no action against Hussite patrons and continued to confirm their priests. On 28 December, 1416 a priest proposed by Lord Čeněk was confirmed by the archbishop's office. This was Čeněk's last presentation of a new priest although he consented to three exchanges involving his priests in 1417 and one in 1418, all of whom were canonically confirmed.[15] Boček of Poděbrady, along with Čeněk, a captain of the league, presented a priest to the episcopal office for the last time on 28 April 1417. His candidate did not have to take the oath against utraquism and Wyclifism, although eight days earlier the archbishop had begun to administer it.[16] The priests of other Hussite barons were also confirmed by the archbishop throughout 1416. The last man to be presented by Hynek Krušina of Lichtenburk was confirmed on 7 August, that of Mikeš of Žampach on 22 September and that of John Sádlo of Kostelec, who was reportedly especially zealous in placing Hussite priests forcefully into office, on 11 April 1416.[17]

In a year like 1416, in which the archbishop and the king pursued a weak and temporizing policy with respect to prosecuting the Hussites, there were accepted ways in which a patron could rid himself of an unwanted priest without violating episcopal procedures. For one thing it was standard practice for priests to exchange offices with one another. Hussite and Catholic patrons could simply have exchanged priests. However even this device was not made use of. From 2 September 1415 until the end of 1416, two such exchanges involving Hussite patrons are recorded in the episcopal records.[18] We cannot say whether or not Hussite politics lay behind these exchanges because the religious views of the patrons of the other two churches affected are unknown.

A related case involved a parish belonging to Albert of Těchobuze, a burgrave of one of the Rožmberk castles hence in the service of Čeněk, the guardian of the Rožmberk children. Albert had indicated his Hussite sympathies by attaching his seal to the 2 September protest letter. On 18 May 1416 the former priest of Albert's parish, Zahoř, was confirmed in Borovnice, vacant by the death of the last rector, whose patrons were the archbishop and a local squire. The priest whom Albert presented to Zahoř also received the archbishop's confirmation.[19] This may have been a normal move on the part of the priests to parishes more to their liking. On the other hand, Albert may have wanted to get rid of his priest for doctrinal reasons and the archbishop then conveniently found for him a vacant parish.

There was one case in 1416 in which a Hussite patron may have expelled a priest without bothering to present his replacement to the archbishop's office, or if he did, he did not receive confirmation. On 12 November, John, the former priest in Hroby, went to the church of St. Adalbert in Prague under the patronage of the Catholic baron, Peter of Šternberk, in what was called an exchange. The patron in Hroby in 1415 had been Hrdibor of Štipoklasy. The Štipoklasy estate belonged to the Zbraslavice domain whose owner, John Podolec affixed his seal to the 2 September letter.[20] It may be that Podolec, as a Hussite enforcing his religious principles, was behind the decision to get rid of the priest in Hroby.

Another way in which a patron could get rid of a priest without violating episcopal procedure was simply to have the office declared vacant by resignation and appoint another priest. Normally a confirmation entry in the records included the reason for the departure of the last rector, namely death or resignation for a variety of reasons. As we saw above, a significant number of entries gave no reason for the resignation, probably because they were forced from the incumbent by the patron. In 1416 this device accounted for twenty-one percent of the vacancies, a rise of seven points from the previous year.[21] Unexplained resignations, did not, however, represent the activity of Hussites. On the contrary, it was Romanist patrons who were declaring offices vacant with no explanation and presenting other priests. Thus known enemies of the Hussite movement, such as Lords Otto of Bergov,[22] and Hynek Berka of Lipá,[23] as well as ecclesiastics such as the abbots of various monasteries,[24] Albík, the provost of the Vyšehrad cathedral,[25] and the archbishop[26] appointed priests after they had had the episcopal vicar-general declare the offices vacant.

Only one such case involved a patron associated with the Hussite cause. This was in Skryje, where the priests resigned on 11 October 1415 without an explanation.[27] The patrons here were Nicholas of Husinec, well known for his Hussite sympathies, his step sons and another local squire. The suspicion that Nicholas presented a Hussite after he had compelled the last one to resign seems inescapable. Why then did the archbishop's general-vicar, who was responsible for confirmations and who pursued a committed course in opposition to the Hussite movement, confirm Nicholas' priest? It was because throughout the years the episcopal office and lay patrons had worked out a *modus vivendi;* the noble patron recognized the archbishop's right to confirm and install his priest and in return the archbishop honoured the noble's choice for priest. This relationship continued until 1417, and other than the two cases where Hussite patrons may have been active, there is no evidence of a general changeover of priests caused by the Hussite noble league in 1416. If the Hussite nobility had already begun a wholesale replacement of Catholic priests with Hussites, including churches over which they did not own the patronage, an act which would have amounted to confiscation, the episcopal office would have objected, as it did later in 1417 when a Catholic patron tried it.

The year 1417, on the other hand, was crucial for the Hussite movement. Early in the year both king and archbishop embarked on a vigorous policy aimed at suppressing Hussitism. At the same time radical tendencies, within the movement, seeking more far-reaching changes in ecclesiastical life, had become more outspoken, alienating some nobles and jeopardizing the much needed support which the university leadership had carefully fostered among the nobility. In this situation, with their movement under attack from the outside and undermined from the inside, the noble friends of Wyclifism and utraquism responded using their authority as patrons. Fulfilling the terms of their 6 September 1415 pact, they defended their priests from ecclesiastical citations and then, in order to bring the radicals into the moderate mainstream of the movement, they provided them with parishes.

Already in December 1416, King Wenceslas, under pressure from the Council of Constance and his brother Sigismund, had forced the university to conform to his policy of a Catholic restoration. Royal decrees of 2 December expressed a settlement between the university and the archbishop, according to which all seized property was to be restored, expelled Catholic priests were to be reinstated, and the reformer lawyer, John of Jesenice, the cause of an interdict, was to leave Prague. As a concession to the Hussites, utraquism was permitted in certain churches.[28] But the hoped for peace was not to be. Most of the Hussites, led by Jakoubek of Stříbro, declined to comply with the king's orders. The Catholic clergy of St. Vitus cathedral refused to return to their offices and resume services, saying that neither churches nor property had been returned to their former owners.

More important for the Hussites was the archbishop's action at the beginning of 1417 which in effect made it necessary for the nobles to defend their clergy. After this they found themselves forced to act in defiance of the archbishop's office. On 10 January the archbishop published the Council's decree condemning utraquism and declared that henceforth he would neither ordain nor confirm into office any utraquist priest. Next, in order to remove those Hussites already in possession of church offices, he ordered his rural deans to convoke assemblies of parish priests for the purpose of ferreting out violators of the Council's instructions.[29] Furthermore, to keep any new Hussite priests from taking office, the archbishop instituted a special oath whereby priests being confirmed swore that they would not administer wine as part of communion nor would they hold the forty-five condemned Wyclifite articles. On 3 March 1417 the first Hussite priests were deprived of office for reasons of faith and on 8 April the oath abjuring Hussitism appeared for the first time.[30]

At the same time that the archbishop adopted his aggressive policy towards the Hussites, various trends developing within the Hussite movement began to threaten its unity. Some of the more radical tendencies with their far-reaching plans for reform had become a concern to the moderate leaders of the university-nobility coalition. The radicals wanted to reduce religious life to its most simple form. They denied the existence of purgatory and the usefulness of giving alms for the dead, and questioned the value of venerating the images of Christ and the saints, as well as a whole series of ceremonial and thaumaturgic rituals connected with the church's worship. Lastly, in keeping with the central position which the ceremony of the eucharist had assumed in the movement, they insisted that infants also partake in communion.[31] The moderate Hussite leadership, the university masters and nobles feared that the radicals, with their espousal of these Waldensian tenets, only obstructed any efforts to get European acceptance for their reforms. Already the radicals had induced some nobles to defect to the opposition thus placing the cause of reform in jeopardy at home.

Lord Čeněk of Vartemberk, at the end of 1416 and the beginning of 1417, took several steps aimed at reconciling the Hussite movement with the church. In a gesture which at the same time was intended for repairing his relationship with the future king, King Sigismund of Hungary, Čeněk accepted his offer, made in March of 1416, to mediate the dispute between the Hussite barons and the Council.[32] Concurrently, in a meeting with the university masters, Čeněk expressed strong disapproval of the ideas advocated by the radicals and urged the masters to seek reconciliation with the church.[33] In response to his prodding, the university on 25 January and 7 February 1417 issued public statements exhorting all to believe in purgatory, to continue to offer prayers, alms, and other suffrages for the dead, and to venerate the images of Jesus and the saints during worship as well as to observe various ceremonies like bell-ringing and blessing of grains, cheeses and eggs.[34]

The archbishop's campaign of suppression, launched at this same time, however, wrecked the hopes for a reconciliation between Hussites and Catholics and compelled Lord Čeněk to take steps to consolidate the Hussite Church by regulating the status of the Hussite clergy, while at the same time bringing the more radical ones into an established Hussitism. There was no dearth of volunteers willing to take up the pulpits in the name of the chalice and the freedom to preach the word of God. The problem was that in addition to spreading acceptable Hussite ideas these priests were also preaching tenets condemned by the university and sometimes indulging in behaviour deemed scandalous by the moderate Hussites. The problem for the Hussites was to regulate their own clergy so that in case of scandal there would not be a bad reflection on the movement. To meet this need for qualified priests, Čeněk on 6 March abducted Herman, the titular bishop of Nicopolis and suffragan bishop of Prague, to his castle Lipnice, where his father-in-law had endowed a collegiate church. Here Herman ordained priests for the Hussite Church including some of the younger men whom Čeněk hoped to draw from their radicalism into a more moderate stance by giving them a regular place and living.[35]

Later, on 17 June, in an effort to strengthen the Hussite position on the extensive Rožmberk domains, where Čeněk's guardianship ran out when the young Ulrich came of age in January 1418, Čeněk announced that henceforth communion was to be administered in both kinds, bread and wine, and that any cleric not willing to accept this would be replaced by one who was.[36] As part of this action Čeněk placed some fifteen priests into vacated Rožmberk parishes, most of whom had been ordained at Lipnice.[37]

After the onset of the archbishop's attack, Hussite priests were no longer confirmed to their parishes, either because their patrons did not present them to the episcopal office or because the officials refused them. Evidence of Hussite patronage can nevertheless be found in the episcopal records. For example, frequently the statement describing the installation of an orthodox priest identified him well enough so that he can be traced to his last office. When the office from which he came had no corresponding confirmation and the patron of that benefice was a Hussite we can be sure that he or she had removed a Catholic priest in favour of a Hussite.

The relatively high number of priests confirmed in 1417 who had left offices where Hussites were patrons supports the claim that 1417 was a decisive year for the Hussite nobility. In that year they expelled those of their priests who cooperated with the archbishop's officials and their attempts to locate Hussite priests for disciplinary action. In addition, on 10 March 1417 the University of Prague officially declared itself in favour of utraquistic communion. Any priest who could not accept this practice was evidently dismissed if his patron was an utraquist. This group of priests expelled from office because of their loyalty to the Roman faith and rite reflect the existence of a group of Hussite nobles who were committed to the reform movement even though it meant open disobedience to the established church and medieval religious order. These nobles played an important role in helping the Hussite movement in a critical period by giving its priests, parishes and security to conduct their ministry. From 1417 to late 1419 their domains were the only lands where Hussites enjoyed a legal existence while the rest of the realm drifted towards reaction.

Two of the priests whom Cenek expelled are identifiable in the episcopal records. In 26 April 1417 the former priest in Sedlčany was confirmed in Kovařov with the consent of the patrons, the abbot of the monastery in Milevsko and the local squires. Sedlčany was a Rožmberk church where Lord Henry had presented Vlaštek in 1407.[38] Similarly we know that Čeněk expelled the chaplain from Velešín, a Rožmberk office, sometime before 20 July 1417 because on that day John, the former chaplain there went to Drahov under the patronage of William of Ústí. As is to be expected, neither of the priests entering the two vacant Rožmberk churches received episcopal confirmation.[39] In addition, Čeněk most likely used the legitimate device of exchange to replace unwanted clerics. To this end he cooperated with Catholic patrons who found themselves with undesirable Hussite priests. Čeněk consented to exchanges involving three of his own churches in northeastern Bohemia. One of the exchanges affected a parish owned by Lord John of Michalovice, who in 1410 had supported the Wyclifites and had in that period placed one of them in that office. After returning to the Catholic fold in 1414 or 1415 he found the presence of a Hussite priest intolerable.[40]

Lord Čeněk was not the only patron active on behalf of Hussites. The episcopal records show that at least ten other Hussite nobles, five of whom had signed the 2 September protest letter, expelled priests for religious reasons and replaced them with Hussites. Sometime before 22 March 1417 Albert of Těchobuze and his co-patrons expelled their priest from his parish in Hodětice.[41] Similarly sometime before 22 April, Boček of Poděbrady released Peter, his chaplain of Náchod castle.[42] By July 21 Ulrich Vavák of Hradec had expelled his priest, Peter from the church in Straž, where he had presented him in March 1415.[43] Similarly Nicholas of Dětenice expelled his priest from Železný Brod (Brodec)[44] and lastly, from the ranks of the signers of the protest letter, John Medenec of Ratiboř expelled the priest from the church in Smilový Hory (Buchberg).[45]

Other nobles not party to the 2 September letter but otherwise known to be friends of the Hussite movement, also exercised their right of patronage on its behalf. Přibek of Klenov, who in the 1420s fought for his radical Hussite neighbours from Tabor, expelled his priest, from the altar of St. John the Evangelist in Týnec sometime before 14 March 1418.[46] So also John Mladenec of Újezdec, a neighbour of the lords of Rožmberk, most likely in connection with Čeněk's action in 1417, expelled the local priest.[47]

In addition there were actions, parallel to but apparently independent of that led by Čeněk, which provided Hussite priests with security. In January or early in February 1417 the squires, Přech of Olbramovice, Herman of Červený Hrádek and John of Leskovec, all from south-central Bohemia, founded a league for the defense of the chalice which had similarities with the baronial pact of 1415. The members promised their subjects, including their priests, protection from anathemas and ecclesiastical citations but also vowed to prevent their priests as well as other church authorities from administering such censures. Referring to the right of lay-people to take wine at communion, the first point reads:

"should they (our priests) try to keep us or our subjects from it, we are to move against them and oppose them, as enemies of the Law of God."[48]

At least two members of the league promptly put those words into effect. Evidently the priest in Olbramovice, Anthony, had tried to implement the archbishop's instructions of 10 January and had prohibited the use of the chalice in communion. Anthony had been presented to the parish in Olbramovice by Přech and his brothers and had been confirmed there on 3 October 1415. Since then however he had experienced a change of heart and by 12 February 1417 his patrons had expelled him.[49]

Similarly Herman of Červený Hrádek ousted a Catholic priest from office. Herman shared the patronage in the parish of Kosová Hora as well as in the chapel of St. Margaret and was sole patron of another chapel there.[50] By 11 August 1417 he had expelled Wenceslas of Sedlec, the altarist of St. Margaret's whom he had presented there in 1412. On the 11th, Wenceslas was confirmed to the church of Bohumilice under the patronage of Conrad of Vimberk, and through the intervention of the archbishop, after the priest there resigned without explanation. Most likely Lord Conrad arranged for his resignation, if indeed the language in the confirmation is not simply a euphemism for expulsion.[51] The other priests to whom Herman had been patron were likely not expelled judging from the fact that they were not confirmed to any new office. Presumably his religious beliefs were not offensive to them, although in the case of the parish Herman may have had to contend with opposition from the co-patrons. The third member of the pact, John of Leskovec, who was also party to the 2 September protest letter, was the patron of two parishes but it appears as though the priests whom he presented in 1412 and 1413 accepted his religious views.[52] Neither of them was confirmed elsewhere.

The pact of the gentry was formed at a time in which to them there seemed to be a vacuum in the leadership of the Hussite movement. The leading baron, Lord Čeněk, had taken up negotiations with the heir-apparent to the throne, King Sigismund, an avowed enemy of the movement, while at the same time he was urging the university masters to suppress the more radical popular expressions of religious renewal. Čeněk had not yet begun to supply the radical priests with parishes. Simultaneously the movement was coming under attack from the archbishop. Thus independent of the barons, these squires sought to provide some leadership and at least defend their domains from the reactionary drift which they felt was developing. Manifestations such as theirs perhaps induced Čeněk to temper his hostility towards the radicals and to embark on the course which sought to bring them into the Hussite Church established along moderate lines under the leadership of the university. They may also have had some influence on the university's decision of 10 March to officially declare itself in agreement with the use of wine for lay people in communion.[53]

Other references in the literature of the period, combined with the data from the records of confirmation show that the nobility's action to defend Hussite priests extended beyond the known members of the leagues and included one noble lady. In 1417 an anonymous writer wrote a series of verses, *Sermones ad Bohemos,* in which he praised those who defended orthodox Catholicism and damned those who fostered the Hussites. In the latter category he placed Lady Anna of Mochov, the widow of John Kamenice of Ústí. Alluding to Biblical and classical characters, he addressed her as: "You most fierce Jezabel, as you did to Elijah, so you now persecute a man as just as Abel, the priest in Ústí, who suffered abuses from you. You shall writhe in Hell."[54]

The incident to which he referred was Anna's removal of Benedict from the chapel near Hradiště, the site of an old castle a little over a mile from Ústí where Tabor, one centre of radical Hussitism was later built. She, with her sons, John and Procop, had presented Benedict there in October 1414. Benedict, in defiance of his patrons, remained true to the Roman faith and lost his position to an utraquist. He however found a church in Pravonín under the patronage of the monastery in Louňovice and was confirmed on 18 February 1417.[55] Since the author of *Sermones* singles out Lady Anna for vilification, and since her sons later that year presented an orthodox priest, she was most likely the moving force behind Benedict's ejection.

Only a small proportion of the over 200 churches to which Hussite nobles owned patronage experienced a change of priest during the religious upheavals which followed Hus' death. To some churches Hussite patrons had earlier appointed men who shared their sympathies for reform. Other priests, sensing the direction their lord was moving, adapted their own religious views accordingly in order to keep their jobs and income.[56] Furthermore not all expelled Catholics necessarily found a patron and thus do not appear in the episcopal records. It is however clear that Hussite nobles made use of their right of patronage on behalf of their own religious goals to the advantage of the movement in general.

The information derived from the episcopal confirmation records, showing the activity of Hussite patrons, puts into more accurate perspective the aristocratic contribution to the Hussite revolution.

Historians have mostly emphasized those forces of the revolution emanating from Prague and the rural non-noble communities. F.M. Bartoš, although he discussed Lord Čeněk's action, interpreted the defection in 1417-1418 of several nobles to King Sigismund's party as the end of effective noble support. Henceforth, he stressed, leadership for the movement came from Prague priests like Jakoubek of Stříbro and John Želivský and similar types from the country.[57] J. Macek discounted the nobles' efforts entirely mentioning only the 2 September protest letter for which he gave the gentry most of the credit.[58] F. Seibt granted that the policy of the Czech nobility was no less dynamic than that of the "masters, nationalists, republicans and brotherhoods [eg. Taborites]."[59] He however left unanalyzed the nobles' policy and contribution to the movement. H. Kaminsky paid due attention to the noble league but restricted himself to the activity of Čeněk of Vartemberk.[60]

The success of the Hussite revolution, both in Prague and the country, owed more to the nobility than has been generally recognized. The assistance of the aristocratic church patrons made possible the later success of Hussitism both in its Prague and rural plebeian setting. Hussite nobles protected their priests on domains in eastern Bohemia, starting from the north around Železný Brod past Jičín, Poděbrady, Hradec Králové, Litomyšl, Chrudim, Čáslav, Lipnice and to the Rožmberk domains just south of Tabor. This was exactly the region where Hussitism enjoyed its greatest strength in the years following. It is no coincidence that in this region were the two main centres of popular and radical Hussitism, Hradec Králové and Tabor, to which flocked the masses in the hope of finding a new world. It was the priests to whom Hussite nobles had given shelter on their domains who awakened these ideas in the masses. It was these people who came to the defense of Prague, besieged by King Sigismund's armies. Just as Hussite nobles used their patronage and power on behalf of their priests, so the Catholics rallied to the support of their church when it was under attack, lending their secular authority for the protection of its priests.

CHAPTER 9

CATHOLIC NOBLES IN DEFENCE OF THE FAITH

The fact that Hus had encouraged the secular lord to take over church lands made Hussite nobles susceptible to the charge that they were greedy for clerical property. The Catholic nobles were working for the Roman Church, an institution which sanctioned the clergy's ownership of land. This fact gave the nobles a greater degree of freedom when they undertook to defend their clergy and when they assumed rights which had previously belonged to the clergy their motives were less in question. In the course of defending the Catholic faith the nobles sometimes acted in cooperation with the clergy but at other times despite its opposition. Among those acting in concert with the archbishop were a number of nobles who had personally supported Hus, but who, as the lines between the radicals and the moderates became more sharply drawn, opted for a return to orthodoxy and submitted Catholic candidates to the archbishop for investment into office.

Although the religious issue, which deeply divided the Czech people for years to come, also affected the nobility, it did not determine the nobles relationship to each other. They retained sight of those interests which united their estate and tolerated each other's religious differences. As each sought to establish security for his or her priest the Catholic noble left the Hussites in peace just as the Hussites did not disturb their counterparts. At most the differences between Catholic and Hussite nobles produced an irresolution which resulted in the noble estate standing by powerlessly as the revolutionary wars raged throughout the land after 1419.[1]

Evidence of a basic unity among the barons can be found throughout the years as the religious dispute over John Hus began to heat up. Lord John Jr. of Hradec, who in the fall of 1415 was a leader of the Catholic league, during Čeněk's dispute with Bishop John of Litomyšl in 1413 intervened with the king on Čeněk's behalf in an effort to get a settlement.[2] Furthermore, Čeněk's Hussite beliefs did not deter Catholic nobles from seeking his aid in their disputes. Two allies in the fight for Catholic Christendom against utraquism, Nicholas Zajíc of Hazmburk and Otto of Bergov, in October 1414 asked Čeněk, after he had openly acknowledged his sympathy for Hus, to supervise the truce with which they had interrupted their feud at that time.[2] Similarly Čeněk was to oversee, and in the event of an infraction, arbitrate, the truce of 18 June 1416 between the king and the archbishop on the one hand, and the lords of Osek and Přimda on the other.[3] Later, on 17 November 1419 the noble officials of the realm, including both Hussites and Catholics, in cooperation with other leading nobles from both camps, closed the land register (zemské desky), ordering that until the new king had arrived in the kingdom no more entries whatsoever were to be made in the books.[4] This action was evidently aimed at preventing any changes of property resulting from the imminent revolution from acquiring the force of law.

The Catholic barons who met at Český Brod at the beginning of October 1415 with the archbishop left no record of their program except to say that they did not wish to be Hussites.[5] They were loyal to King Sigismund of Hungary, whom they expected to become king after his brother Wenceslas' death. When he wrote them that it was very improper for them to hold meetings and form associations without their monarch's permission they apparently acquiesced and allowed him and the archbishop to take the initiative in their respective spheres. To the archbishop they probably indicated that they intended to see to it that the Catholic order of worship was observed on their domains and that they were prepared to enforce his instructions to that end. The Catholic nobles, however, made no effort to reverse or counter what the Hussites were doing on their own lands and there is no evidence of violence or tension between the two baronial groups.

In the years 1417-1419, noble patrons, in helping the Roman Church maintain its doctrine and rite, permitted the clergy to intervene in their appointment of priests to office. When the archbishop detected an utraquist priest, and deprived him of an office to which a Catholic noble was patron, the latter supported this and presented an orthodox candidate. Expulsion from a church benefice was not new although it became more frequent after 1416.[6] From 3 March 1417, when the first reference to deprivation occurs, to 28 March 1419, the last mention, eight priests were expelled by the archbishop and at least two by lay patrons. All but one of them lost their offices in the period of little over a year, as expulsions virtually ceased after 14 May 1418.

It was mostly nobles who were affected by dismissals as seven of the eight priests had had noble patrons. Three involved barons: Hynek Berka of Lipá, Henry of Elsterberk and Procop and John of Ústí, men who may have regretted their presentation of reformist priests.[7] In the case of the lords of Ústí we know that their cooperation with the archbishop in installing a priest faithful to the church represented a change of policy.

Earlier in 1417 they had cooperated with their mother in expelling a Catholic priest from Hradiště. The author of *Sermones ad Bohemos,* writing in the fall of 1417, evidently did not know of the lords of Ústí's return to the fold because he denounced them all, except Ulrich, as Hussites.[8] In late October 1417 Procop and John, without their mother, Anna of Mochov, presented an orthodox priest to the church in Kamenice who was confirmed on 19 November 1417 after the archbishop had deprived the previous rector of the office.[9] Had they still been in the Hussite camp they would not have consented to the expulsion of a Hussite priest.

The degree of cooperation between Catholic nobles and clergy extended to the point that nobles accepted not only the archbishop's supervision but also that of the local priests. Thus on 16 January 1419 the altarist of the chapel of St. Mary in Načerač was confirmed after the incumbent had resigned without explanation. The parish clergy there had intervened, apparently pressuring him out, and the local squires, Přibek and Hynek of Machlov, the patrons, had consented. In 1419 the episcopal official mentions the clergy's consent. In 1406 at the last confirmation it had not been required.[10]

In some cases the Romanist nobles did not wait for the church to act. At least two members of the gentry took the initiative and expelled their priests whom they suspected of heresy. The archbishop's aggressive pursuit of Hussites was spreading as lay noble patrons began to select only orthodox priests. On 5 July Amcha of Vesele withdrew his presentation of a Maršík of Muta who was accused of having deserted his church, preaching errors in several parishes and celebrating communion with both wine and bread. Amcha feared that he would lose his right of patronage so he relinquished Maršík's candidacy.[11] Whereas late in 1415 the episcopal office had accepted the presentation of a known Hussite, Nicholas of Husinec, to a church whose former rector had had to leave under pressure, in 1417 the archbishop's forceful policy had made some nobles like Amcha timid and unwilling to take the risk of losing rights of patronage.

In a stronger case of independent action, Leopold Kraselov of Žimutice, who along with his brothers John and Hrdoň, affixed his seal to the 2 September letter,[12] signalled his defection from the Hussite cause on 31 July 1418. Just before this he had removed Stephen, the altarist of the alter of 10,000 Knights in the Žimutice parish, just south of Tabor. The confirmation of his replacement asks that Stephen's resignation be approved because he had celebrated communion in both kinds in the presence of his patron.[13] Stephen had come there in 1414 with Leopold's consent. Perhaps Leopold's change of religion came as a result of pressure from his recently come-of-age baronial neighbour, Ulrich of Rožmberk. Lord Ulrich did not share the commitment to the reformers' cause which had marked the policy of his former guardian, Čeněk of Vartemberk. These examples show that Catholic nobles were willing to work with the church insuring that Romanist priests controlled parishes. The Catholic nobility was however also willing and able to make the defence of the faith its own affair going as far as taking over rights and property belonging to the clergy if need be. By the end of 1416 it had become increasingly difficult to maintain order. The literature of the period reflects the fact that the common people were expressing their hatred for the clergy by storming monasteries and churches which they then usurped or destroyed.[14] In the east shortly after Hus' death the nobility had attacked the property of Bishop John of Litomyšl but in the west the populace was at the forefront of the violence. Reflecting the turbulent situation the nobleman, Nicholas Zajíc of Valdek, owner of a castle between Plzeň and Prague, on 21 October 1416 wrote to the Chapter of St. Vitus in the Prague castle, excusing himself for not coming to see them because it was not safe to ride to Prague. He promised to come as soon as possible saying that he had served them gladly and would continue as before.[15] The situation had deteriorated to the point that some regions were described as being in a state of war. Thus King Wenceslas absolved the monastery in Chotěšov of the royal tax on 5 February 1417 because the fighting had reduced it to poverty.[16]

Other nobles who shared Nicholas Zajíc's eagerness to serve the church in these tumultuous circumstances did so by accepting guardianship over ecclesiastical property. The nobility's takeover of church property has scandalized observers past and present. Andrew of Brod did not differentiate between Hussite and Catholic lords when he charged them in 1421 with acting with the intent of acquiring the property of clergy and townspeople. More recently F. Bezold observed that the behaviour of the nobility in Sigismund's party, based on considerations of what would bring them the most material gain, must have cast a peculiar light on those who had cast themselves as the foremost defenders of the threatened church.[17]

The record shows however that at least at the beginning the clergy in general entered into such arrangements voluntarily. They knew that a noble was in a better position than were they to keep their property from falling into the hands of rebels and heretics.[18] For example, Bohuslav of Švamberk on 12 January 1417 accepted wardship over three villages belonging to the dean and the canons of the chapter of St. Vitus for which he was to receive seventy-two groschen annually and the obedience of the inhabitants.[19] The lords of Švamberk also received a revenue of 15,000 groschen from the Chotěšov monastery granted them by the king on 5 February. The nobles were expected to defend the monastery, which was also in their interest if they wanted to collect the income. Later on 19 May 1420 William Zajíc of Hazmburk and his sister Anna, the widow of John of Milheim, Hus' patron in 1402, took custody of some property near Prague belonging to John of Kralovice, a prelate who went into exile with part of the episcopal consistory. In this case the nobles' care was to last for their lifetime as they promised that their heirs would return it assuming that the danger was over by then.[20] Lady Anna's switch to the Catholic cause reflects the radicalization of the reform movement since the beginning of the century. Events had evidently not progressed as she and her husband had hoped when they provided Hus with the means to preach his ideas. Similarly accepting money from the church were the lords Henry of Elsterberk and John of Lestkova who on 26 February 1420 got part of the promised 18,000 groschen from the Chotěšov monastery.[21] There was no mention for what the payment was given but most likely it was in return for protective services rendered by the nobles. Church property could also be used to purchase the loyalty of Hussite nobles. Thus in 1421 King Sigismund entrusted two ecclesiastical villages to the brothers Buzek and Henry of Dráhov, men who in 1415 had joined the letter protesting Hus' death. In exchange for the villages they promised to serve the king with eight horses for one year.[22]

Sometimes such protective services meant that the nobility assumed patronage over churches belonging to others. In some cases Catholic townsmen and clerics were threatened in their patronage rights by the local population and called on noble assistance. Thus for example, Henry of Elsterberg on 2 April 1417 presented a priest to the church in Chotikov with the approval of Thomas Pabiak of Plzeň after the archbishop had deprived Nicholas Mníšek of that office. Previously, in 1394, the patronage in Chotikov had been owned solely by a Plzeň burgher.[23] Chotikov was about twelve miles from the war-troubled monastery in Chotěšov, and Mníšek, one of the radical Hussite preachers, had evidently persuaded his parishioners of his beliefs and may even have incited the violence against the monastery. In any case the decision by a townsman in nearby Plzeň to install an orthodox priest evidently did not gain the latter entrance into a parish whose members were angered by the archbishop's removal of their priest. The added authority of a baron, who had the power to enforce it, was supposed to provide security and assurance that the Catholic priest could indeed function.

Lord John Chotěmice of Vlaším also assumed the administration over church property and intervened on behalf of its patrons in order to add his authority to ecclesiastical confirmations. Twice he replaced the archbishop as patron, on 15 April 1418 in Vyskytna and on 6 May 1418 he was one of the patrons of the altar of Corpus Christi in Řečice.[24] Similarly he presented to two other towns, Rovna and Dřevčice, in 1417 and 1418 where earlier two prelates had been the patrons.[25] Lastly in March 1419 he was the patron in Hořepník "with the special permission of the lord Conrad, archbishop of Prague."[26]

All of these churches except Dřevčice were scattered throughout the Kouřím archdeaconry in southeastern Bohemia which was heavily represented by Hussite gentry in the 1415 protest letter. Dřevčice was just northeast of Prague. All were hence in areas hostile to the church. The goal of a landowner was to have his property in a compact unit to facilitate and economize its administration. The fact that the churches in question were scattered suggests that John took over the lands from the clergy not so much for the purpose of building up an estate as to protect them from Hussites and to give force to the archbishop's confirmations of Catholic priests to church office.

The assumption by barons of patronage over parishes belonging to ecclesiastical institutions was not always appreciated. The actions of Lord John Vartemberk of Ralsko are instructive in this respect. Notorious for stealing and violence but under the influence of John Hus in 1405 he promised to mend his ways. He however disappointed Hus a few months later by ending his penitence with a renewed outbreak of violence when he found out he was not to get the royal domain of Bělá at the death of Margrave Procop.[27] The habitation from which the demons had been cast, was filled with them many times over (Matthew 12:43-45), in that it was said of John that he resumed robbing and stole everything which he had been unable to lay his hands on previously. Although not named in the complaint, it seems that Ralsko (also called Chudoba, i.e. The poor), a member of the Catholic league in 1415, in 1417 took over both property and patronage belonging to the Cistercian monastery in Hradiště in northeastern Bohemia. On 12 February 1417 and 15 April 1418 he was patron in Hlavice whereas in 1412 it had been the abbot of the Hradiště monastery.[28] John, the abbot after 1415, in a letter to another abbot wrote that at the monastery "they had been placed in maximum danger and penury from the fact that the noble lords of Vartemberk, the successors of our founders, to the detriment of us and our order, hold and usurp our property and the chattels of our monastery."[29] Lord John of Ralsko, by presenting orthodox priests to the consistory for confirmation, could appear as a loyal son of the church while at the same time requiring suitable payment for his services. He also appeared as the patron in Žibřidice for the first time on 23 May 1418, which suggests a change of property of some sort since the previous patron here had been the squire John of Zarov.[30]

Similarly the Duchess Anna of Osvětim, a zealous Catholic who submitted her priests for confirmation as late as 7 April 1419, that is as long as the consistory functioned, tried to wrest patronage in Solnice from an ecclesiastical institution. In September 1417 she, with her son Půta of Častolovice, was accused of opposing the confirmation of Laurence, presented by Martin, the prior of the House of St. Bartholemew in Pardubice. Půta had earlier been party to the Hussite protest letter but in June 1417 had joined the king's service, the terms of which he renegotiated with King Sigismund in 1420.[31] Disregarding the verdict of the episcopal court which gave the right to the Order, Lady Anna, violently installed her own priest, obstructing the installation of Laurence. This is the only case recorded by the episcopal records where a noble was accused of having occupied a church belonging to an ecclesiastical institution. This along with other evidence outlined above suggests that as early as 1417 the nobility had begun to exact a price for its service to the church. After the revolution broke out in late 1419 the nobles' requirement, that they be paid in property, either royal or ecclesiastical became a regular feature and eventually a source of wealth and power.

While the Catholic nobility defended the church, the situation in Bohemia had developed to the point where nobles who at one time had supported the Hussite movement became increasingly unwilling to do so. For one thing the objectionable radical tendencies, advocating beliefs long condemned as heretical and harder to defend than the more limited and conservative Wyclifite-Hussite principles, had not been removed. Furthermore, some noble friends of Hus may have been opposed to the university's declaration on 10 March 1417 officially approving the chalice. In addition, in the spring of 1418 the newly elected pope, Martin V, took the offensive and sent King Wenceslas, whom the pope accused of harbouring heretics, a list of 24 demands to be executed in order to bring Bohemia back into the fold of the church and for him to recognize the Roman Church as the only true one. The fulfillment of the pope's demands naturally amounted to a reversal of Hussite gains. All of these developments made the prospect of defending Hussite ideas on church reform less appealing.

King Sigismund, whose zeal for the Roman faith was well known, was expected to provide the secular force to implement the pope's policy. By the fall Sigismund was on his way eastward preparing to intervene with the help of the papal legate John Dominici. At Passau, in Bavaria, a delegation from King Wenceslas met him and was told that Sigismund's intervention on behalf of his brother keeping the Council and pope from proceeding against the royal family was coming to an end.[32] Several Bohemian barons met Sigismund there as well and at least one of them, Peter of Šternberk, openly declared himself prepared to help the king defend the Roman faith by entering his service.[33]

From the point of view of Wenceslas, still king of Bohemia, but now threatened by his brother who was acting in league with the barons, a situation which to Wenceslas recalled the baronial confederations at the beginning of the century, it was time to end his toleration of the Hussites and reverse their recent advances. All the parishes and altars in the royal cities he therefore returned to their Catholic owners and by 26 February 1419 Catholic services were resumed. The king permitted utraquistic services in four churches in Prague and at those altars to which Hussites could gain access.[34] The noble leadership, as well as the university masters, decided not to oppose the king. The nobles were not bothered on their estates and in any case were not prepared to take a step which meant rebellion against their recognized monarch. While some, like Čeněk, practicing utraquism on their lands, were content to wait until the death of Wenceslas and the outcome of negotiations with Sigismund, others, judging the cause of moderate Hussitism to be futile, returned to the church.

One sign of a noble's defection from utraquism was his patronage of an orthodox priest confirmed by the archbishop. The episcopal records reflect the fact that eleven of the signers of the letter protesting Hus' death in 1415 had in this way deserted the Hussite cause. The fact that six of them took the step in October and November of 1417 indicates that this was the crucial period and perhaps they were reacting to the fact that the Hussite leadership in the summer had decided to make the chalice the focal point of the movement.[35] In other words they could support a program whose ideals, a pure moral life, were abstract enough to be safe, but when the symbol became a concrete one, easily identifiable, they hesitated and eventually abandoned their earlier course.

John of Běstvina was one of the earliest defectors. On 25 June 1417 he consented to an exchange between his priest and the one in Heřmanice.

Both priests swore that they did not hold any Wyclifite doctrines and that they would not offer wine to lay communicants. John later in May 1419, again presented a priest to the episcopal office after his priest had left for another office.[36] John of Landštejn and John of Zdebuzeves, who both affixed their seals to the September protest letter, by 23 October 1417 had both left the movement. On that day their priests exchanged parishes and testified to their orthodoxy by taking the oath against the forty-five ecclesiastically condemned articles of John Wyclif.[37] The author of the *Sermones ad Bohemos* was aware of the defection of the lords of Landštejn and included them in the section—Praise of Barons. The Landštejns, he wrote, were at first not able to perceive properly the stench of the Hussite schism but having taken sound counsel they emerged from the affair with their banner, the white rose, unstained.[38]

The defection of others who had been party to the 1415 protest letter warrants brief mention. On 25 October 1417 Jost of Zhoř consented to an exchange between his priest in Michalovice and the one in Čerňcice.[39] Then on 3 November 1417 and August 1418 the priests of Naršik of Alberovice were confirmed to the chapel in Křivsoudov, a town owned by the archbishop. On 10 November Wenceslas of Sulevice and his co-patron had their priest confirmed to the chapel in Křešín and on 13 November Leon of Mnich presented a priest to Mnich who took the oath of orthodoxy at his confirmation.[40] The outgoing priests of the three confirmations in November 1417 were said to have resigned, but no explanation was given as to why or where they went. The evident answer is that in returning to the Catholic Church these former Hussite patrons got rid of undesirable priests who had refused to go along with their conversion.

Furthermore in September 1418, two priests patronized by John Podolec of Zbraslavice were confirmed to office. Similarly Albert of Stojice, whom we met in connection with expelling a Catholic priest in 1417, was back in the Catholic camp by 25 February 1419 when he consented to an exchange involving his priest in Těchobuze. Albert, as the burgrave of the Rožmberk castle Příbenice, was most likely affected by the fact that Ulrich of Rožmberk had reached majority and was not strictly following Čeněk's lead on the question of religion. Lastly, Vitek of Žehusice and his brother John presented the local priest who was confirmed on 16 May 1419.[41] There may have been others who defected but since they were not patrons or because their priests changed religion with them they do not appear in the episcopal records.

In addition several men who had not signed the protest letter but had had a connection with the reform movement also presented to the

Catholic consistory in 1417 and after. Diviš of Říčany, one of the lesser noblemen who sent a letter to Sigismund's court at Constance on Hus' behalf appeared twice as a patron: in September 1417 and June 1418.[42] Similarly Menhart Velhartice of Hradec, the son of John Sr., a prominent Hussite baron, had rejected his father's policy when he took over the estate at his father's death in 1417. Menhart testified to being an orthodox Catholic by presenting priests to the episcopal office for altars in Hradec in January and May, to an altar in Velhartice in March and to the parish in Prachen in April 1418.[43]

Ulrich of Rožmberk cannot be considered a defector from Hussitism since he only reached the age of majority in January 1418. His decision to present orthodox candidates to the archbishop's office did however mean a departure from what seems to have been the policy of his father, and certainly that of Čenek of Vartemberk. Henceforth utraquists could no longer expect the sixty parishes on his domains to be open to them. Ulrich's first act as patron was his consent to two exchanges on 25 April 1418 involving his own parishes of Bavorov and Strunkovice. From that day until 23 December 1419, shortly before the records ceased to be kept, he exercised his right five additional times.[44] One of these was his presentation of a priest to Mlazov in January 1419 after Master Thomas of Lysá, to whom his father Henry had been patron in 1407, had resigned. The confirmation states that the church is vacant "by the voluntary resignation of Master Thomas of Lysá" which shows that that formula was simply a pro forma statement necessary before a new priest could be confirmed. Thomas was obviously not resident in Mlazov or he would have shared the fate of his fellow Hussite, John of Jesenice, who having ventured onto the Rožmberk domains, was placed into a dungeon where he died.[45]

The record of Queen Sophia's confirmations during this period also reflects her return to the Catholic fold. Her pattern of presentations conforms to the scheme of events outlined in this and the preceding chapter. As part of the Hussite coalition she stopped submitting candidates to the consistory at the beginning of 1417 after the archbishop began his concerted attack on the Hussites by withholding confirmation from their priests. Then in 1419, under pressure from the pope, who cited her to answer charges that she had persecuted priests, as well as from King Sigismund, she returned to presenting orthodox priests.[46] Just as the people in south Bohemia had taken to the fields and hills to hear preachers recently turned out of office by patrons like Ulrich of Rožmberk, so in the east where lay the queen's landholdings, among those who gathered on hilltops were many who had lost their regular priests as a result of her return to Catholicism.

Both Catholic and Hussite nobles undertook the defence of their religions on their domains. By using their rights of patronage both groups were instrumental in determining what would be the religion in their region. In general for the Hussites this was the east and for the Catholics the west. Neither group tried however to extend its faith onto the estates of the other. This basic respect for the seignorial rights persisted even though for many in Bohemia the struggle over religious issues had become a matter of life and death. It was precisely because the issues were being discussed in apocalyptic terms and the struggle as the final one between good and evil, that the moderate leadership no longer satisfied those most convinced of the need for reform. As a result of the Hussite nobility's hesitancy in the face of the reaction in 1419 the radicals came to dominate the direction of events towards their hoped for revolution. It took the nobility fourteen years before it could achieve enough agreement on a policy giving them the strength to defeat the revolution.

When the moderate Hussites declined to take vigorous action on behalf of the ideas and adherents of the reform movement the initiative passed to the forces of the revolution. With its coming the paramount task of the nobles was to re-establish order in the country, an order of which they had been the arbiters. Their goal therefore was to undermine the support which the radical leaders of the revolution had among the people. Although erratic and disunited at first this was the policy around which Catholic and Hussite nobility eventually coordinated their efforts.

In Prague the insurrection was led by the former monk, John Želivský, who in the course of the year aroused the masses to protest the king's policy by marching through the streets attacking their foes through polemical songs. Among their enemies the radicals regarded also the Hussite university masters, the allies of the Hussite nobility who in response to the royal opposition had counselled the people to obey the king's orders in the hope that a better time was at hand.[1] The most momentous popular demonstration was the one on 30 July 1419. In an action which was probably previously discussed with the radicals in the rural countryside, Želivský led a procession from his church to the Town Hall of New Town Prague. They invaded the building and in an act of defiance to the king, threw the recently installed anti-Hussite town councillors to their deaths on the street below.[2]

Just as in Prague, so in the country the suppression of Hussitism through the removal of their priests from office, which we illustrated in the preceding chapter, permitted the radicals to seize the initiative. Former parish priests like Peter Hromádka and Vaněek, beginning at Easter 1419, were instrumental in organizing the assemblies of people who wished to practice utraquism, but who were shut out of their churches. These people met under the open sky to hear the preaching of the word of God, and took communion with both bread and wine.[3] Their leaders, who interpreted the oppression by the authorities as a sign of the end times, called the people to gather in five cities which they said had been selected by God as places of security. Many responded, left home, property and family and provided a vast reservoir of human beings which was tapped by the radicals to give power to their ideas.

The revolutionary events of 1419, especially those on 30 July, placed the king into a tight situation. Confronted by the power of the Hussite movement he gave in to the demands of their priests and appointed city councillors sympathetic to them. On the other hand he was under pressure from his brother, King Sigismund who was in touch with leading Bohemian barons, to take action to suppress the Hussites. The tension was too much for him; two weeks after the defenestration, his body, weakened by gout and heavy drinking throughout his lifetime, suffered a stroke and the king died at the age of fifty-eight.[4]

Wenceslas' death vacated the throne to which Sigismund was heir. All that blocked Sigismund from ascending was that his known opposition to Hussitism had made him enemies in Prague who resolved to block his ascension unless he granted them religious freedom. It was the same people responsible for the removal of the hated town councillors and for gathering the people in the countryside who led the resistance to Sigismund. The Czechs and the heir-apparent did not reach agreement on this issue until 1436 so that until then Bohemia existed in a state of revolution and illegitimacy.

With respect to the question of restoring legitimacy the Bohemian policy was divided into three groups: the party of King Sigismund, the Polish party and the radicals. Through the course of the sixteen years some members drifted from one group to another. But it was not until 1427, after the Polish candidacy had proved to be untenable and the desire for peace among the people began to outweigh their revolutionary fervor, that the Sigismund group became representative enough to begin effective negotiations with the king.

The Polish party consisted of Hussites who wanted to retain the old social-political order but who were angered by King Sigismund's refusal to protect Hus and to grant their religious wishes. As a king he was therefore unacceptable to them. They wanted an end to violence and at the head of an ordered society they wanted a king whom they sought in the neighbouring kingdom of Poland, a country where the people spoke a related Slavic language. Since the end of the fourteenth century there had existed such a party in Bohemia, which, sometimes with and sometimes without support from King Wenceslas, had aided the Poles in their struggle with the Teutonic Knights. Until their search for a Polish king proved ephemeral no serious approach to Sigismund was undertaken by them. The religious program of this group was one of moderate reform embodied in the Four Articles of Prague: communion was to be celebrated with both bread and wine, the word of God was to be freely preached, all priests were to give up lordship over temporal property and live model lives and "public mortal sins" were to cease and the

Bohemian realm cleansed of slander. This group included some radicals but in general was made up of the moderate Hussites of Prague and those noblemen associated with the city.[5]

The radicals consisted of that part of Prague controlled by Želivský and in general the Taborites of south Bohemia and the Orebites from the east. For them the primary question was not one of restoring legitimacy but one of defending their concept of the truth. For this they were willing to fight, even to the point of taking the initiative against their enemies, attacking both baronial and urban fortresses in order to destroy the nests of their Catholic enemies before the latter did the same to them. As far as the Taborite priests were concerned the monarchy was not needed for the organization of society. At Klatovy, in 1424, they expressed the principle that if the legitimate powers were remiss in their duties the people themselves, moved by God's spirit, could take over the functions of government.[6] If this group had any particular person in mind for its king it did not push his candidacy very strongly. Judging from a statement, which a Prague poet attributed to Nicholas of Husinec, one of their military captains, they would have accepted a native born Czech as king.[7] John Žižka, perhaps the most prominent military commander among the radicals, accepted the idea of seeking a candidate in Poland although when such one arrived in the person of Prince Sigismund Korybut of Lithuania, nephew of the King of Poland, Žižka did not always cooperate with him.[8]

For the religious program of the radicals, the Four Articles were only the point of departure. To them the true church was one patterned on that of the New Testament, which for them meant a great diminuation of the power of the clergy. They disagreed with the Praguers on the importance of the sacraments, wishing to dispose of them insofar as they were not present in the original church. In addition they insisted that Christ was not corporeally present in the Eucharistic bread. They stood for a greatly simplified life, objecting to any signs of luxury such as the ornate vestements worn by the moderate Hussite priests as well as to the rich fineries and elegant mustaches of the burghers of Prague. They justified the destruction of such church buildings which according to them were no more than dens of thieves and simoniacs and they asserted that it was permissible to steal valuables from the churches when these were used to help the poor.[9]

The Sigismund party, to which most of the nobility belonged, was split in its religious program. Most of its members were orthodox Catholics who sought a return to one church in Bohemia practicing the rites and doctrines of Rome and obedient to their lawful king, King Sigismund.[10]

There were however also Hussites in this camp whose religious program was moderate like that of the Polish party. Although sincerely committed to a policy of safe guarding the practice of utraquism, the Hussites of both groups did not want to do this at the expense of the rights of their estate. To cooperate with the revolutionaries in defence of the Chalice meant a subordination of their privileged status and fighting alongside peasants whose ferocity in battle was distasteful to them. To some Hussites, however, for example Čeněk of Vartemberk, a Polish king was not really a viable alternative. Čeněk could not conceive of calling a king without the support of the nobility as a whole. And because he knew of the loyalty which Sigismund commanded among the nobles he never seriously considered a Polish candidate. His efforts rather, were directed at trying to create a united front which could confront the king with a list of demands.[11]

After the death of King Wenceslas, the moderate wing of the Hussite movement led by the nobles tried to regain control of events in order to carry through the reformation on their own terms. To this end, in September 1419, Čeněk initiated a pact in alliance with the Catholic barons, the city of Prague and some prelates whose goals were to secure freedom for utraquism while at the same time to support the queen in maintaining order while they awaited the arrival of the king. At the same time, to show to all that they were the spokesmen for utraquism, the Hussite nobility, together with Prague, and in the name of the estates of the Czech kingdom, issued a series of requirements including guarantees for their religion and the Czech language to Sigismund, which he was to accept if he wanted to be king in Bohemia.[12] The next step was for the noble leadership to regain control of Prague which had fallen to the radicals as a result of the defenestration in August. In November the nobility tried to surround the city in an effort to block the rural multitudes from joining their radical friends in the city whom they wished to help. To the city itself they issued letters of challenge, which was like declaring war, unless the city joined them.[13] Still in pursuit of their goals to attain recognition for utraquism under Sigismund's reign, the nobles went to Brno in Moravia to attend the king's court. There at the end of December both Hussite and Catholic barons swore obedience to the king. From Brno they accompanied the king to Wroclaw, which at that time belonged to the Bohemian crown lands.

Events which followed doomed the efforts of the moderate Hussites to failure. In Wroclaw Sigismund took two steps in mid-March 1420 which illustrated to all concerned that he intended to cooperate fully

with the church's program of exterminating the Hussite heresy. On 15
March he permitted a Prague merchant, John Krása, a Hussite at that time
in Wroclaw, to be executed as a heretic by the local bishop. Two days
later he participated in the publication of a papal bull which announced a
crusade against all heretics, Wyclifites and Hussites.[14]

The combined episodes compelled Čeněk and his party[15] temporarily
to desert King Sigismund. The king had at about the same time, as arbi-
trater of a dispute between the Polish king and the Order of the Teutonic
Knights over the south eastern part of Lithuania, ruled against the Pole.
Hoping to take advantage of the Polish anger towards Sigismund, Čeněk
sent a delegate to the Polish court who was to ascertain the chances of
King Vladislav accepting the Bohemian crown. The effort was fruitless
but it established an unforgotten precedent.[16] Čeněk himself returned to
Prague where he allied himself with the radicals and replaced the royal
garrison of the castle with one loyal to the Hussite city. On 20 April he
and Ulrich of Rožmberk, in the name of the lords, the cities of Prague,
the knights, squires and other towns, issued a declaration admonishing
all estates of the kingdom of Bohemia not to obey Sigismund, who was
neither elected nor crowned. The man, they said, was an enemy of the
Czech tongue and realm for which they cited the evidence of his behaviour
in Wroclaw. As further indication that he intended to do battle with
Sigismund, Čeněk had his banner displayed on the tower of the Prague
town hall.[17]

By early May, Čeněk had again reversed himself and returned to Sigismund's camp. Except for his close circle, the nobility had not supported
his call to defy Sigismund, and any resistance without significant support
from his fellow barons was unthinkable. Through the mediation of two
baronial friends in Sigismund's camp, Ernest Flaška of Richenburk and
William Zajíc of Hazmburk, he reached agreement with the king. Sigismund promised not to interfere with the practice of utraquism on the
noble's estates and consented to a hearing on the religious question for
Prague. In return Čeněk was to place Prague castle at the disposal of royal
troops. Despite this gain, Sigismund's forces, drawn from all over Europe
failed to conquer Prague. After several unsuccessful attempts to storm the
city, the Bohemian nobility urged the king to send the foreign troops
home and offered him the crown. On 28 July 1420, in the Cathedral of
St. Vitus, in Prague castle, Sigismund was crowned by Archbishop Conrad
in the presence of princes, prelates and barons.[18]

Čeněk's defection removed all that remained of the trust which he had
built up in his defence of the Hussite cause. His credibility had been put

to the test by his counsel of acquiescence towards King Wenceslas' reactionary policy but his latest action destroyed it completely. To symbolize how low his prestige and leadership had sunk the people of Prague removed his banner from the tower of city hall and placed it in the pillory in the town square. The feeling of having been deserted by the nobility, especially after it consented to Sigismund's coronation was expressed by a Prague poet, who in the name of the Czech crown reproached the nobles for their ingratitude towards that crown in making the singularly unqualified Sigismund king. Having described Sigismund's various offenses, he wrote:

> Thus you, my Czech lords,
> to whom these evils are known,
> having been honourably betrothed to me,
> and to my Czech land,
> and called to this task
> that you should protect us,
> and with powerful hand protect our honour,
> and should keep property and people secure,
> you have chosen this evil man,
> whom God has damned, . . .[19]

However not all the barons had deserted Hussite Prague. Members of two families, related through marriage, whose hostility to King Sigismund went back to the time of King Wenceslas' second captivity in 1402, did not join Sigismund during the Hussite wars. Hynek Krušina of Lichten-burk, whose father John and Boček Sr. of Poděbrady had earlier fought for King Wenceslas' release from Sigismund, was elected military captain of Prague after Čeněk left. Apparently judging the outlook for Prague not to be favourable when Sigismund and the crusaders attacked in July 1420, he left the city, but in November, he and the baron Viktorin of Poděbrady, Boček's son, were the only lords of substance who fought alongside Prague at the battle over the Vyšehrad castle at the edge of the city.[20]

After the nobility defected, the Hussite cause became the affair of the revolutionary masses from town and city, the peasants and the gentry led by men like John Žižka, John Želivský, Nicholas of Husinec and later Procop the Shaven and John Čápek of Sány. These had the resolve and more important the military success enabling them to defend Hussitism where the nobility had failed. Twice in 1420, Prague, with the assistance of her rural allies defeated Sigismund's armies. In the south at the same time Žižka's armies defeated those of the nobles Ulrich of Rožmberk and Bohuslav of Švamberk and then in the course of the wars achieved further military successes at the expense of King Sigismund and the nobles. The result was that the field armies of the Oreb and Tabor brotherhoods had almost unobstructed passage to spread the political and religious revolution where ever they went.

Despite these setbacks the Hussite nobility never gave up its policy of trying to isolate the radicals. The means towards this goal were straightforward, to put Prague in control of the conservative patricians and university masters who shared the nobility's aversion for the masses and with whom they were sure they could negotiate a settlement with Sigismund and the church. A detailed account of the events leading to Sigismund's ascension is beyond the scope of this study and is accessible elsewhere.[21] It will suffice here to chart several occasions where the nobility in cooperation with the conservative Prague circles sought to remove the radicals from the positions of dominance which their military successes had granted them.

In an attempt to create a provisional government and discuss a future king for Bohemia the nobles with the two cities of Prague, Old and New, on 18 May 1421 called for a meeting of a diet at Čáslav, to which Catholics were also invited. It had been a long time since a general diet had been called in Bohemia. In their absence during King Wenceslas' reign, the land court had operated as a governing body and this as we saw was dominated by the barons. At Čáslav they took second place to the city of Prague. Barons representing the full political spectrum, from the Catholic, Ulrich of Rožmberk, to the moderate, Čeněk of Vartemberk and the radical Taborite, John Roháč of Dubá were present.

The major issue confronting the diet was the question of a king. Some Hussites were carrying on negotiations with the Poles and the more radical among them wanted the diet to officially repudiate Sigismund's kingship. As it was, it was awkward to offer the crown to the Pole when it had been placed on the head of the King of Hungary. The nobility however demurred and since a resolution of a diet without the nobles' consent would have meant very little in Poland, the radicals toned down the language of the statement. The resolution declared that they will not accept the unworthy Sigismund as king unless by "the will of the Lord God" the various estates should vote to do so. In other words the coronation of 1420 was undone, but the road was not closed to further negotiations with Sigismund. The remaining resolutions were fundamentally hostile to Sigismund, blaming him for the violence and disorder in the land. The radicals at this time were still too strong and the nobility failed to make any headway on behalf of his candidacy. Furthermore the nobility, including the gentry, got only ten of the twenty seats on the regency council created by the diet.[22] Because of John Želivský's influence in Prague the hoped for alliance between the nobles and the city at the expense of the brotherhoods had failed to materialize.

Hoping to undermine Želivský's power, Lord Čeněk and Ulrich of Rožmberk in August called for another meeting to be held in Český Brod to discuss Sigismund's return. Because Želivský was absent on a campaign in the north the nobility was able to prevail upon Prague to send a delegation. But Želivský suspected they wanted to undo the work of Čáslav so he quickly returned, denounced the nobles, charged them with deception and treason and persuaded the officials to recall the delegates. As a sign of the nobility's frustration, John Sádlo of Kostelec rebuked him saying that as a priest he ought not to intervene in secular affairs. Prague eventually did send a delegation when its request that the meeting be held in Kutná Hora was met. Unfortunately there is no record of the meeting except that many discussions with much disagreement were held. Želivský renewed his efforts to rid Prague of the influence of the moderates by expelling several university masters, Christian of Prachatice, John Příbram and Procop of Plzeň from their respective church offices. In the same spirit of suspicion they captured and beheaded the noble, John Sádlo, who had ventured into Prague not suspecting the extent of Želivský's power.[23]

On 5 February 1422 with the help of the more staid citizens of Prague, the nobility succeeded in removing Želivský from power. The nobility had returned with Žižka from a successful campaign in the east and expected that their success on behalf of Hussitism justified them in asking for a stronger role in the government. As a result they forced the election of new town councillors and appointed a military captain from among the nobility.[24] A month later, having tricked Želivský into coming to a meeting in Old Town Prague, the home of the moderates, the new councillors executed him. But the fury and rioting which this act evoked among his followers compelled the officials, for the sake of peace, to include them in the government. In addition, the university masters, seen as accomplices in his death were exiled to Hradec Králové in eastern Bohemia.[25]

With the most dynamic personality among the radicals removed the nobility could proceed. The diet of St. Gall, held in Prague in late 1423 was the outcome of maneuvers by the Hussite and Catholic barons, in league with the conservative elements in Prague to reach agreement with

King Sigismund and end the disorder in the country. The time was opportune for the nobility because Prague was in a dispute with Žižka who was away in Moravia on a campaign. The diet's resolutions were directed against Žižka and the radicals, whom they blamed for the land's difficulties. The expenses of war had been especially hard on the nobility and cities, who therefore desired stability in order to rebuild their economies. The diet called for a year long truce in accordance with the wishes of the party of Sigismund. All estates were to be returned to their original owners. All roads were to be kept open for trade and commerce and the minting of money was to be strictly regulated. For governing the land, the diet established a council of twelve members divided equally between Catholic and Hussite nobles. The towns and the brotherhoods of the radicals were to be excluded.[26] All of this was but the preliminary to the establishment of peace in which the nobles could negotiate with Sigismund his accession.

Their effort failed however because of the king's intransigence and because of Žižka's military skill. Sigismund refused to grant the hearing which the diet had called for Brno in which Hussite theologians were to debate Catholics. More important for the failure of the governing council was Žižka's hurried return from Moravia. Early in 1424 he pursued a personal grudge against two leading royalist Catholic barons, John Městec of Opočno and Půta of Častolovice, who had hired someone to assassinate him. At Jaromír he thoroughly defeated their armies. He next turned against some Hussite barons and his generally successful warfare in the east made effective government by the council impossible.[27]

The moderates were equally unsuccessful in their efforts to stabilize society under a Polish king. Their attempts bore partial fruit with the arrival of Prince Sigismund Korybut, the nephew of King Vladislav and the Grand Duke Vitold, who had sent him to act as governor of the realm while negotiations continued. Korybut arrived in Prague in May 1422 shortly after the violence which accompanied the death of Želivský broke out and was warmly welcomed by the Praguers as one who might bring reconciliation. Prague raised money for his army, allowed him to choose new councillors and permitted the expelled university masters to return. Korybut failed however to gain the extremists. His call for the leading Catholic baron, Ulrich of Rožmberk, to obedience was ignored and the support of the radical brotherhoods was reluctant and suspicious at best. When however his first regency came to an end in March 1423 it was because the Duke, not wishing to oppose the church and King Sigismund any longer with his implied support of the Hussites, ordered him home.

In June 1424, Korybut returned to Prague in defiance of his uncles and in response to the Czechs' invitation that he come and be their king. One of his first acts was to send a letter of challenge to his opponent, Sigismund of Hungary. He then devoted himself to the task of bringing peace and stability to Bohemia hoping eventually to re-unite it with the church. He was not however capable of dealing with the complexities facing him and the Czech people. The lack of support from large segments of the population made his job especially difficult. His failure came to a head in 1427 when he aligned himself with those forces in Prague which sought reconciliation with the church on almost any condition. In April his and the university masters' secret efforts to this end were uncovered and after being imprisoned for a year he was allowed to return to Poland.[28]

After Čeněk's death in 1425 Menhart of Hradec assumed a more prominent role and directed the moderate Hussites onto a more conservative if not reactionary path. Menhart was the son of John Sr., a member of the 1415 Hussite league. As we saw, in 1418 he opted for orthodoxy and presented Catholic priests to the archbishop's office for confirmation. His lands were near the Taborite stronghold in south Bohemia and most likely it was for tactical reasons and fear of their vengeance that he occasionally fought on their behalf.[29] In any case he was to play an important role in bringing the efforts to form a Catholic-Hussite coalition to a successful conclusion and undermined the power of his Taborite neighbours.

When the collapse of Korybut's second regency ended all hope for a viable Polish candidate, there was a general movement among the Hussite lords towards King Sigismund. Lord Menhart even persuaded the Taborite leader, Procop the Shaven, to enter negotiations with King Sigismund. After Old Town Prague was defeated by a Hussite noble army in October 1428, only Prague New Town, under the influence of Želivský's successor, Jacob Vlk, and the Orebite brotherhood from the east remained opposed to such negotiations except on the most stringent terms.[30]

By March 1430, when all Hussite parties, including the nobles, met in Prague to prepare for the hearing which the Elector Frederick of Brandenburg was trying to arrange, all agreed on the need for an open hearing with Catholic Europe for the purpose of making peace even though they still differed on the nature of their religious demands. Similarly, on 11 February 1431 all Hussite factions participated in the diet of Kutná Hora which elected a twelve member government administration and prepared a delegation for a meeting with the pope which the Polish king was trying to arrange. Later in May all Hussite parties agreed to refuse the king's and the church's requirement that they submit to the Council and enter a truce for the duration of the negotiations.[31] Despite this general agreement the more extensive religious demands of the brotherhoods made negotiations with the Council difficult.

Eventually the nobility lost patience and undermined the Hussite negotiating position by leading the Council to believe that there was less resolve in the Hussite camp than in fact there was. Thus when Tabor, at the diet of 10 February 1432, where the Hussites were making preparations for going to Basel, demurred on the ground that the previously agreed upon program did not go far enough, the angry nobles contacted the Catholic city of Plzeň saying that they were one with them except on the matter of the Chalice on which they were prepared to submit to the Council. Similarly, in June 1433, the impatient nobility, led by Menhart of Hradec, and in cooperation with the university masters met secretly with the Council's delegation and offered a weaker version of the Four Articles. They told the Council that Tabor was the cause for the delay and that the majority of Prague's priests wanted unity with the church as long as the freedom of the Chalice was granted.[32]

The Council's representatives, aware of where their opposition was the weakest,   sought to exploit the nobility's impatience. First they asked that more lords be members of the panel with which they were in discussion. Then on 25 June 1433, having asked for a private meeting with some of the lords, they tried to separate the nobles from Tabor by appealing to their class feeling. It was not, they said, proper for them to be subordinate to people whom they would scarcely have as servants. To this the nobles however responded that they wanted to remain united with their nation and not negotiate on their own.[33] Before the delegation left, Lord Menhart, with Master John Příbram met with it once again. The contents of their talk are not known but most likely Menhart shared some of his plans for facilitating union with the church. As a culmination to these developments Menhart, along with some other lords and university masters reached his own reconciliation with the Catholic Church.[34]

Just as the Hussite lords subordinated support of their religious movement to the interests of their estate, so the Catholic nobles hedged their efforts on behalf of the church and the king. Before the Catholic nobility undertook the defence of their king and the church they required payment in money and property. Most of this came from church lands as King Sigismund exercised his prerogative as its guardian using its property to pay for the struggles to re-establish its unity in Bohemia.[35]

F. Kavka illustrated that one of the basic reasons that it took the Catholic nobility so long to get their king the throne, despite the fact that they held approximately 200 castles, compared to the Hussites' ninety, was the lack of a unified sense of purpose in the Catholic camp. One example of this was the personal hostility between several of the Catholic lords and the officials of the royal cities. The lords of Kolovraty, Burian of Gutštejn and Hynek Krušina of Švamberk quarreled with the city of Loket in the west, Henry and John Berka of Dubá and Sigismund Vartemberk of Děčín with Žitava in the north and Ulrich of Rožmberk with Budějovice in the south.[36]

Similarly the nobility often worked at cross purposes with the king's goals. The king regarded his nobility as a voluntary aid to help him regain the crown and rebuked them if they followed an independent policy. For their part, the Catholic nobility wanted to put the king on the throne in such a way that it would be clear he owed his place to them. Thus in 1420, at the siege of Prague, they urged him not to attack the city, because a triumph over the capital with the help of the German crusading armies would weaken their own position. They assured the king that within a month they would bring Prague under his dominion adding that they were the Czech crown and not those farmers holding the city.[37]

Furthermore, there was a wide gulf between the nobility's stated intention and their actual performance. For example, the Plzeň Landfrieden, an association of Catholic nobles in western Bohemia, and Ulrich of Rožmberk on at least four occasions pursued policies and actions directly in opposition to the interests of the king. In the fall of 1424, as part of the Zdice agreement with the Hussites, the Catholic nobles agreed not to obstruct anyone, including their own subjects, who wished to join the Hussite campaign into Moravia. A year later the same group of nobles again made a truce with the Hussites as they embarked on a campaign eastward thus securing the Hussite rear. Then in 1427, instead of joining the Fourth crusade against the Hussites, Lord Ulrich made and kept his truce with Tabor, freeing it to conquer Tachov and lay seige to Plzeň. Ulrich similarly kept his truce with Tabor in 1430, allowing the brotherhood armies free reign on their campaign in the east.[38] Honouring their agreements with the radicals did not mean however that the nobles were not looking for an opportunity to overcome them.

As the period of the Hussite wars drew to a close the similarity in goals of the nobility in both camps became ever more clear so that in the fall of 1433 both sides decided to act together for the sake of re-establishing their hegemony over the realm. In November the nobility, including lords who had fought in the armies of the brotherhoods, proceeded with their plans to put an end to the violence and lawlessness in the country. To this end they called a diet and elected the Orebite lord, Aleš Riesenburk of Vřeštov, of a venerable but poor family, as administrator of the realm with wide-ranging powers and incomes.[39] Before Aleš could function effectively the nobility needed to put an end to the operations of the armies of the brotherhoods. The radicals were at one of the lowest points in their popularity. Their sustained military activities required them to live off the countryside requisitioning cattle and grain to feed themselves. In addition personality conflicts within their leadership had surfaced resulting in a split between their eastern and southern factions. Thus while the Catholic nobles met at Kouba in Bavaria, the utraquists met somewhere in the eastern part of Bohemia to plan military action. Lord Menhart of Hradec, as the go-between co-ordinated the attacks. First on 5 May 1434 they defeated the radical forces controlling Prague New Town. Then on the 8th, at Lipany, the hastily regrouped armies of the Taborite and Orebite communities were defeated by a Hussite-Catholic coalition of nobles thus ending their role as the effective power brokers in the realm.[40]

For years the Czech people had defeated the efforts of the crusading armies of King Sigismund and the church who had sought thus to establish their rule in the realm. These wars gave the Czechs a great sense of self-assurance. The nobility had not been at the forefront of these struggles and had mostly obstructed them. Now with their victory over the brotherhoods they had proven themselves masters in Bohemia and could therefore reap the fruits of the earlier victories and the resulting feeling of pride.

CHAPTER 11
CONCLUSION:
NOBLE GAINS IN THE HUSSITE REVOLUTION

In the short run the victory of the nobility over the lower classes meant also a victory for the king whose fiercest opponents were thus eliminated. However, in longer terms the nobility's success meant a further decline of monarchical power, a process which the nobility had begun in the 1390s. In 1436 and especially during the reign of George Poděbrady after 1458 the towns and the gentry shared in the increase in power which the Hussite wars had brought the estates, but by 1471, after George's death, the barons had taken control at the expense of the towns, peasants and king.

The power of the estates was reflected in the fact that they elected their king, switching from family to family without regard to the individual's nationality. In the first place, after the battle of Lipany, several diets representing all parties including the defeated radicals, were held at which the Czechs decided upon the conditions which they would offer Sigismund. Eager to take the throne he gave in to their demands, which consisted primarily of the moderate Hussite religious program, including their right to elect an archbishop. In July 1436 he signed the agreement granting the Bohemians their freedoms and privileges. Only after this was he permitted to assume the throne.[1] After Sigismund's death in December 1437, his son-in-law, Duke Albert of Austria had the strongest claim to the throne. He was supported by the diet dominated by the barons, Ulrich of Rožmberk and Menhart of Hradec. A strong minority, predominantly Hussite, invited the Polish king to take the throne but he did not care to contest the matter. Albert died shortly, in October 1439 and the whole question of the succession was up in the air again, made complicated by the fact that a son, Ladislas, was born four months after his death.[2] By the beginning of 1440 the nobility had decided what their priorities were, namely that the supervision of the establishment of peace in the land and the election of the king should be in their hands. The Catholic lords accepted the Hussites' right to their religion as they pushed aside the religious question for the time being and formed a solid front. The barons were, however not able to overcome the insistence of the towns and gentry that they too participate in determining who should be king. As a result a body of electors was organized, in which the barons had eighteen seats and the gentry and royal towns each fourteen. These elected Albert, Duke of Bavaria, who to the Czechs' surprise, rejected the offer. The Czechs then turned to Ladislas, the four year old son of the former duke of Austria.[3] The guardian of the child-king was Frederick III of Austria. He had no desire to become involved in Bohemian politics despite invitations from the nobility to establish some sort of administration there. As a result the parties in Bohemia had to fight out the establishment of hegemony among themselves. The first victory went to the eastern nobility led by Hussite nobles like Hynek Ptáček of Pirkštejn and George of Poděbrady. George in 1448 defeated the Catholic Menhart of Hradec whom King Sigismund had made chief burgrave and who was a friend of Ulrich of Rožmberk. In the process Prague was brought into the Poděbrady camp. The voice of the Czech people was most strongly expressed when they elected George of Poděbrady in 1458 after he had served as effective administrator for ten years during Ladislas' short life. In an election which according to one historian had almost a modern democratic character, in that the masses made their support for George known to the three curia of the estates, the Czechs chose him, a native nobleman, to wear the crown of St. Wenceslas.[4] Finally, for our period, after the death of George in 1471, the Czech estates chose Vladislav II of Poland from four candidates, after he promised, among other things, to protect the Hussite religion.[5]

The estates in general benfited from the increased authority which the land diet had achieved. Previously the land court controlled by the barons, had acted as the highest court of justice as well as the law making body. After the Hussite wars, the land diet, meeting twice yearly, took over legislative functions. The diets had three curia, made up of towns, gentry and barons. This separation gave the towns and gentry more opportunity for independent action. In addition the gentry gained the right to sit on the panel of jurists, getting eight on the expanded twenty-member body.[6] Although King George had come to power with the help of the barons, with whose interests he identified, as king he concluded that royal interests represented better those of the land than did the barons'. In order to weaken their power in the government, he used such well tested devices as appointing members of the gentry to high offices such as chief justice of the land court and the chancery. Furthermore, burghers whom he used in his administration he raised to the status of gentry and both classes were used in the regional defence forces which he established in 1470.[7]

In addition to the increased status gained by the barons as part of the estates, they also made specific advances of their own. In the settlement reached with King Sigismund in 1436 the barons had already begun to put distance between themselves and the other estates. Having decided that their interests differed from those of the gentry and the towns they did not support their more stringent demands that Sigismund himself accept the chalice and that Catholics be excluded from the land court and governing council. As a result Sigismund could ignore these conditions when he granted his acceptance charter. Neither gentry nor barons assisted the towns in their desire for self-government, hence Sigismund could likewise evade their request that they be allowed to choose their own military captains.[8]

Perhaps the most significant gain made by the nobility was the increase in their landholdings. Some bought out those whom the wars had brought low, but mostly their prosperity came at the expense of the church. Two of the better examples of noble success were John of Smiřice and Jakoubek of Vřesovice whose property acquisitions resulting from the wars raised them from the status of the gentry to the baronage. Smiřice took over the estates of Roudnice, Hoštka and Helfenburk all belonging to the archbishop and the Prague chapter. In addition he got Jestřebí, which before the wars had belonged to a branch of the Catholic Berkas of Dubá.[9] In the north-west, Vřesovice, who had come from Moravia to assist the Hussites, accumulated large holdings ranging in the north from Kostomlaty, formerly an estate of a noble family, and reaching south as far as Toužím, which had belonged to the monastery in Milevsko.[10] In the east the Kostkas of Postupice improved their position when they got the extensive domains of the bishopric of Litomyšl including Landšperk after 1451.[11]

Barons similarly added to their holdings. Hynek Krušina of Lichtenburk came into the possession of the Častolovice estates by purchasing some from the orphans of Půta, and the rest by marrying Půta's widow, Anna of Koldice. The lords of Náchod, earlier an impoverished branch of the Berkas of Dubá, expanded their holdings at the expense of the monastery in Broumov. Similarly, Ulrich of Rožmberk compensated for what he lost to the Taborites through annexing the nearby property of monasteries like that of the Golden Crown, the ones in Milevsko, Zvíkov and Sedlčany.[12] When the nobility's enrichment came at the expense of the church, it meant a corresponding diminuation of the royal power since the crown, as the church's guardian had administered and disposed of its property in times of need for its own ends. In the same vein the king's prerogative suffered further during Vladislav's reign when his right to dispose of estates whose owners had died heirless was abolished and his rights to the incomes of the silver mines, which had always been royal income, were limited to the advantage of the nobility.[13]

It was the peasantry which perhaps suffered the most as a result of advances which the Hussite wars brought the nobility. In 1437 their freedom was restricted when the land court ruled that a lord could force those who had fled to the city during the wars to return to his land. Because King George depended largely on the support of the lower classes this remained largely unenforced during the first year of his reign. However, during the rebellions of the Catholic nobility in the 1460s George had to grant further rights to the nobility at the expense of the lower classes.

Some of the leading baronial families envied George, one from their ranks who ruled as king over them. Foremost among his opponents were Zdeněk of Šternberk and the lords of Rožmberk. In the summer of 1465 when King George called a diet of the Czech estates this party remained away sending a delegation with a list of twelve demands, all relating to the status of the barons in the land government, which they alleged had suffered under George's reign. Their aim was to draw more nobles away from their support of the king. The time was not yet ripe for them so that their attempt failed. The nobility backed King George and reprimanded the absent barons for presenting their grievances without consulting the diet.[14]

At the end of 1466 the discontented nobles were aided by developments abroad. In December, Pope Paul II officially excommunicated King George, making explicit that hereby the king's subjects, vassals and allies no longer owed him allegiance. It was a device which the papacy had frequently used in order to bring recalcitrant secular rulers into line although by the later middle ages it had mostly lost its effect. However when applied to a ruler such as George who protected known heretics and who had important enemies it could be very dangerous. In June 1467, the Catholic barons, meeting in Jihlava in Moravia, operating under the assumption that they had no legitimate king, extended an invitation to Casimir of Poland to come and assume the throne, or if he were unwilling to let his son come. George lacked the military might to put down the noble league with force. He therefore accepted the offer of Casimir, who himself did not wish to take on the task of opposing George let alone ruling the country, to mediate a solution.[15]

It was in the midst of these developments that King George made concessions to the baronial estate in order to rally whatever support he could. At a diet held in Prague in February 1467, he agreed to restore to the barons some of their ancient rights and economic privileges. The most important grants had to do with property rights which in the 1390s had also been the nobility's main concern. Whereas earlier they had been concerned with limiting royal prerogatives on their property this time they sought to extend theirs downward over the inhabitants of their lands. The lords were again allowed to apply the law of devolution and claim estates of their subjects who had died intestate; a right which the nobles during the reformatory period of the late fourteenth and early fifteenth centuries had been willing to give up. In addition, George permitted them to purchase estates belonging to townspeople and peasants and insert titles into the land register without special royal permission. Without the king's supervision over these transactions the lower estates were more susceptible to pressure from nobles to sell or to yield disputed claims.[16]

The nobility during this period also increased its control over the administration of the land. During the Hussite wars the offices of the district justices (*popravci*) had all but disappeared. Again in this sphere George's need for the support of the nobles brought them what they wanted. In 1451 George, as governor of the land, defeated the league of Strakonice, consisting of nobles from the southwest. In an effort to conciliate his adversaries, as well as consolidate the support of his baronial friends, he re-introduced the office of the district justices placing them in noble hands. At the same time the sessions of the noble controlled land court were re-established on a regular basis. Henceforth it was to be the sole recourse for litigants seeking justice. During Vladislav's reign the royal influence in the land court was almost completely eliminated and the royal court (*dvorský soud*) practically ceased to function. Furthermore the nobles had come to control access to the king's council, which in the late fourteenth century had been a sort of royal privy council but by the late fifteenth century had become an institution directed by and serving the interests of the barons.[17]

The fact that the goals for which the nobles had fought in the 1390s, to curb the growing power of the king and the rise of the town classes, had been achieved by 1471 despite temporary reversals indicates a certain cunningness in the nobility itself or if not in them in the movement of ideas and events. Their success raises the suspicion that the nobles agreed beforehand to separate into two camps, encourage Hussitism, and then try to hang on while all other parties exhausted themselves, at which point they could take the spoils. Such an over simplified scenerio, although it has its appeal also has its difficulties.

For a man like Čeněk of Vartemberk it would have had little meaning. He and others like him joined the Hussites, moved by new and compelling ideas about society, religion and themselves, preached by skillful university trained reformers. They were aware of the dangers which support for heresy meant to their social, economic and political positions. Individuals have been known to give up their lives for others but it is doubtful that Čeněk risked his own political position just so that his estate might twenty or forty years later acquire so much more. Rather Čeněk and his allies sought to promote a particular brand of moderate reform. When their program proved not to please the masses these nobles found themselves broken by the sweep of events as the lower classes brought them literally to their knees. For the family of Čeněk of Vartemberk, which died out with the death of his son Henry in 1434, the wars were a calamity. For others, like the Poděbrady, they represented only a temporary decline from which they rebounded to positions undreamed of earlier. Such a fate was more representative of the nobility as a class.

If the nobility's temporary loss of power resulting from their support of Hussitism was not a deliberate act of self-denial perhaps their ultimate fortune was the effect of the operation of a subliminal force in man's make-up. The nobility acted as men who knew almost instinctively that a certain course of action must eventually work out to their own benefit even though in the short run events may develop which have the opposite effect. For the Marxists such a hidden force is the interaction and struggle between the classes. For religious people it is God leading mankind according to His Will. The result for both belief-systems is a utopia beneficial to all in the end. We may not know whether either of the above moved the nobility to support the Hussite movement in the fifteenth century. In any case after a short catastrophy, the force which moved them brought them many benefits.

APPENDIX I
COMMODITY PRICES IN PRE HUSSITE BOHEMIA

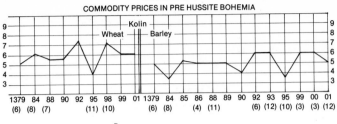

1379 84 88 90 92 95 98 99 01 1379 84 85 86 88 89 90 92 93 95 99 00 01
(6) (8) (7)   (11) (10)   (6) (8)   (4) (11)   (6) (12) (10) (3) (3) (12)

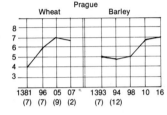

Prague

Wheat — 1381 96 05 07 (7) (7) (9) (2)

Barley — 1393 94 98 10 16 (7) (12)

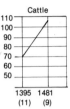

Cattle — 1395 1481 (11) (9)

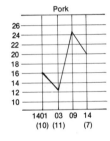

Pork — 1401 03 09 14 (10) (11) (7)

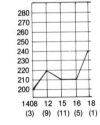

Cider — 1408 12 15 16 18 (3) (9) (11) (5) (1)

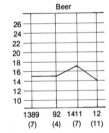

Beer — 1389 92 1411 12 (7) (4) (7) (11)

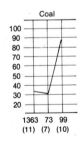

Coal — 1363 73 99 (11) (7) (10)

Building lime — 1372 74 75 76 77 78

NOTES TO APPENDIX I

1. The prices on the left hand vertical axis are in groschen. The numbers enclosed in brackets on the lower horizontal axis designate the month during which the prices were recorded. The grain was sold in measures called, strych i.e. about 2.5 bushels, the animals by the head, the cider by the "laga", about 36 pints, the beer by the "vas", the coal by the wagon, and the lime by the basket.

2. The source for the information is Graus, *Dějiny venkovského lidu,* 406-433 and his *Chudina městská,* 189-195.

APPENDIX II

FAMILIES HOLDING IMPORTANT LAND OFFICES 1404-1410

Symbols: R=Royalist during revolts
BL=member of baronial league

	District	Traditional Justice[1]	Justice in 1405[2]
I	Kouřim	Prague burgrave, Kunštát, Dubá, Šternberk.	Andrew of Dubá (R)
II	Slany	Zajíc-Hazmburk	unknown
III	Žatec	Šumberk, Boreš (Osek)	burgrave of royal castle Kadaň
IV	Plzeň	Skála, Švihov, Švamberk.	Ulrich Zajíc of Hazmburk and of Přimda (R)
V	Pracheň	Velhartice, Strakonice, Rožmitál	John Hradec of Velhartice (BL), Zdeněk of Rožmitál
VI	Pisek	Lord of the Rose,[3] Ústí.	unknown
VII	Bechyně	Rožmberk, Hradec, Landštejn	Henry of Rožmberk (BL), Ulrich of Hradec (BL) John Kamenice of Ústí (BL)
VIII	Čáslav	Lichtenburk, Chlum	Vitek Landštejn of Lipnice, Nicholas Kolovraty of Zruč.
IX	Hradec Králové	Chustník, Opočno, and Veselé.	John Krušina of Lichtenburk (BL), Theodore of Náchod and the burgrave of Hradec (royal).
X	Chrudím	Lacembok, Chlum or Boskovec	John Krušina of Lichtenburk (BL), Sdeslas Šternberk of Zaječice.
XI	Boleslav	Michalovice, Zviřetice, Berka of Dubá, Valdštejn, Vartemberk.	William of Zviřetice, John of Michalovice (BL), and Aleš Škopek of Dubá.
XII	Litoměřice	Berka of Dubá, Děčin, and a Škopek.	Herbert of Kolovraty, John Vartemberk of Děčin (BL). Hyenk Berka of Honštejn (BL) and Ulrich Hazmburk of Přimda.
XIII	Mýto	unknown	John Krušina of Lichtenburk (BL).

APPENDIX II

Lords at the Court of the land (*zemský soud*), December 1404[4]

Boček Sr. and Jr. Kunštát of Poděbrady, Albert of Šternberk, Wenceslas of Dubá and Wenceslas Leštno of Dubá.

Ulrich and William Zajíc of Hazmburk.

––––––––––––––––

Půta of Skála, John and Raček of Švamberk and Břeněk Sr. Skála of Švihov.

––––––––––––––––

––––––––––––––––

John Jr. and Ulrich of (Jindřichův) Hradec.

Albert of Kolovraty.

Jaroslav Opočno of Dobruška, Beneš of Chustník, John Krušina of Lichtenburk, John Vartemberk of Veselé, Čeněk Vartemberk of Veselé and Theodore Náchod of Janovice.

Sdeslas of Šternberk

Aleš Škopek of Dubá, John Vartemberk of Kost. Henry Berka of Jablonná, Henry Vartemberk of Valdštejn, Peter Vartemberk of Děvín and William of Zvířetice.

Hynek Berka of Honštejn, Hynek Berka of Houska and Herbert of Kolovraty.

NOBLE FAMILIES AND THEIR POLITICS

	Baronial[1] Revolts 1394-1405	Hussite[2] League 1415	Catholic[3] League 1415	Challenged[4] Prague 1419-1420
1	Bergov, Otto Sr. & Jr.		Otto	Čeněk
2	Častolovice Puta (d.1403)	Puta, (son)		
3	Dubá, Berkas Hynek of Honštejn		Hynek	
	Hynek Hlaváč of Lipy		Hynek Hlaváč	Hynek Hlaváč
	Hynáček of Vizmburk (d.1401)			Henry of Jestřebí
4		Dubá, Henry Škopek	Aleš Škopek (brother)	
5	Hradec, Henry (d.1398)			
	Ulrich (son)	Ulrich	John Jr. (brother)	
6		Janovice-Chlumec, Peter		
7		Košmberk-Chlum John, William & Diviš		
8	Landštejn William (d.1398)	Herman & John of Borotín		Herman & John
9	Lichtenburk John Krušina (d.1407)	Hynek Krušina (son)		John Krušina Hynek's (brother)
10		Lomnice, John Košík		John Košík
11	Lopata Herman			William

	Baronial Revolts 1394-1405	Hussite League 1415	Catholic League 1415	Challenged Prague 1419-1420
12		Milčina-Kostelec John Sádlo		
13		Mochov-Roždalovice Nicholas		
14		Opočno-Městec John		
15	Michalovice John		John	
16	Osek, Boreš Sr. (d.1403) & Jr.			
17	Poděbrady-Kunštát	Boček, Sr. & Jr.		
18		Potštejn, Bavor		
19		Potštejn Žampach Mikeš William		
20	Pardubice-Richenburk Smil Flaška (d.1403)	Ernest (son)		
21	Rožmberk, Henry (d.1412)			Ulrich (son)
22		Rožmitál John & Zdeněk brothers		John & Zdeněk
23	Skála, Puta I, (d.1401) Břeněk (son, d.1407) Puta II			
24	Šternberk-Konopiště Albert (d.1405)	SmilŠternberk of Holice	Peter (nephew of Albert)[5]	

	Baronial Revolts 1394-1405	Hussite League 1415	Catholic League 1415	Challenged Prague 1419-1420
25	Švamberk Busek (d.1395) Bohuslav (d.1401)			Bohuslav (son)
26		Týnec, Zdeněk Medek		Zdeněk Medek
27	Vartemberk Peter of Kost (d.1402) John of Děčín (d.1412) Henry of Valdštejn	Henry		Beneš & Sigismund of D. Henry
	Wenceslas			
		Čeněk of Veselé		Čeněk
			John of Ralsko	John
28		Valdštejn Vok & Nicholas		
29		Vlašim, John		
				Janek Chotěmice of Vlašim
30	Ústí John Sr. (d.1403) John Jr. of Kamenice (d.1414) Sezema (d.1397)			
31		Zviřetice, William, Wenceslas, Peter & Sdislas		Wenceslas, Peter & Beneš brothers.
32			Elsterberk Henry	Henry
33			Hazmburk William Zajic	William and Nicholas Hazmburk of Kost.
34			Koldice, Albert	Albert

NOTES TO APPENDICES

APPENDIX I

1. Palacký, F., "Pomůcky ku poznánj staročeského práwa i řádu saudnjho," *Časopis českeho museum*, IX (1835) 446. These families traditionally held the office.

2. Those appointed by King Wenceslas to the office at the settlement of 1405. See Rieger, B., *Zřizení krajské v Čechách*, I (Prague, 1894), 52, n. 14, cf. *Čechy*, 211.

3. The lords of Landštejn-Borotín had a white rose as their emblem while those of Rožmberk had a red rose.

4. *RT*, II, 10., Others present were: John Šternberk of Holice, Hynek of Třebechovice, Hynek Hlaváč of Lipy, John of Vizmberk, Hynek of Červená Hora, Hynek of Aberspach, Hynek of Milštejn (Last six members of Berka Dubá clan) Hynek of Pihel, Jenek of Peterspurk, John of Janovice, Předbor of Žandov, Henry of Elsterberk, Beneš Ryzmburk of Krčín, John of Rotštejn, Henry of Dubá and Paul of Vintmberk.

APPENDIX II

1. Members who participated are found in *AČ*, I, 52, 54-56, 59-61, 65-66 and *Čechy*, passim.

2. *Šlechta, Documenta*, 580ff and *Úvahy*, 89ff.

3. *Documenta*, 572, 602, *DNČ*, III, 188 and Kejř, J., *Husitský Právník*, 100, n.28.

4. *AČ*, IV, 375-381.

5. Peter was not in the league but was a known Catholic. See *Documenta*, 696.

An Utraquist Compact among the squires of the Vltava District—1417. Printed in *O Stavu Rytjrskem a rozmnozeni geho yak dawno a odkud ktery Rod a Erb do tohoto Kralowstwi prissel.* Kniha treti. by Bartholomeo Paprocki (Prague, 1602). (Translated by John Klassen.)

We Přech of Olbramovice, John Leskovec, Herman of Hrádek, etc., squires of the Vltava District. We with this letter declare before all who will read it or hear it, that we have entered, and through this letter do enter into the following agreement.

First: That our priests, who are under us, shall not accept any letters of citation or of anathema, and that they shall freely preach the word of God without any interference, and speak freely in their churches. As indicated, they shall not accept any anathema of any kind which might be placed on us or on our subjects unjustly and contrary to the law of God, as is now being done regarding the communion with the body of Christ and his precious blood. Should they try to keep us or our subjects from it, we are to move against them and to oppose them, as enemies of the Law of God.

Second: Should any priest want to anathemize one of our priests—of us who have joined in this compact—he whose priest takes this action must stop him. And if he should be a priest of someone else, who has not joined our compact, we shall send to this priest, that he cease and desist; should he refuse, then he would be our enemy and unjust defamer, and a letter is to be written to his lord in order that he instruct him to desist from such actions. Should the lord not do this, we would understand it as meaning that he too is an enemy of us and of the Truth of God.

Third: Should anyone want to oppress us with such anathemas, taking to aid the secular arm as is published in those anathemas, in this we want to be of help to each other, so that we not be oppressed by them with anathemas and citations contrary to our knightly rights.[1] And in such a case we all the above signed, as we have written in this letter, promise to help each other and to stand by each other, on pain of forfeiting our trust, honour and property.

Fourth: Should one of us withdraw and not help us in this, as the above Přech, John Leskovec and Herman of Hrádek have outlined it, he at that time will forfeit his trust and honour and even his property he will forfeit to those who stood together and helped each other in the above articles. They may take over his property by force or by law and he is not to oppose this, neither through word nor deed. And should any of the above squires withdraw from us and not hold to that which stands written above and the other two learn this about him: he is to suffer the forfeitures described above. Similarly, should two withdraw and not hold to what is written above, and the others learn this about them, both have to suffer the forfeitures described above. And should the three above named withdraw and a fourth remain after them in their place, the above described forfeitures shall have full force, as if all four were together.

Fifth: Should someone want to join us, and should give us a written instrument binding himself, we are obliged and liable to help him as if he had signed this letter with us, with the above described penalties. Also, should it be necessary that we help each other against someone, we are to do this under the direction of the four above mentioned squires. Should one of the squires die, then those remaining have full authority to co-opt another in the place of the deceased, from all the above mentioned squires and any who might later have joined us, as often as this might be necessary, for the definition of forfeitures and the direction of mutual help.

Finally, this compact between us is to last six years successively and after six years it is to have no authority unless we renew it. For the confirmation, stability and certainty whereof, all of us above mentioned have affixed our seals to this letter which is given in the year of our Lord, 1417.

---

1   Members of the lower nobility were subject to the lesser land court (*soud menší*) unless the case involved more than 10 marks, in which case it was heard in the regular Court of the land (*zemský soud*). Brandl, *Glossarium,* 386. Tomek, *DMP,* III, 622 makes reference to an older law, approved by the Court of the land, which forbade the citation of laymen outside of the realm especially by clergy.

NOTES
CHAPTER 1

1. See his *Autopsy of a Revolution* (New York, 1971), 21-22.

2. As recently as 1975 William Wright discusses peasant conditions in pre-Hussite Bohemia without reference to the latest scholarship. See his "Neo-Serfdom in Bohemia", *Slavic Review*, 34 (1975), 239-242.

3. Klecanda, V., "Přijímaní do rytířského stavu v zemich českých a rakouských na počatku novověku", *Časopis archivní školy* IV, (1928) 6, and McFarland, K.B., *The Nobility of Later Medieval England* (Oxford, 1973) 6.

4. Graus, F., *Dějiny venkovského lidu v Čechách v době předhusitské*, II, Prague, 1957) 66-67. (With French résumé).

5. His, R., *Zur Rechtsgeschichte des thuringischen Adels* (Darmstadt, 1967; first published in 1903), 11-12 and *Glossarium*, 220, 306 and 365, and *DNC*, II, 667 n.199.

6. Graus, *Dějiny venkovského*, 66, 69, 199.

7. *Ibid.*, 200.

8. *Ibid.*, 201-205.

9. *Ibid.*, 198. The size and measurements of fields in the middle ages was inexact and depended on the amount of ploughing one team and plough could do in one day. This in turn depended on the type of soil, the endurance of men and animal and other variables. See Duby, G., *Rural Economy and Country Life in the Medieval West* (Columbia, 1968), 116-119.

10. Graus, *Dějiny venkovského*, 209-211.

11. *Ibid.*, 238, 242, 249. Cf. Duby, 227.

12. Graus, *Dějiny, venkovského*, 84-90 has shown that this phenomenon was not the result of German colonists but of the dynamics of resettlement in general. Cf. Krofta, K., *Dějiny selského stavu* (Prague, 1949), 38.

13. Graus, *Dějiny venkovského*, 145-147.

14. For the archbishop see Weltsch, R.H., *Archbishop John of Jenstein 1348-1400* (The Hague, 1968) 312-140. Cf. Graus, *Dějiny Venkovského*, 255-56.

15. For the charters see Haas, A., ed., *Codex juris municipalis regni Bohemiae*, IV, (Prague, 1954), 133 ff.

16. Graus, *Dějiny venkovského*, 19-20 and Duby, 238.

17. *DNČ*, II, 375, 402-403 and 440. Krofta, K., "Začátky české berně," *ČČH*, 36, (1930) 1-26, 237-257, 437-490 traces the development of the tax.

18. Graus, *Dějiny venkovského*, 174.

19. *Ibid.*, 177-179. See below p. 28 for a more complete discussion of the tithe.

20. Graus, F., *Chudina městská v době předhusitské* (Prague, 1949), 179, 189. (With French résumé).

21. Duby, 294-311, McKisack, M., *The Fourteenth Century 1307-1399* (Oxford, 1959) 339-340, Žižka, 38 and Graus, *Dějiny venkovského*, 75-76.

22. Graus, *Dějiny venkovského*, 437-438. The list of wages paid over these years was published by Krejcik, A.L., *Urbář z r. 1378 a účty kláštera třebonského z let 1367-1407 (Historický Archiv* 52 (Prague, 1949). The wages of women were half that of men.

23. Graus, *Dějiny venkovského*, 102-105, 434-442.
24. *Ibid.*, 106.
25. Mendl, B., "Hospodářské a sociální poměry v městech Pražských v letech 1378-1434", *ČČH*, 22 (1916) 436 and Graus, *Chudina*, 116.
26. Mendl, "Z hospodářských dějin středověké Prahy", *Sborník příspěvku k dějinám hlavního města Prahy* V (1932), 263.
27. Graus, *Chudina*, 55-57.
28. *Ibid.*, 54.
29. *Ibid.*, 36-40.
30. *Ibid.*, 64.
31. *Ibid.*, 67, 106.
32. *Ibid.*, 86-88, 98.
33. *Ibid.*, 176-77.
34. *Ibid.*, 77-79 and *Dějiny venkovského*, 441.
35. Sedlák, J., *Studie a texty k náboženským dějinám českým*, 4 vols. (Olomouc, 1914) I, 288, 299, Graus, *Chudina*, 81-84.
36. Graus, *Chudina*, 189-195. The tables in the appendix are mine.
37. Šusta, J., *Karel IV za císařskou korunou* (Prague, 1948), 206.
38. Graus, *Chudina*, 177. The text of the synods decree is in Hofler, C., ed., *Concilia Pragensia 1353-1413* (Prague, 1862), 49.
39. Mendl, *Hospodářské ČČH*, 23 (1917), 355-57.
40. Mendl, *Z hospodářských dějin*, 259-61, 266-68 and Graus, *Chudina*, 128-130.
41. Mendl, *Z hospodářských dějin*, 165.
42. *Ibid.*, p. 267 includes the table comparing European cities.
43. Graus, Chudina, 203-204.
44. Yoder, J.H. *The Politics of Jesus* (Eerdmans, Grand Rapids, 1972).

CHAPTER 2

1. Schmid, H.F., "Die rechtliche Grundlagen der Pfarrorganisation auf westslavischem Boden," *Zeitschrift der Savigny-Stifting für Rechtsgeschichte, Kanonistische Abteilung*, XV, (1926), 154.
2. Nový, R., "K sociálnímu postavení farského kléru v Čechách v době předhusitské," *Sborník historický*, VIII (1961), 160-165, F. Fiala, "Správa a postavení církve v Čechách od počátku 13. do poloviny 14. století," *Sborník historický*, III (1955), 69, Schmid, *Grundlagen*, 151-153, Schlenz, J., *Das Kirchenpatronat in Böhmen* (Prague, 1928), 57, Feine, H.E., *Kirchliche Rechtsgeschichte* I (Weimar, 1955), 234 and for England see Ault, W.O., "Manor Court and Parish Church in 15th Century England," *Speculum*, XLII (1967), 62.
3. Schlenz, *Kirchenpatronat*, 79-82 and Krofta, K., "Kurie a církevní správa zemí českých v době předhusitské," *ČČH* X (1904), 275, n.1.
4. *DMP*, III, 218. If the qualifications of the candidates themselves were not the issue the archbishop decided questions of patronage on the basis of who had title to a village in the land register; on rare occasions patronage disputes were settled by casting lots. *LC*, VI, 1 and V, 181.

5. Grey, J.W., "The 'Ius presentandi' in England from the Constitutions of Clarendon to Bracton," *The English Historical Review*, LXVII (1952), 492-493.

6. DMP, III, 158, Schlenz, *Kirchenpatronat*, 89-91 and Vyskočil, J., *Arnošt z Pardubice a jeho doba* (Prague-Vyšehrad, 1947), 342-43. The LC mention the tax only rarely before 1422. Although Hus in his tract, "On Simony," in Spinka, M., trans., *Advocates of Reform from Wyclif to Erasmus* (London, 1953) 258, mentioned a tax of 240 groschen for the letters, the highest I was able to find was 60. LC, VI, 96 and SA, II, 127, 167.

7. See Hledíková, Z., *Úřad generalních vikářů pražského arcibiskupa v době předhusitské* (Prague, 1971) 68, n. 38 and LC, VI, 184, 235, 231 and 258.

8. Feine, *Rechtsgeschichte*, 360, Schlenz, *Kirchenpatronat*, 114ff. Schmid, *Grundlagen*, 72-73 mentions that some patrons required honoraria from their priests in the form of bread, fish or fowl. For England see Grey, *Ius presentandi*, 485.

9. SA, I, 116, 78, 79, and LC, VII, 212.

10. Schlenz, *Kirchenpatronat*, 114-116.

11. LC, VI, 285 and Kalousek, J., "Zášti ve vychodních Čechách," *Časopis českého musea*, LXXVII (1903), 270.

12. Weltsch, R., *Archbishop John of Jenstein 1348-1400* (The Hague-Paris, 1968), 44ff.

13. Kallen, G., *Die oberschwäbischen Pfrunden des Bistums Konstanz und ihre Besetzung 1275-1500* (Amsterdam, 1955; repr. of Stuttgart, 1907 edition), 271.

14. See LC, VII, 51-Modřejovice, cf. *Hrady*, VIII, 111, 113; LC, VI, St. Nicholas in Prague, 134, Mechlov, 71, Lipa 77, Kydliny 123 cf. *Hrady*, IX, 167, Tachov 276, Němcice 271 cf. *Hrady*, VII, 176, Hradec Králové 183, Horšice 183, Libchova 200 cf. *Hrady*, II, 116, 146 and Okunov 212 cf. *Hrady*, XIII, 246.

15. LC, VII, 152 Benešov and VI, Stříbro 77, 124, Budějovice 280, Pavlovice 92, Čermná 117, Kadaň 131, Kosová Hora 24, Kutná Hora 50, Uhostany 57, Tachov 58, Rynoldvilla 68, Křivsoudov 279, Bor 279, Podolí 280, Sedlčany 280, Božejov 283, Lužice 284, Ždar 284, Opočno 259, Jiřetín 261, Stropnice 239, Časlav 235, 240, Náchod 243, Velenky 245, Libochovice 236, Visočany 117.

16. LC, VII, Espentor 161, Vlčí pole 121. In VI, Nezvěstice 132, Běstovice 30, Mýto 42, Divišov 53, Neděliště 247, Novosedly 257, Černilov 270, Chřibska 240, Kolin 222 and in IV, Kolin 141.

17. Examples abound throughout the LC. See VII, 84, 140, 209, 107 as well as V, 221 and VI, 242.

18. In Prague the Hospital of St. Anthony was reserved for those priests, especially of the cathedral, no longer able to perform divine services because of old age or sickness. DMP, III, 258.

19. The number of confirmations recorded annually ranged from a low of 156 in 1410 to a high of 290 in 1407.

20. The desertion of parishes started as early as 1413. See HHR, 163ff. We know of one priest who was absent from his parish for the purpose of spreading Hussite ideas and that in 1417 he was deprived of his church in Domaslav. LC, VII, 233. The format used in the unexplained resignations was "data est commissio ad d. pleb. ecclesiae in Miza (ie. to the executor), ut recepta resignatio a d ...." VII, 107. The wording of the case in Újezd in December 1415 suggests that this was the formula used when compelling resignations. ". . . commissum est d. plebano ecclesiae in N. quod recepta resignatio juris, quod pretendabat se habere ad dictam ecclesiam . . .Johannes. . ." VII, 141.

21. Barraclough, G., *Papal Provisions* (Oxford, 1935), 92-94.
22. Fiala, *Správa,* 84-85.
23. Krofta, *Kurie,* 292-294.
24. Eršil, J., "Správní a finanční vztahy avignonského papežství k českým zemím ve třetí čtvrtině 14. století, " *RČSAV* (1959), 79. For a description of the type of people who went for chapter prebends see Thompson, A.H., *The English Clergy and their Organization in the Later Middle Ages* (Oxford, 1947), 72-73.
25. Haller, J., *Papstum und Kirchenreform* (Berlin, 1903) 36 and Kallen, *Pfrunden,* 267.
26. Eršil, *Správní,* 79 and *LC,* VII, 264.
27. *LC,* V, 261.
28. *LC,* 164.

CHAPTER 3

1. *DMP,* III, 144-147 and Kurka, J., *Archidiakonáty kouřimský, boleslavský, hradecký a diecese litomyšlská* (Prague, 1914).
2. *Čechy,* 234-25. See also Kurka, 713, Schlenz, *Kirchenpatronat,* 50-52 and Eršil, *Správní a finanční vztahy,* 45.
3. *DNČ,* II, 655-56.
4. For the papal tithes see Tomek, V.V., ed., *Registra decimarum papalium* (Prague, 1873) and for the ecclesiastical map showing churches not on the papal list see Kalousek, J., *Výklad k historické mapě Čech* (Prague, 1874).
5. The records were resumed in 1422 by the archbishop's chancery, which had not followed him into the Hussite camp. Its members fled to Žitava in northern Bohemia. There under the protection of the Catholic city and feudality they resumed the business of the church including recording what confirmations came their way after 1422. *LC.* VIII-X.
6. If a priest took office in 1375 or shortly thereafter at the age of 20 (the canonically prescribed age was 24 but exemptions were frequently given) he could still have been alive in 1419 having reached the age of 65.
7. For example, *LC,* VI, 106. In IV, 148, twenty-eight folia are missing involving a gap from 1 October 1380 to 31 March 1383. See also p. 47 for a gap of four months.
8. For example the parishes in Police and Broumov belonging to the monastery in Břevnov. Kurka, 589, 591.
9. Nine of these recorded no confirmation whatsoever.
10. Sedláček's *Hrady* and *Úvahy,* and Kavka's *Strana.*
11. Brunner, O., *Land Und Herrschaft* (Darmstadt, 1970; repr. Vienna, 1965) 407. See *Hrady,* XII, 329 and *AČ,* I 61 for Wenceslas Vundevein of Radim, a man enjoying rights of citizenship in a royal city, but who as the owner of an estate participated in the noble unity in its war against the king in the 1390s.
12. Actually the figure is on the high side since many of the 70 churches in the Share column were shared by members of several lay estates. Rarely did a monastery share with secular clergy. All averages exclude the numbers in columns *Sh* and *NC.*
13. The king and the nobility had four each. Five churches belonged to townspeople who also shared two with secular priests. One church was shared by its

parishioners and the archdeacon. *DMP*, III, 144-145. For the elections of the chapters see Vyskočil, *Arnošt z Pardubice*, 342-343.

14. For south-west Germany see Kallen, *Die oberschwäbischen Pfründen*, 250 and for England, Thompson, A.H., *The English Clergy*, 116-117.

15. *Hrady*, III, 24, 128.

16. Spinka, *John Hus: "On Simony,"* 272 cf. 258.

17. *HHR*, 150.

18. Höfler, C., *Geschichtsschrieber der hussitischen Bewegung in Böhmen. Fontes rerum Austriacarum*, erster Abteilung, VII, (1866), 36, 85 and Schlenz, *Kirchenpatronat*, 125.

19. Slavík, J., *Husitská revoluce* (Prague, 1934), 44-45 and Macek, *Tábor*, I, 72, 78ff and 87.

20. *HHR*, 152-154.

21. See his *Geschichte des Hussitenthums und Prof. Constantin Höfler* (Prague, 1868), 140.

22. For the royal records see Friedrich, G., ed., *Desky dvorské království českého*, 2 vols. (Prague, 1929, 1941 or *AČ*, XXXI, XXXV, XXXVI and XXXVII. The remnants of the land records are in *RT*.

23. *HHR*, 152-154.

24. For England see McFarlane, K.B. *Lancastrian Kings and Lollard Knights* (Oxford, 1972) and McKisack, *The Fourteenth Century*, 510-515.

25. *Hrady*, XII, 206, *Úvahy*, 98. His sons, one of whom with his father signed the protest letter of 1515 against Hus' death later established their right to the church.

26. In counting the gentry families I used the material collected by Sedláček in *Hrady*. Normally I counted one family per fortress or estate unless he specifically stated that several owned it. The question is made complex by the fact that several individuals occur named after a given fortress at about the same time but we do not know whether or not they were of one family.

27. The barons owned patronage more proportionate to their number. The 33 barons made up 22.7 percent of the baronial population (145 individuals of baronial status lived in the period 1415-1434 according to the names compiled by Kavka in *Strana* and augmented by those in the 1415 protest letter) and owned almost 20 percent of the parishes to which the barons as a class owned patronage. This excluded the 60 Rožmberk churches to which Lord Čeněk acted as patron while Ulrich was a minor that is until 1418.

28. *Hrady*, I, 112, 242.

29. Nějedlý, Z., *Dějiny města Litomyšle a okolí* (Litomyšl, 1903) 216, 242.

30. *Šlechta*, 31, Bartoš, F.M., "Vznik a osudy protestu proti Husovu upálení," *JSH*, XXII (1953) 55-57.

31. *DMP*, III, 349.

32. Quoted in Kaminsky, H., "The University of Prague in the Hussite Revolution: The Role of the Masters," *Universities in Politics*, ed., Baldwin, J.W. and Goldthwaite, R.A., Baltimore, 1972), 90.

33. *DMP*, III, 557 and *HHR*, 160.

CHAPTER 4

1. Bean, J.M.W., *The Decline of English Feudalism 1215-1540* (Manchester, 1968), 8-14, Cf. McFarlane, K.B., *The Nobility in Later Medieval England* (Oxford, 1973).

2. Kapras, J., *Přehled právních dějin zemí české koruny* (Prague, 1920; 2nd ed. 1922) Pt. I, 60-64.

3. Brunner, O., *Land und Herrschaft* (Darmstadt, 1970; reprint of 1965 Vienna edition) 181-194. One could use the term territory as do historians of the sixteenth century. *Terra* and *Territorium* have identical meanings in medieval sources. However by the sixteenth century territorial state and territory had acquired the meaning of a dynastic state with a unified administrative system unknown to the earlier centuries. Cf. *Ibid.*, 169, 172, 178. Cf. also Seibt, F., "Land und Herrschaft in Böhmen," *Historische Zeitschrift*, CC (1965).

4. Brunner, 358-64. Hence the term revolt, inasmuch as it implies resistance to authority by people not having it and acting illegally is inaccurate. This meaning is conveyed by Bartoš in *Čechy*, 113, by Šusta, J., *Karel IV za císařskou korunou* (Prague, 1948) 395 and Seibt, F., "Die Zeit der Luxemburger und der hussitischen Revolution," *Handbuch der Geschichte der Böhmischer Länder*, ed., Bosl, K., (Stuttgart, 1967) 481. The nobles had authority and acted lawfully. It was a question of whose concept of law would prevail, the king's or the nobles'.

5. Kapras, 32-33 and Seibt, *Land und Herrschaft*, 305-307.

6. Graus, F., in *Přehled československých dějin* (Prague, 1958) Pt. I, 119-121.

7. *Čechy*, 114.

8. *Glossarium*, 44 and *DNČ*, II, 647-48, 658.

9. Palacký, F., "Pomůcky ku poznání staročeského práva i řadu soudnjho," in *Časopis českého musea*, IX, (1835) 442. The same terms, *judicium terrae, provinciale*, or *terrestre* and *colloquium, consilium* or *conventus baronum* or *dominorum*, were used for both diet and court. See *Glossarium* 316, 386.

10. *Glossarium*, 386.

11. See *Ibid.*, 286 for his functions and *DMP*, V, 42 for the holders of the office, and *Čechy*, 120-121 for the beginning of the revolts.

12. *Glossarium*, 102. Henry Škopek of Dubá held the office from 1381-1387 and after a brief interruption until 1395. *DMP*, V, 40.

13. *Glossarium*, 325. The position was held by Andrew of Dubá until 1394, *DMP*, V, 41.

14. *Glossarium*, 230, *DNČ*, II, 652. See *DMP*, V, 41 for the holders of the office.

15. *Glossarium*, 96 and *DNČ*, II, 649-652.

16. Rieger, B., *Zřízení krajské v Čechách* (Prague, 1894), 33-42. See appendix II below for the names of the families who traditionally held these offices.

17. Kapras, 62-66 and Chaloupecký, J., "Inaugurační diplomy krale Jana z roku 1310 a 1311," *ČČH*, L-II (1947-1949), 98ff.

18. Šusta, *Karel IV*, 185-186 and Seibt, *Die Zeit der Luxemburger*, 401.

19. Šusta, *Karel IV*, 401-403 and Seibt, *Die Zeit der Luxemburger*, 398.

20. The text for the charter for Plzeň is in Čelakovský, J., *Sbírka pramenů práva městského království českého*, Pt. II, *Privilegia královských měst venkovských z let 1225-1419* (Prague, 1895) 734-735. The other towns are given in subsequent pages.

21. The dating is Bartoš' in *Čechy*, 58, n. 1. See also Daňhelka, J., *Nova rada Smila Flašky z Pardubice, Památky staré literatury české* (Prague, 1950).

22. *AČ*, I, 56-58.

23. *Čechy*, 58-60.

24. *AČ*, I, 56-58.

25. *AČ*, I, 61-63. For Radím see *Hrady*, XII, 329.

26. *AČ*, I, 57. The requirement that the lords be native born was moderate in comparison to those made to King John in 1310 and 1311 and to those made to King Sigismund in 1420 and 1435. See Chaloupecký, *Inaugrační diplomy*, 98ff, *AČ*, III, 206-208 and 419-420, cf. *Žižka*, 70-71 and Smahel, F., 'Nation', 213-214. See also Gerlich, A., *Habsburg-Luxemburg-Wittelsbach im Kampf um die deutsche Königskrone* (Wiesbade, 1960), 150. For Hus' patriotism see *MJHN*, I, 82-83.

27. *AČ*, I, 56.

28. *Ibid.*

29. *Ibid.*, 52.

30. *Ibid.*, For the archbishop's relationship to the nobles see Weltsch, *Archbishop John*, 40-78 esp. 54 and *Čechy*, 50, n. 1.

31. Cohn, H.J., *The Government of the Rhine Palatinate in the Fifteenth century* (Oxford, 1965) and Spangenburg, H., *Von Lehnstaat zum Ständestaat* (Munich-Berlin, 1912), esp. 77-80 and 88-91 discuss the struggles of the nobility with townspeople and royalty in late medieval Germany. See also Pirenne, H., *Belgian Democracy* (Manchester-Longon, 1915) which is older but still useful.

32. Quoted in *DNČ*, II, 605, n. 112.

33. See his *Nobility in Later Medieval England*, 248-267 first published as a Ford lecture in 1953.

34. See his "Had the Burgundian Government a Policy for the Nobility?" in *Britain and the Netherlands*, edd., Bromley, J.S. and Kosemann, E.H., Groningen, 1964).

35. Bartoš in *Čechy* has treated the period in question the most throughly. Palacký's *DNČ* II also contains valuable material as does Seibt's *Die Zeit der Luxemburger*. See also Fiala, Z., *Předhusitské Čechy 1310-1419* (Prague, 1968).

36. See his *Hrady*.

37. *AČ*, I, 56-58.

38. *Hrady*, X, 32-33.

39. For a discussion of joint-tenancy in the English setting see Bean's *Decline of English Feudalism*, 152. In Bohemia it was called a *spolek* and *unio* or *congressus bonorum* and was a device whereby the co-owner gained the right to inherit the property, thus avoiding devolution to the king. *Glossarium*, 319. In the case of Velešín, Peter agreed that if Margaret should die before he, his family would retain what had been an allodial estate although he would hold it in fief from the king. For this he had to give up the allodial status of two estates, Ratný and Úštěk. *Hrady*, III 223-226. Cf. *Hrady*, XIV, 105, *RT*, I, 445 and for John of Michalovice's relationship to Albert of Koldice see *AČ*, I, 402.

40. *Čechy*, 49-50.

41. *Hrady*, IV, 104.

42. *Čechy*, 120, *Hrady*, XII, 70.

43. *Čechy*, 58-60.

44. For Smil see AČ, I, 54-55, for Vznata, *Hrady*, X, 303, I, 34.

45. *RT*, I, 547-548, *Hrady*, I, 80.

46. *Hrady*, X, 199, XII, 78 and *Čechy*, 123, n. 2.

47. The immediate cause of the dispute was the refusal of several royal towns to pay damages to Lord Marquart in 1382. *Čechy*, 86. According to Palacký, *DNČ*, II, 566 the land court refused to rule in Marquart's favour. He cites no source for this.

48. *DNČ*, II, 636-642, *Čechy*, 203-204, *DMP*, V. 42. For the history of Lopata see *Hrady*, XIII, 72-73 where Sedláček, on the basis of testimony given under torture by a Henry Zelený in 1402 to the officials of the chief burgrave, suggests that Procop was attacking someone who had taken Lopata from Herman. Zelený confessed that he and friends, being in the castle with a Hroch as their captain, had stolen cattle from Herman and robbed on the highways. The chief burgrave in 1402 was Henry of Rožmberk, one of the king's chief enemies. The king himself was in his brother Sigismund's captivity from 6 March 1402 until 11 November 1403. It is more likely that what actually happened was that Zelený was part of a garrison placed in Lopata by Procop after he had taken the castle from Lord Herman on behalf of the king and that Zelený had somehow fallen into the hands of the king's enemies. The torturor elicited a suitable confession from him; namely that he had committed criminal acts so that the burgrave was justified in punishing him for actions done while in the king's service against one of Rožmberk's fellow leaguers. His punishment then could be seen not as a reprisal from Rožmberk to a royal servant but rather as the legitimate carrying out of justice.

49. *Hrady*, XIV, 171, XIII, 219.

50. *Čechy*, 121.

51. *Hrady*, XIII, 167-168.

52. *Hrady*, XIII, 72-73.

53. For Škopek see *RT*, II, 41, *Čechy*, 461 and *Hrady*, XIV, 105, 111, 204.

54. For example on 25 August 1394, see *Čechy*, 126-129 and *AČ*, I, 53-54. The nobility scored especially great gains on 2 April 1396 when a thirteen member council was formed with only one member, aside from the archbishop, loyal to the king; namely Henry Škopek. *Čechy*, 140 *DNČ*, II, 601. For a similar settlement of 15 June 1399 see *AČ*, I, 61-65 and *Čechy*, 163.

55. Only Olbram had been loyal to the king.

56. The king agreed that "into these offices we have to place well behaved gentry (zemany)." *AČ*, I, 67.

57. *Ibid.*, *Čechy*, 188-189, *DNČ*, II, 627.

58. *Čechy*, 191-203.

59. *RT*, II, 6, 10, cf, Rieger, *Zřizení*, 51-52.

60. *Čechy*, 218-219, *AČ*, I, 52, *RT*, II, 6, 10. For example, the king's friend and chancellor, Wenceslas Kralík in 1407 guided the fruitless attempt to aid Henry Topler, the burgrave of the Rothenburg castle in Swabia in his fight with Prince Ruprecht.

61. *Čechy*, 210.

62. *AČ*, I, 61, *Hrady*, I, 97, XII, 211.

63. *Hrady*, IX, 174.

162   NOTES

CHAPTER 5

1. See for example Pekař, J., Žižka a jeho doba, 4 vols. (Prague, 1927-1933) II, 35-38, III, 2, and Seibt, F., Hussitica, Zur Struktur einer Revolution (Cologne-Graz, 1965), 187-188 and HHR, 147. Cf. the Bishop of Lodi's speech at the Council of Constance in 1416 quoted in Betts, R.R., "Jerome of Prague," University of Birmingham Historical Journal, I (1947) 88.

2. HR, I, 19.

3. Strana, 21. He names Otto of Bergov, Hynek Berka of Honštejn, John of Michalovice and John Vartemberk of Ralsko (Chudoba). In fact Ralsko did not participate in the baronial leagues. Kavka likely confused him with John Vartemberk of Děčín who was not in the Catholic league of 1415 but who had joined the baronial league in 1400. AČ, I, 65. Děčín died in 1401. Ralsko quarrelled with the king in 1394 but did not join the other nobles and made peace with the king. By 1402 the king considered him his friend and entrusted a castle to him in order to keep it out of the hands of his enemies. Hrady, X, 143, 13, 22.

4. They were the first three mentioned by Kavka above plus Hynek Hlaváč of Lipy.

5. Ulrich of Hradec, Boček of Poděbrady and Henry Vartemberk of Valdstejn.

6. The Hussite sons of former rebels were, Půta of Častolovice, Ulrich of Hradec, Hynek Krušina of Lichtenburk, Boček Jr., of Poděbrady and Ernest of Pardubice. The Catholic son was John Jr. of Hradec, brother of Ulrich. DNČ, III, 188.

7. William Zajíc of Hazmburk, Albert Koldice and Aleš Škopek of Dubá whose brother Henry was a Hussite.

8. Novotný, V., Náboženské hnutí české ve 14 a 15.století (Prague, 1915) 185-186 and Kolářová-Císařová, A., Žena v hnutí husitském (Prague, 1915) 49. See also Kybal, V., "Étude sur les origines du mouvement hussite en Boheme. Matthias de Ianov," Revenue historique, CIII (1910), 1-31.

9. HHR, 7-20, Kolářová-Císařová, 32-35 and Novotný, Náboženské, 57-69, 179-207.

10. MJHN, II, 392, n. 4, Betts, R.R. Essays in Czech History London, 1969 114-120 and Spinka, M., trans., The Letters of John Hus (Manchester, 1972).

11. Šmahel, F., "The Idea of the 'Nation' in Hussite Bohemia", Historica XVI, (1969), 163-178, Seibt, Hussitica, 84 and Kaminsky, H., "The University of Prague in the Hussite Revolution: The Role of the Masters," Universities in Politics, eds. Baldwin, J.W. et al., (Baltimore, 1972), 90.

12. HHR, 25-34 and Spinka, John Hus: On Simony, 272-273.

13. HHR, 98ff.

14. Ibid., 273-75, 369.

15. Ibid., 440-444, 467-476, 486.

16. Brock, P., The Political and Social Doctrines of the Unity of Czech Brethren, (The Hague, 1957) 56-65 and HHR, 321-323, 422-425.

17. See the case of John Vartemberk of Ralsko below p. 200-1 and Spinka, The Letters of John Hus, 12-20.

18. Šmahel, F., The Idea of the Nation, 177-178.

19. Šlechta, 63-64.

20. Bartoš, F.M., "Vznik a osudy protestu proti Husovu upálení," JSH, XXII (1953), 53-55 and HR, I, 49.

21. Čechy, 120, DMP, III, 383, DNČ, II, 583.

22. Hlavaček, I., Urkunden- und Kanzeleiwesen des böhmischen und römischen König Wenzel (IV) 1378-1419, Monumenta Germaniae Historica Schriften XXIII, (Stuttgart, 1970) 136-137, cf. Čechy, 214, Hrady, III, 191 and ČČH, XXX (1924), 312.

23. Čechy, 227ff.

24. AČ, III, 295.

25. Ibid.

26. Rynešová, B., Listář a Listinář Oldřicha z Rožmberka, I (Prague, 1929), iii calls her an ardent professor of utraquism. For Maurice's letter see AČ, III, 299-300. For more on Henry's patronage of students see below chapter eight.

27. Čechy, 215, HR, I, 49 and below chapter six for details of his dispute with Čeněk.

28. LC, VI, 65, Čechy, 54, 269-270, 472, cf. Nějedly, Dějiny města Litomyšle, 185-186.

29. RT, II, 6, 10.

30. AČ, III, 486, Hrady, XIII, 8-10, 147 and DMP, III, 619.

31. AČ, I, 196 and VI, 3ff.

32. Pozůstalosti, CLXXV, 661 and CXXIV, 54.

33. DMP, III, 544, Hrady, IX, 173, XI, 222; AČ, I, 52, 65-66; RT, I, 98.

34. Strana, 84-85.

35. See Hrady, X, 66-67; AČ, III, 278-279 for the 17 October truce; Kalousek, J., "Zášti ve vychodních čechách," Časopis českého museum, LXXVII (1903), 270; Documenta, 580, 584, 590 & AČ, I, 7.

36. For the meeting of the royal council and the murders see Čechy, 147-148, DMP, III, 398, DNČ, II, 606, Gerlich, Habsburg-Luxemburg, 149-150.

37. MJHN, I, 82-83.

38. Čechy, 215, Hrady, XII, 6 and Heymann, F., George of Bohemia King of the Heretics (Princeton, 1965), 13-14.

39. Pozůstalosti, LXXXIV, 13, 19; Čechy, 197.

40. AČ, I, 5 for Sigismund's intervention on the queen's behalf and III, 277-278 for the truces and arbitration conducted by Čeněk. Čechy, 199 for the destruction of the Poděbrady estates by Sigismund.

41. Nějedlý, Dějiny, 216.

42. DMP, IV, 108.

43. Bartoš in Čechy, 120 calls Henry Berka of Honštejn one of the leading barons of the revolts. The text of the league of 1394 refers to a Berka of Holštein as a member. AČ, I, 52. The owner of Honštejn after 1380 was Hynek whose uncle Henry Berka of Houska had been his guardian until then. Hrady, XIV, 242-244. As far as is known the lord of Houska did not participate in the royal feuds, Hrady, X, 249-250. Hynek is a derivative of Henry but in order to distinguish the lord of Honštejn from the lord of Houska, of which only the former fought against the king (AC, I, 59) I use Hynek as the owner of Honštejn. For the latter I use Kavka's spelling rather than Bartoš' Hohenštejn.

CHAPTER 6

1. Palacký in DNČ, II, 594 said that among those who joined the noble unity in 1395 were Čeněk of Vartemberk and Hašek of Lemberk. Neither of them are

mentioned in the source he cited. (AČ, I, 54) The fourteen other members are. The older Čeněk died in 1396 and the younger is first mentioned in 1400. (Hrady, V, 256) Čeněk was present among the nobles on the land court on 20 December 1404 which made several decisions prejudicial to the king but so were known friends of the king like Beneš of Choustnik, Ulrich and William of Hazmburk. (RT, II, 10) Neither Bartoš, Čechy, nor Tomek, DMP, mention Čeněk's participation in the wars. See also Čeněk's disavowal of participation, below ad. n. 23. Sedláček, Úvahy, 90 stated that Čeněk in 1405 held the honourary office of the king's butler, but Tomek, DMP, V, 51 does not so list him. Henry of Rožmberk was a friend of Čeněk's in-laws judging from the fact that Henry was guardian of the Lipnice children in 1403. LC, VI, 13.

2. For Čeněk's mother see AČ, II, 363 where is indicated that the older Čeněk forfeited Kačna's dowry and Hrady, I, 34. However in Úvahy, 89 Sedláček held that Čeněk was the son of Princess Bolka of Bozel.

3. Bartoš, HR, I, 17 calls Henry Čeněk's uncle, ie. stryc. Perhaps he used the term in its old Czech sense: relative, (Glossarium 325) as Sedláček evidently did. (Hrady, V, 255) According to the data found throughout the Hrady, volumes the two were in fact cousins. Čeněk's father had had a brother Beneš who had three sons, two, Wenceslas and Peter are named in V, 319. In X, 60 Henry is called the brother to this Wenceslas which makes him the son of Beneš and Čeněk's cousin.

4. In Úvahy, 89-90, Sedláček wrote that he was 50 years old in 1415. The first reference to him, however is in 1400. (Hrady, V, 256) Cf. Pekar, J., Žižka, III, 43 who wrote that Čeněk was scarcely 30 years old in 1420.

5. Hrady, X, 66-67 and above n.2.

6. Ibid., V, 305.

7. RT, II, 30, 45 and Hrady, X, 47.

8. SA, Pt. VI, 205-206, Hrady, V, 306.

9. Novotný, V., Ed., M. Jana Husi, Korespondence a dokumenty (Prague, 1920), or Spinka, M., trans., The Letters of John Hus (Manchester, 1972), 13-19. For a list of the charters see Haas, A., ed., Codex juris municipalis regni Bohemiae, IV, (Prague, 1954), 133ff. For Čeněk's charter see Kapras, J., ed., Kniha svedomí města nového Bydžove z 1311-1470 (Nový Bydžov, 1907), vii-viii.

10. Hrady, X, 60.

11. Hrady, V, 187, 254-55, 165, 319, cf. Úvahy, 89. While the queen was deciding the Vartemberk dispute, Čeněk was arbitrating one between her and Hynek of Lichtenburk. AČ, III, 277-278.

12. According to a report of a French knight passing through Prague at this time the fight among the nobility related to the religious issue around John Hus. Čechy, 376-377. The most detailed account of the Dubá-Malovec dispute can be found in Nějedlý, Dějiny městalitomyšle, 217-220. He also relates the quarrel, albeit not concretely, to the Hussite issue.

13. AČ, II, 518-519.

14. Ibid., 520.

15. John of Hradec on 20 February wrote Čeněk that the king regarded Malovec as disobedient to the findings of the court. Ibid., 524-25, 529. Čeněk's repeated assertion that he was prepared to have Malovec stand before the full court suggests that a court hearing was never held. Also the bishop wrote Čeněk 11 March that

when no restitution was forthcoming he had written to the king's council. The latter had members hostile to Čeněk and perhaps the decision of the lords against Malovec was one of the royal council. *Ibid.*, 528.

16. *Ibid.*, 525.

17. *Ibid.*, 520, 523.

18. *Ibid.*, 524.

19. See below chapter 7, ad. n.18, 19 for a fuller discussion.

20. *Ibid.*, 526, 529. Actually at the time Conrad functioned as the administrator of the archbishopric not being confirmed until July 1413. *DMP*, V, 104.

21. *AČ*, II, 523. The bishop urged Čeněk to take action because Malovec was his and the orphans' man. 522.

22. *DMP*, IV, 49.

23. *AČ*, II, 517.

24. *Ibid.*, 528.

25. *Ibid.*, 530.

26. *Hrady*, IV, 206.

27. For a discussion of the relationship between the ownership of patronage and noble Hussitism see above chapter 3. For the Bydžov patrons see *LC*, VII, 249.

28. For the reform efforts of the archbishop, Weltsch, *John of Jenstein*, 162ff. Also three works by Hledíková, Z., "Die Visitation des weltlichen Klerus im vorhussitischen Böhmen," *Mediaevalia Bohemica*, II (1969), "Synody v pražské diécezi v letech 1349-1419", *ČsČH*, XVIII (1970) and "Korektoři kléru pražské diéceze," *Pravně historické studie*, XVI (1971).

29. The letter including the names of the signers is published in *Documenta*, 580-590 and in *Šlechta*, 59ff. See also below.

30. *HHR*, 369-370. Čeněk was not concerned about the fourth point which called for the purgation of public mortal sins in which name the radicals were calling for an end to fancy dress and were destroying beautiful works of art in churches and monasteries.

31. *Tábor*, II, 218, cf. *Anděl, R., Husitství v severních Čechách* (Liberec, 1961), 41.

32. *DMP*, IV, 39.

33. "K otazce polské kanditury," *Sborník Žižkův*, ed., Urbánek, R., (Prague, 1924), 102.

34. *Žižka*, III, 44-45.

35. *Strana*, 121. Included are all his shifts including those brought on by force when defeated on the battlefield by the troops of John Žižka. The changes refer to political and tactical ones; he seldom changed his religion, practicing the utraquistic communion until his death. Heymann, *Žižka*, 217 and *DMP*, IV, 332.

36. Schlenz, *Kirchenpatronat*, 130-131 gave some of the names of the priests who thus found livings, cf. *HHR*, 247-249 where more are added and they are identified as radicals.

37. *HR*, I, 35.

38. In May 1420 there was still some question if perhaps some nobles, eg. Hynek Berka of Dubá, who before had supported the Catholic cause, might not yet join Čeněk. See Pekar, *Žižka*, IV, 30, n. 2.

39. *HR*, I, 67.

CHAPTER 7

1. McFarlane, K.B., *Lancastrian Kings and Lollard Knights* (Oxford, 1972), 225-226. See also Aston, M.E., "Lollardy and Sedition 1381-1431," *Past and Present*, XVII (1960), 5. For the Cathars See Strayer, J.L., *The Albigensian Crusades* (New York, 1971).

2. *DMP*, III, 447-449 and *MJHS*, 103-107, *MJHN*, I, 142-150.

3. *MJHS*, 137-142, *MJHN*, I, 243, 283-285, 314-325.

4. *Čechy*, 291-314, *HHR*, 66-67.

5. *Čechy*, 352-353, *HHR*, 80, *MJHS*, 240.

6. Thus John Náz, an enemy of Hus testified. *Documenta*, 312, *DMP*, III, 518, *MJHN*, II, 122.

7. *DMP*, III, 348, *HHR*, 14ff, and Kybal, V., "Étude sur les origines du mouvement hussite en Boheme. Matthias de Ianov," *Revue historique*, CIII (1910), 1-31.

8. *Hrady*, IV, 122. Thomas had a second daughter, Peltra, who worked in a hospital in Třebon and made several monetary gifts to ecclesiastical institutions. *Pozůstalosti*, CV, 176 and CLXXV, 624.

9. Other noble ladies living in the community were Kunka of Vartemberk, Ludmila and Catharine of Pasovary, Strežka of Čejkovice, Margaret of Ostrý, Petra of Říčany and Margaret of Peruce. It is not known to which of the two branches of the Vartemberk clan which supported Hussitism, Veselí or Zvířetice, Kunka belonged if to either. Petra most likely was related to Diviš and Bartoš of Říčany who sent letters to Constance on Hus' behalf. For Hus' friendship with Petra see *Documenta*, 101, 102, and the English, Spinka, M., trans., *John Hus at the Council of Constance* (New York, 1965), 256.

10. Quoted in *DMP*, III, 439. The St. Vitus gift is in Borový, C., ed., *Libri Erectionum*, V, 561-562.

11. Quoted in *HHR*, 71.

12. He came from the fortress near Čáslav in eastern Bohemia where the Hussite representation among the gentry was strong. He is not mentioned among the patrons of the local parish who had appointed a university student there, perhaps a Hussite, by name of Bohuněk. See *Hrady*, XII, 62, *Monumenta Historica Universitatis Carlo-Ferdinandae Pragensis*, Vol. II, Pt. I, (Prague, 1834), 54, *LC*, V, 187.

13. *MJHN*, I, 347, *DMP*, III, 459. F. Šmahel, "Pražské universitní studentsvo v předrevolučním době: 1399-1419." *RČSAV*, No. 3 (1967), 42-44 omitted both John and Hroch from among noble students. According to Sedláček, *Úvahy*, 95 and R. Cikhart, "Šlechta na Táborsku proti upálení M.J. Husi," *JSH*, III (1939), 24-25 John owned Borotín and Prčice in south-West Bohemia and was a member of the Hussite baronial league in 1415 and a student at the University of Prague.

14. *MJHN*, I, 411, *DMP*, III, 480-481, *MJHS*, 167-169. Also *Documenta*, 396. *Hrady*, VI, 112 does not mention Gallus as an owner of Knin.

15. *Documenta*, 412-14. The Michalovice family history is in *Hrady*, X, esp. 214-216.

16. Hus had a personal acquaintence with Henry's wife and servants as reflected in a letter of Hus. *Documenta*, 118, cf. Bartoš, F.M., "Husuv přitel a hostitel Jindřich Škopek z Dubé," *JSH*, X (1937), 34-35.

17. For the options open to the Valois party to intervene on the Maid's behalf see Perroy, E., *The Hundred Years War* (London, 1951), 289.

18. *Documenta,* 22-23, *MJHN,* II, 223-224, Čechy, 363-364.
19. For the summoning of the synod see *Documenta,* 473-474.
20. See above Ch. four.
21. *RT,* II, 80.
22. *Ibid.* 86. Here it is called the council of nobles.
23. *Ibid.,* 110-114.
24. The chief burgrave was not present at the 1411 and 1412 sessions of the court. John of Hradec was named to the office sometime in 1412 so can be assumed to have been present in November. The office may have been vacant just before this. *DMP,* III, 6.
25. For Nicholas see *Čechy,* 220-221, 356.
26. *Ibid.,* 370, n. 1. CF. *Hrady,* IV, 144ff.
27. *Hrady,* IV, 146.
28. *Ibid.,* VIII, 102, n. 14. For Lefl's friendship with Hus see *Documenta,* 147, 692.
29. *Čechy,* 375, *DMP,* III, 551, *HHR,* 137.
30. *Čechy,* 379-380, *MJHN,* II, 347. Novotný, in *Šlechta,* 6, however wrote, "nobody gave it a thought that Hus might be condemned." Cf. *MJHS,* 358, that the Council was not bound by Sigismund's promise in any case.
31. *HHR,* 137-138, Kejř, *Husitský právník,* 89. Zbyněk's earlier charges were ignored.
32. They were William of Zvířetice, his son Peter, Hlaváč of Ronov, Wenceslas of Lnaře, Oneš of Mikovec, the burgrave of the royal castle Lichtenburk, Stibor of Bohdáneč and William of Doupov. *Documenta,* 243, DMP, III, 554. The inquisitor's note is also in Spinka, Council, 151-152. The lords of Zvířetice were party to the September letter as was Stibor's brother, Milota. *Úvahy,* 90, 94, *Hrady,* XII, 113.
33. *Documenta,* 531, *HHR,* 138, Kejř. *Husitský právník,* 89 and Spinka, *Council,* 151-153. William and Čeněk were distantly related Marquart (1197-1228), six generations earlier was their mutual ancestor.
34. The moderate group included Michalovice, Aleš Škopek, John of Frimburk, Peter Vartemberk of Veliš and perhaps Peter of Šternberk. The last three I hypothesize as supporting Hus because they had family ties with nobles of the Hussite league. Frimburk was the uncle of John of Opočno, Veliš was dominated by his brother Henry (above Ch. 6.) and Peter of Šternberk was married to Perchta of Kravare of the Moravian magnate family which was among the foremost adovcates of Hus.
35. *Šlechta,* 5, *HHR,* 138.
36. *Šlechta,* 6, *Documenta,* 253.
37. *Šlechta,* 7.
38. *Ibid.*
39. The threat of being tainted with paganism was one by association. Hus himself had supported the Poles against the Order. The German princes in 1400, as part of their complaint against King Wenceslas, rebuked him saying that in being against the Order he was against Christianity and in alliance with pagans and Tartars. Goll., J., *Čechy a Prusy ve středověku* (Prague, 1897), 110, and Pekař, *Žižka,* III, 4.
40. In Prague the author of the drafts was most likely John of Jesenice and in Constance Peter of Mladoňovice. *HHR,* 139, n. 148.
41. *Šlechta,* 44-45. English text is in Spinka, *Council,* 153-154. See *Documenta,* 22-23 where Hus in a letter to the nobles agreed to accept fitting punishment as long as he had been granted a public hearing.

42. Čechy, 408-409.

43. Boček of Poděbrady signed it on the basis of property in Moravia.

44. Šlechta, 56, Spinka, Council, 158-159.

45. Šlechta, 56.

46. Ibid., Spinka, Council, 159-162. Unfortunately the names of the 250 signatories are missing. We can assume that they were by and large the same group which was joined by an additional 200 for the September 2 letter for which we have some 450 names.

47. Šlechta, 53-54.

48. Ibid.

49. The others were Paul of Jenštejn, John of Dubá, Aleš Hřic of Pozno, Henry of Vlaším, Diviš and Bartoš of Řičany and John Hřic of Dradenice. Ibid., 56. F. Seibt, Hussitica. Zur Struktur einer Revolution (Cologne, 1965), 110 exaggerated when he called them "some of the most influential lords." Only Jenštejn and Vlaším could be properly classed as barons and they had very modest land holdings and no official capacity.

50. Šlechta, 56, Documenta, 555 for latin text.

51. Šlechta, 52, contrary to Novotný's inscription.

52. Ibid., 53-54.

53. Ibid., "We believe and place hope in you that you will induce His Royal Grace to this, that Master John Hus be released and not imprisoned anymore. And as he freely went to Constance under his safe-conduct, so let him again freely return to us in Bohemia under the same safe-conduct."

54. HR, I, 11, HHR, 141. See Čechy, 447-449 for an account of Hus' condemnation and death.

55. Nějedlý, Dějiny Litomyšle, 243 claimed Bishop John was meant.

56. Šlechta, 64.

57. Bartoš, Čechy, 434 recounts how Sigismund expressed his sentiments to the prelates. The king spoke freely of his disdain for Hus because he thought Hus'friends from Bohemia had left the room whereas in fact they had merely stepped to the window, out of view.

58. Šlechta, 64. MJHS, 356.

59. Úvahy, 85-109, 310-352. Not all Hussite supporters were on the list. Peter Zmrzlik, Chval of Machovice, Přech of Olbramovice and Herman of Hrádek, to name a few, are missing. On the other hand not all on the list necessarily supported Hus. One from Moravia denied having done so. HHR, 144, n. 9. Nevertheless the list represents an important measure of Hussite strength among the nobility.

60. "Vznik a osudy," 57, HHR, 147.

61. As did Bartoš, Ibid., and Kaminsky, Ibid.

62. It was for this reason that Sedláček Úvahy, 326-327 left open the possibility that the Hermanice in question was near Časlav rather than Litomyšl, even though William appears on the Chrudim list rather than on the Čáslav. In Hrady, I, 25 he placed this William on a fortress just north of Litomyšl.

63. Úvahy, 104.

64. In order to determine the number of owners of estates in these regions around 1415 I counted all which had a gentry owner after 1400. It is an arbitrary approach but necessarily so given the paucity of sources for that period. For example an estate like Morašice, Hrady, I, 186 was excluded from the count. Its owner is mentioned

in 1394 but then not again until 1430, (when he was a different individual) although a squire may well have lived here in 1415. On the other hand Jehneď, *Hrady* , I, 28, whose only known owner in the middle ages was mentioned on 1404, and others like it were counted, even though the estate may have devolved to the king before 1415, it may have been bequeathed to an ecclesiastical estate or sold to a baron, all not uncommon occurrences in that period.

CHAPTER 8

1. *Documenta*, 601. Bartoš, *Do čtyř pražských artikulů*, 486 says that the meeting was presided over by John of Hradec. John was not listed as present. The Council did however expect John to play a leading role in the defence of the Church. See *Documenta*, 572. For the text of the Hussite pact, with latin translation, see *Documenta*, 590ff and *HHR*. 144-145 for partial English translation.

2. *Documenta*, 618Cf. *HHR*, 155.

3. Goll, J., ed., *Fontes rerum Bohemicarum* V, (Prague, 1893) 338ff, cf. *HHR*, 155. For the university chronicle, *DNČ*, III, 184.

4. *DNČ*, III, 184, *HR*, I, 20-21, *HHR*, 146ff.

5. see n. 3 above. the attack on the monastery in Opatovice at the beginning of November 1415 may have appeared to the Council as an act of the Hussite politics since Otto of Bergov a member of the Catholic league, and John Městec of Opočno, a Hussite, cooperated in the attack. See Kalousek, J., "Zášti ve vychodních Čechách," *Časopis českého museum*, LXXVII (1903), 275-279.

6. The number of Masters is approximate, since it includes two M. Peters, two M. Stibors, and one M. Stephen (along with three other Stephens identified by place of origin), who were not well enough identified for me to tell if the name represented one or more individuals. Only two students without degrees are identified as such. The remaining non-matriculated students were found registered in the law faculty identified as a priest in a given church office, (See *Monumenta Historica Universitatis* II, i.) whose patron was found in the *LC*. Mostly these were not presented to office as a student but became students after confirmation. The term student includes post-graduates.

7. *MJHS*, 193-194. Of those present, four were known enemies of the reformers, Nicholas Cacabus, Gregory of Prague, Procop of Kladruby and John of Beroun. 26 were known Hussites. The stance of the rest is not known. The list of names is published in Ryba, B., ed., *Magistri Iohannis Hus Quodlibet. Disputationis . . . a. 1411 habitae Enchiridion* (Prague, 1948), 219-220.

8. Boček of Poděbrady in Jeseník, *LC*, VI, 207, Peter Janovice of Chlumec in Janovice, *LC*, VII, 100, John of Vlašim in Kondratice, *LC*, VII, 131 and two squires, Leonard of Luky and Peter Malovec of Pacov, *LC*, VI, 215 and VII, 12.

9. Peter Malovec presented M. Jacob whom I take to be M. Jacob of Soběslav a friend of Hus. *MJHN*, I, 453.

10. *LC*, VI, 226, cf. *Hrady*, V, 207.

11. *LC*, VI, 26.

12. Four of these were masters: 1402-Sedlčany, 1407-Mlazov, 1407-Nezvěstice, 1408-Sviny, *LC*, VI, 75, 225 (cf. 160), 220, 247. Two other students, to Ledenice-1404 and Chiška-1407, VI, 133, 202. The seventh, Andrew, the priest in Chotovice was in the Law Faculty, *Monumenta Historica Universitatis*, II, i, 41.

13. Peter's patron in 1413 was a squire John of Střimelice. *LC*, VII, 100. Peter probably attended the university but did not receive a degree. See *HHR*, 281, n. 60. In addition there were other forms of patronage as when John of Jesenice in 1409 got the right to collect an annual revenue on one of Lord John of Chlum's estates. Kejř. *Husitsksý, právník*, 94-95.

14. See above no. 1.

15. *LC*, VII, 214. The three exchanges, confirmed after 2 March 1417 when the baron and the archbishop parted ways, occurred in northeastern Bohemia, on Čeněk's own domains which may account for the fact that these confirmations appear in the episcopal records even though Čeněk's placements in the Rožmberk churches do not. It was in the south that Čeněk followed an active policy on behalf of the Hussites. For the exchanges see *LC*, VII, 232-Vapno, 227-Skalice, 255-Koleš.

16. *Ibid.*, 225.

17. *Ibid.*, 207, 209, 199.

18. For more details on this and other points made in this chapter see Klassen, J.M., "The Czech Nobility's Use of the Right of Patronage on Behalf of the Hussite Reform Movement," *Slavic Review*, 34 (1975).

19. *LC*, VII, 202-203.

20. *Ibid.*, 211, cf. *Hrady*, VII, 177.

21. The highest percentage was 25% in 1407. See above p. 32.

22. *LC*, VII, 205.

23. *Ibid.*, 201-202.

24. *Ibid.*, 186, 191, 192, 196, 202, 203, 204.

25. *Ibid.*, 206.

26. *Ibid.*, 209, 2 times.

27. *Ibid.*, 177.

28. Kejř, *Husitský pravník* on Jesenice and *HHR*, 224-225.

29. *HHR*, 227 esp. n. 21.

30. *LC*, VII, 220, 224, *HHR*, 240-41, ns. 53, 54.

31. *HHR*, 230-234.

32. *HR*, I, 35-36.

33. *Documenta*, 633ff, *HHR*, 234, n. 35 and Kejř. *Husitský právník*, 108.

34. *Documenta*, 654, 656, *HHR*, 230ff.

35. *HHR*, 242-244 and *Hrady*, XII, 70-71.

36. *HHR*, 244-246.

37. *Ibid.*,

38. *LC*, VI, 198, VII, 230.

39. *LC*, VII, 235.

40. See above n. 15.

41. *LC*, VII, 77, 146.

42. *LC*, VII, 224-225, *Hrady*, V, 11.

43. *LC*, VII, 152, 235.

44. *Ibid.*, 102, 260.

45. *Ibid.*, 179, 273.

46. *Ibid.*, VI, 261, VII, 253, cf. *Hrady*, IX, 156.

47. *LC*, VI, 47, VII, 242, *Hrady*, XI, 262.

48. For the complete translated text see below appendix IV. Anthony's expulsion suggests the pact was formed either in January or early February.

49. *LC*, VII, 176, 217, *Hrady*, XV, 245.
50. *LC*, VI, 24, 260, VII, 21, 56.
51. *Ibid.*, VII, 56, 236.
52. *Ibid.*, 43, 79.
53. Kejř. J., "Deklarace pražské university z 10 Března 1417 o přijímaní pod obojí a její historické pozadí," *Sborník historický*, 7 (1961), 133-145, *HHR*, 239 and *passim*.
54. *Documenta*, 697, cf. *HHR*, 247 n. 78.
55. *LC*, VII, 131, 218.
56. The names of 52 persons, including priests, who later regretted their abdication from the Catholic faith are given in *SA*, VII, 116-123. CF. Schlenz, *Kirchenpatronat*, 131.
57. *HR*, I, 56-59.
58. *Tábor*, I, 178.
59. *Hussitica*, 186-187.
60. *HHR*, 240-153.

CHAPTER 9

1. *AČ*, II, 524-25, 529.
2. *AČ*, III, 278-279.
3. *AČ*, III, 279.
4. *AČ*, III, 309-310.
5. *Documenta*, 602. "Eodem anno in Broda Bohemicali in die S. Remigii (1 Oct.) congregati sunt ad archiepiscopum Pragensem Conradum domini terrae contra Hussitas: D. Berka de Hohenstein, D. Hlawacz, D. Koldicz, D. Michalczo, D. Joannes Ralsko, D. Elsterbach, D. Wilhelmus Zajiec et alii quamplures, qui nolunt se proscribere cum aliis dominis oppositam partem tenentibus."
6. Seven of the eight deprivations in this period occurred in little over a year, between March 1417 and May 1418. The basic wording was "the church is vacant because lord Nicholas, the last rector, by way of sentence, has been deprived of the said church by archbishop Conrad" ie. ultimus rector, eadem ecclesia per d. Conradum archiep. Prag. sentencialiter privatus existet." *LC*, VII, 223. The wording was not substantially changed from that of the previous period. After 1416 the archbishop himself did the expelling rather than his vicar-general. Cf. Hledíková, *Úřad generálních vikářů*, 87-88. Given the events and the spirit of the times it can be safely assumed that the later deprivations involved the Hussite heresy.
7. Those from the gentry whose priests were deprived of office and who then resubmitted orthodox priests were: Chval of Hertvikov, *LC*, VII, 220, Amcha of Vesele, 233, Henry of Ach, 252, John of Světec, 260. In addition the priest in Libyně was deprived of office, 246. The patron here was John Janovice of Petersburk, 165, but he was not mentioned in the confirmation in 1417. In 1422 he was a member of the Catholic Plzeň Landfrieden and in 1433 he apparently joined the Taborites. *Strana*, 96. Whether the fact that he is not mentioned as the patron (no patron was mentioned)means he did not approve of the deprivation is not known.
8. *Documenta*, 697, "Sed de Usk, pridem nobiles, in hoc regno spectabiles, nimium infamati. Vestra rosa est polluta, vituperio induta istis nunc temporibus, . . . Ulricum militem excludam, . . ."

9. *LC*, VII, 247. For Anna's action see above Ch. 8 ad n. 54.

10. For 1406, *LC*, VI, 193, for 1419, VII, 280.

11. *LC*, VII, 233.

12. There were five brothers who shared the family estate as well as part of Žimutice. Leopold and John were in Rožmberk service. *Hrady*, XI, 139-140, III, 196, Cf. *Úvahy*, 310-311.

13. *LC*, VII, 266, for 1414, 132. The 10,000 Knights most likely recalled the 10,000 "soldiers" who according to legend were crucified with their leader Akakios by the Emperor Hadrian. *Lexikon für Theologie und Kirche*, X, (Freiburg, 1965), 1322.

14. See Pekař, *Žižka*, III, 22-23 for the contemporary literature alluding to such violence. For Litomyšl see *Hrady*, I, 6.

15. *AČ*, VI, 35.

16. *Pozůstalosti*, CXXIV, 54. "Wenceslaus rex cum mon. in Chotessow per querras pervenit in inopiam idem mon. ab summis berne regalis subsidus absolvit ad annos durante sexenimo."

17. Bezold, F., *König Sigmund und die Reichskriege gegen die Husiten*, 3 vols. in 1, (Munich, 1872-1877) I, 42. For Andrew see *HHR*, 150.

18. Technically the property in question was sold for a limited period, as for example six years in the following case or for the person's lifetime. Cf. *Pozůstalosti*, CVI, 27-28.

19. The villages were Chachov, Timochov and Mokrusov. *Ibid.*, LXXVII, 55. The terms describing the nobles' relationship to the property were *poručenství, oprava* and *naprava*. The first two were equivalent to wardship and protection, and *naprava* to benefice. *Glossarium*, 254, 204, 169.

20. *Pozůstalosti*, LXXVII, 59.

21. *Ibid.*, 58.

22. *Hrady*, IV, 338. This does not exhaust the list of men accepting royal or church property even at this early date.

23. *LC*, V, 187, VII, 223.

24. *LC*, VII, 258, 173, 259, cf. *Hrady*, IV, 252, 276.

25. Dřevčice-*LC*, V, 287, VII, 266; Rovná-VI, 81, VII, 242.

26. In 1403 the patrons had been Přibek Tluxa of Bořejov and a Peter Lunoněpas. *LC*, VI, 87, for 1419, VII, 289.

27. Procop on 6 June 1402 entrusted Běla to Ralsko in order to keep it out of King Sigismund's hands, which is why Ralsko expected it at Procop's death. It is doubtful if Ralsko's repentence had anything to do with opposition to the king. *MJHN*, I, 178, n. 1 and Pekař, *Žižka*, IV, 3, n. 2.

28. *LC*, VII, 61, 217, 256.

29. *Pozůstalosti*, CXXI, 3. The original was not available to me. Sedláček's copy is undated but includes two glosses—"(saec. 15 c. 1440-1470)" and "Littera e tempore regis Venceslai?" The fact that John of Ralsko acted as the patron of a church belonging to the monastery points to the earlier dating, during the time of King Wenceslas who died in 1419.

30. *LC*, VII, 157, 261.

31. *Ibid.*, 240-241. In 1359 John and Vznata of Skuhrov gave the patronage in Solnice to the Order of the Cyriaks. *Hrady*, II, 203. For Půta's service to the kings see Kalousek, *Zástí*, 280-281.

32. *HHR*, 266-267.

33. *AČ*, I, 147.

34. *HHR*, 268.

35. King Sigismund's letter to the nobles on 4 September and the Council's suppression of the university's functions likely also put pressure on them. *Ibid.*, 245-247.

36. *LC*, VII, 231, 291, and *Úvahy*, 105.

37. *LC*, VII, 243-244. Since both priests took the oath it is difficult to see how R. Cikhart in "Fara podoboji v Borotíně," *JSH*, VII (1939), 85-86 could conclude that the priest involved was an utraquist.

38. *Documenta*, 697. Both brothers, John and Herman had been party to the September protest letter and members of the Hussite league. Herman was not mentioned in the 1417 confirmation and likely remained a Hussite.

39. *LC*, VII, 244, *Úvahy*, 107.

40. *LC*, VII, 245-246, *Úvahy*, 99, 104, 313.

41. *LC*, VII, 271, 283, 291 and *Úvahy*, 100, 102, 319. The 11th defector was Leopold of Kraselov mentioned above.

42. *LC*, VII, 238, 264.

43. *Ibid.*, 100, 247, 253, 262, 288.

44. *Ibid.*, 256, 279, 289, 291, 292, 294.

45. *LC*, VI, 255. He was not identified as Thomas of Lysá in the 1406 exchange, but simply as Thomas the former altarist in Klatovy. But when he was confirmed to this latter office in 1405 he was called Lord Thomas of Lysá, Master of Arts, preacher for the Czechs. 160.

46. She stopped submitting candidates after 28 December 1416 and resumed on 21 June 1419. *LC*, VII, 214, 293, Cf. *Documenta*, 640-641 and *HHR*, 267.

CHAPTER 10

1. *HHR*, 273-275.

2. *Ibid.*, 293-295.

3. *Ibid.*, 278ff.

4. *HR*, I, 63-64, cf. Heymann, *John Žižka*, 66 for a vivid description of the king's death.

5. *HHR*, 369. The barons in this camp were Hynek Krušina of Lichtenburk, the lords of Poděbrady and Hašek and Hynek of Valdštejn, brothers of an impoverished family from northern Bohemia. Except for one or two estates in Bohemia their property was in Moravia. During the Hussite wars they hired themselves to Prague. Cf. *DMP*, IV, 101ff. Čeněk joined the party in moments of disillusionment with Sigismund. For a fuller discussion of Czech-Polish relations in the period see Goll, *Čechy a Prusy*.

6. *HHR*, 484-485.

7. Novotný, V., "K otazce polské kandidatury na český trůn" in *Žižkův Sbornik*, (Prague, 1925) 104-105.

8. Pekař, *Žižka*, III, 159-160. According to him Žižka's support was merely passive and soon turned into enmity. According to Heymann, *John Žižka*, 334-335, Žižka fully supported Korybut's goals from the beginning.

9. *HHR*, 512 and Heymann, *John Žižka*, 77, 125 and *passim*.

10. The Sigismund party has been treated most completely by F. Kavka in his unpublished dissertation at the Charles University, 1947—*Strana Zikmundová v husitské revoluci*. He tends to identify the party of Sigismund with the Catholics and includes the Catholic towns as well, p. 20. Pekař, *Žižka*, III, 43-45 and Kaminsky, *HHR*, 304 saw the party of Sigismund as made up of both Catholic and Hussite barons.

11. This lack of noble support was a major obstacle from the point of view of the Polish king. *HR*, I, 127.

12. *AČ*, III, 206-208, Mezník, J., "Dva problémy z počátku husitské revoluce," *ČsČH*, XV (1967) 198-199 showed that the first fifteen demands represented the interests of the nobility and that the conservative Praguers added some of their own. He also pointed out some of the similarities between those demands and those given to King Wenceslas in the 1390s. Heymann, *John Žižka*, 70 supposed the demands to be the product of a general diet summoned by Čeněk. Bartoš, *HR*, I, 72 gave the leading role to Prague.

13. *AČ*, IV, 375-377, cf. *DMP*, IV, 20.

14. Heymann, *John Žižka*, 110.

15. At his time the group included those who were both members of the Hussite league of 1415 and who in 1419 sent letters of challenge to Prague: Henry of Vartemberk, Herman and John of Landštejn, John and Zdeněk of Rožmitál, Wenceslas, Peter and Beneš of Zvířetice, Nicholas of Mochov, Zdeněk Medek of Týnec and Beneš Košik of Lomnice.

16. Novotný, *K otazce*, 102.

17. Heymann, *John Žižka*, 113-115. I do not agree with his assertion that a majority of the Czech nobility accepted the chalice. See also *DMP*, IV, 41-42. See Keen, M.H., *The Laws of War in the Late Middle Ages* (London-Toronto, 1965), 107-108 for the significance of banners in medieval warfare.

18. Heymann, *John Žižka*, 117-119, 143-144, *DMP*, IV, 46-48, Bartoš, *HR*, I, 102 de-emphasizes the significance of the coronation.

19. Daňhelka, J., *Husitské skladby budyšinskeho rukopisu* (Prague, 1952), 66.

20. Both Hynek and Hašek of Valdštejn were in Prague's service going to Poland to negotiate with the king in this role. Hynek's main residence, Kolštejn, was in Moravia. Hašek eventually turned to Sigismund and was rewarded with land in Moravia. Pekař, *Žižka*, III, 282. Hynek of Poděbrady, Viktorin's brother, was an ally of the Orebite brotherhood until May 1425 at which time he left them for Prague and died shortly in battle against his former allies. Hynek Krušina of Lichtenburk was related to the lords of Poděbrady through marriage, *AČ*, XIV, 560. Boček Sr. of Poděbrady died in 1414 leaving three sons, Hynek, Viktorin and Boček. The latter lived in Moravia. *Hrady*, XII, 2. Another baron, Herman of Borotin, fought in Žižka's army but not as an independent commander of his own troops.

21. See for example, Pekař, *Žižka*, Heymann, *John Žižka* and Bartoš, *HR*. The older *DMP*, IV has many useful details omitted by the others.

22. Heymann, *John Žižka*, 220ff (or his "The National Assembly of Čáslav," *Medievalia et Humanistica*, VIII, (1954) attributes to Prague the leading role whereas Pekař, *Žižka*, III, 99-105 gives it to Lord Čeněk. Cf. *HR*, I, 134-38.

23. Novotný, *K otazce*, 120, *DMP*, IV, 181, 208-215.

24. The nobles John Puska of Kunštát, Viktorin of Poděbrady and Hynek of Kolštejn were involved in this putsch. Heymann, *John Žižka*, 311ff and *DMP*, IV, 228-231.

25. *DMP,* IV, 239, 240.
26. Heymann, *John Žižka,* 394ff and *HR,* I, 187.
27. Heymann, *John Žižka,* 398 and *DMP,* IV, 296-293.
28. *DMP,* IV, 360-362, Heymann, *John Žižka,* 460.
29. Pekař, *Žižka,* III, 145 says Menhart was a utraquist in 1421 and that he joined the Taborites after his release from captivity. In 1424 he was a member of the Taborites when they signed a truce with the Plzeň Catholics. *Ibid.,* 154. Cf. Odložilík, O., *The Hussite King* (New Brunswick, 1965) 8.
30. *HR,* II, 43, *DMP,* IV, 406-407, 425-426.
31. *DMP,* IV, 474-476, 479-481.
32. *Ibid.,* 579-580.
33. *Ibid.,* 583-584.
34. *Ibid.,* 586-587, 627.
35. Bezold, *König Sigmund,* I, 42.
36. *Strana,* 17-18, 29-30. His numbers did not include the roughly 1500 gentry fortresses.
37. *Ibid.,* 26-27, Pekař, *Žižka,* III, 57.
38. *Strana,* 58ff.
39. *AČ,* III, 412, Heymann, *John Žižka,* 467.
40. *DMP,* IV, 628-647, Urbánek, R., *Lipany a konec polních vojsk* (Prague, 1934).

CHAPTER 11

1. *AČ,* III, 446-449, Heymann, *John Žižka,* 472-473.
2. Urbánek, R., *Vek Poděbradský,* 4 vols. (Prague, 1915-1962), I, 227, Heymann, *George,* 12, Odložilík, O., *The Hussite King* (New Brunswick, 1965), 23-24.
3. Odložilík, *Hussite King,* 26-29, Heymann, *George,* 13, Urbánek, *Věk,* I, 514-542.
4. Heymann, *George,* 156-160. See also Urbánek, *Vek,* III, 223-280.
5. Heymann, *George,* 588.
6. Heymann, *John Žižka,* 593, *HR,* II, 231-232. See also Hlaváček, I., "Husitské sněmy," *Sborník historický,* IV (1956).
7. Heymann, *George,* 388-389, 557.
8. *AČ,* III, 446-449, Heymann, *John Žižka,* 472-473, *HR,* II, 197.
9. Urbánek, *Věk,* I, 150-151, *Hrady,* XIV, 100, 113.
10. Urbánek, *Věk,* I, 147, *Hrady,* XIV, 336, 417, XIII, 219.
11. Urbánek, *Věk,* I, 161.
12. Urbánek, *Věk,* I, 154, 156, 167.
13. Heymann, *George,* 597-598.
14. *Ibid.,* 390-405.
15. Odložilík, *Hussite King,* 191-201.
16. Heymann, *George,* 442-444.
17. *Ibid.,* 598.

BIBLIOGRAPHY

Dictionary and Geographical Aids.

Brandl, V., *Glossarium illustrans bohemico-moravicae historiae fontes* (Brno, 1876).
Kalousek, J., *Vyklad k historické mapě Čech* (Prague, 1874).
Palacký, F., *Popis králowstwí Českého* (Prague, 1848).
Profous, A., *Místní jména v Čechdch*, 4 vols. (Prague, 1947-1957).

Archival Material

Pozůstalosti of A. Sedláček are a collection of some 200 volumes of copies from various Czech, German and Austrian archives now stored in the Institute of Czech and World History in Prague.

Fourteenth and Fifteenth Century Sources

Borový C., ed. *Libri erectionum archidioecesis Pragensis 1358-1407*, 5 vols. (Prague, 1875-1889).
Brandl, V., ed. *Codex diplomaticus et epistolaris Moraviae*, Vols. XII-XIII (Brno, 1890, 1897).
Čelakovský, J., Friedrich, G., Haas, A., edd. *Codex juris municipalis regni Bohemiae*, 4 vols., (Prague, 1886-1954).
Daňhelka, J., ed. *Husitské skladby budyšinského rukopisu* (Prague, 1952).
Emler, J., ed. *Reliquiae tabularum terrae regni Bohemiae a. MDXLI igne consumptarum*, 2 vols. (Prague, 1870-1872).
——— and Tingl, F., edd. *Libri Confirmationum ad beneficia ecclesiastica Pragensem per archidioecesim 1354-1436*, 10 vols. (Prague, 1865-1889).
Kapras, J., *Kniha svědomí města nového Bydžov z 1. 1311-1470* (Nový Bydžov, 1907).
Monumenta Historica Universitatis Carlo-Ferdinandeae Pragensis Vol. II, Pt. i (Prague, 1834).
Novotný, V., ed. *M. Jana Husi, korespondence a dokumenty* (Prague, 1920).
Palacký, F., ed. *Documenta Mag. Joannis Hus vitam, doctrinam, causam in constantiensi actam* (Prague, 1869).
———, ed., *Über Formelbücher zunachst in Bezug auf böhmische Geschichte* (Prague, 1847).
———, Kalousek, J., Friedrich, G., edd. *Archiv český*, 37 vols. (Prague, 1840-1944).
Ryba, B., ed. *Magistri Iohannis Hus Quodlibet* (Prague, 1948).
Rynešová, B., ed. *Listář a listinář Oldřicha z Rožmberka*, I (Prague, 1929).
Sedláček, A., ed. *Zbytky register kralů římských a českých z let 1361-1481* (Prague, 1914).
Spinka, M. trans. "John Hus: On Simony," *Advocates of Reform from Wyclif to Erasmus, The Library of Christian Classics*, XIV (London, 1953).
———, trans. *The Letters of John Hus* (Manchester, 1972).
———, trans. *John Hus at the Council of Constance. Records of Civilization*, vol. 73 (New York, 1965).

Tadra, F., ed. *Soudni Akta konsistoři pražské, (Acta judiciaria consistorii Pragensis)* 7 vols. (Prague, 1893-1901).
Tomek, V.V., ed. *Registra decimarum papalium* (Prague, 1873).

Seventeenth Century Source

Paprocki, B., *O stavu rytjrskem a rozmnozeni geho yak dawno a odkud ktery rod a erb do tohoto kralowstwi prissel* (Prague, 1602).

Nineteenth and Twentieth Century Sources

Anděl, R., *Husitství v severních Čechách* (Liberec, 1961).
Barbarová, E., "Purkrabí rožmberkských hradů a panství," *JSH*, XXXIX (1970).
Bartoš, F.M., *Čechy v době Husově 1378-1415* (Prague, 1947).
———, "Do čtyř pražských artikulů. Z myšlenkových i ústavních zapasů let 1415-1420," *Sborník přispěvku k dějinám hlavních města Prahy* V (1932) First published separately in 1925.
———, "Husův cititel na faře v Trhových Svinéch," *JSH*, XII (1939).
———, "Husův přitel a hostitel Jindřich Škopek z Dubé," *JSH*, X (1937).
———, *Husitská revoluce 1415-1437*, 2 vols. (Prague, 1965-1966).
———, *Literární činnost M.J. Husi* (Prague, 1948).
———, "Musejní sborník s Husovným kvodlibetem," *Časopis Národního musea* CXII (1938).
———, "Vnik a osudy protestu proti Husovu upálení," *JSH*, XXII (1953).
———, "Zaniklá pamatka z doly husitských táborů r 1419," *JSH*, XXIII (1954).
Betts, R.R., "The Social Revolution in Bohemia and Moravia in the Later Middle Ages," *Past and Present*, II, (1952).
———, "Jerome of Prague," *University of Birmingham Historical Journal*, I, (1947).
Bezold, F., K dějinám husitství (Prague, 1914) Original in German (Munich, 1874).
———, König Sigmund und die Reichskriege gegen die Hussiten, 3 vols. (Munich, 1872-1877).
Brunner, O., *Land Und Herrschaft* (Darmstadt, 1970, Rep. Vienna, 1965).
Chaloupecký, J., "Inaugurační diplomy krale Jana z roku 1310 a 1311," *ČČH* L-ii (1947-1949).
Cikhart, R., "Fara podobojí v Borotině, *JSH*, XII (1939).
———, "Husitští kneži v okolí Tábora," *JSH*, XII (1939).
———, "K rodupisu vladyk z Chelčic, "*JSH*, XVIII (1949).
———, "Šlechta na Táborsku proti upálení M.J. Husi." *JSH*, XII (1939).
———, "Vladkove z Udine,"*JSH*, III (1930).
Cinke, V., "Organizace českých klašterů ve 13. a 14. stoleti na pokladě provincním," *ČsČH*, XVI (1968).
Eršil, J., "Správní a finanční vztahy avignonského papežství k českým zemím v třetí čtvrtině 14. století," *RČSAV*, LXIX, no. 10 (1959).
Feine, H.E., *Kirchliche Rechtsgeschichte*, I, (Weimar, 1955).
Fiala, Z., "Správa a postavení církve od počatku 13. do poloviny 14. stoleti," *Sborník historický*, III, (1955).
Flajšhans, V., "O stižních listech šlechty," *ČČH*, XLIV, (1938).
Frind, A., *Die Kirchengeschichte Böhmens*, II (Prague, 1866).

Frinta, A., "O stižném listu z roku 1415," *JSH*, XXXVI (1967).

Gerlich, A., *Habsburg-Luxemburg-Wittelsbach im Kampf um die deutsche Königskrone* (Weisbaden, 1960).

Goll, J., *Čechy a Prusy ve středověku* (Prague, 1897).

Graus, F. *Chudina městská v době předhusitské* (Prague, 1949).

⸻, *Dějiny venkovského lidu v době předhusitské*, II (Prague, 1957).

⸻, "Das Spätmittelalter als Krisenzeit," Supplementum to *Mediaevalia Bohemica*, I (1969).

Heymann, F.G., *George of Bohemia King of Heretics* (Princeton, 1965).

⸻, *John Žižka and the Hussite Revolution* (Princeton, 1955).

⸻, "The National Assembly of Čáslav," *Medievalia et Humanistica*, VIII (1954).

Hlaváček, I., *Das Urkunden-und Kanzeleiwesen des böhmischen und römischen Königs Wenzel (IV) 1376-1419. Monumenta Germaniae historica-Schriften*, XXIII (Stuttgart, 1970).

⸻, "Husitské sněmy," *Sborník historický*, IV (1956).

Hledíková, Z., "Die Visitation des weltlichen Klerus im vorhusitischen Böhmen," *Mediaevalia Bohemica*, II (1969).

⸻, "Korektoři kléru pražské diecézi," *Pravněhistorické studie*, XVI (1971).

⸻, "Synody v pražské diecézi v letech 1349-1419," *ČsČH*, XVIII (1970).

⸻, *Úřad generálních vikářů pražského arcibiskupa v době předhusitské* (Prague, 1971).

Höfler, C., *Geschichtsschreiber der hussitischen Bewegung in Böhmen. Fontes rerum Austriacarum* erster Abteilung, VII (1866).

Kallen, G., *Die oberschwäbischen Pfrunden des Bistums Konstanz und ihre Besetzung 1275-1508* (Stuttgart, 1907).

Kalousek, J., *České státní právo* (Prague, 1871).

⸻, "Zášti ve vychodních Čechách," *Časopis českého museum*, LXXVII (1903).

Kaminsky, H., *A History of the Hussite Revolution* (Berkeley, 1967).

⸻, "The University of Prague in the Hussite Revolution: The Role of the Masters," *Universities in Politics*, edd. Baldwin, J.W. and Goldthwaite, R.A., (Baltimore, 1972).

Kapras, J., *Přehled právních dějin zemí české koruny*, I (Prague, 1922, 2nd ed.)

Kavka, F., *Přehled dějin československa v epoše feudalismu*, II (Prague, 1955).

⸻, *Strana Zikmundova v husitské revoluci* (Unpublished dissertation in Charles University, Prague, 1947).

Kejř, J., "Deklarace pražské university z 10 března 1417 o prijimání pod obojí a její historické pozadí," *Sborník historický*, VIII (1961).

⸻, *Husitský právník M. Jan z Jesenice* (Prague, 1965).

⸻, "Stát, církev a společnost v disputacích na pražské universitě v době Husově a husitské," *RČSAV*, LXXIV, no. 14 (1964).

Klecanda, V., "Přijímání do rytířského stavu v zemích českých a rakouských na počatku novověku," *Časopis archivní školy*, IV (1928).

Krofta, K., "Kurie a církevní správa zemí českých v době předhusitské," *ČČH*, X (1904), XII (1906), XIV (1908).

Kurka, J., *Archidiakonáty kouřimský, boleslavský, hradecký a diecese litomyšlská*, (Prague, 1914).

Kybal, V., "Étude sur les origines du mouvement hussite en Boheme. Mathias de Ianov," *Revue historique*, CIII (1910).

Loserth, J., "Die Krönungsordnung der Könige von Böhmen," *Archiv für österreichische Geschichte*, LIV (1876).

Macek, J., "K počatkům husitství v Pisku," *JSH*, XX (1953).

_____, *Tábor v husitském revolučním hnutí*, 2 vols. (Prague, 1952-1955).

Mezník, J., "Dva problemy z počátku husitské revoluce," *ČsČH*, XV (1967).

Molnár, A., "The Crisis of the Parish," *Communio Viatorum*, (1970).

Nějedlý, Z., *Dějiny města Litomyšle a okolí* (Litomyšl, 1903).

Novotný, V., *Hus v Kostnici a česká šlechta* (Prague, 1915).

_____, "K otazce polské kandidatury na český trůn," *Sborník Žižkuv*, ed., Urbánek, R., (Prague, 1924).

_____, M. *Jan Hus Život a učeni*, I, *Život a dilo* i-ii (Prague, 1919-1921).

Nový, R., "K socialním postavení farského kléru v Čechách v době předhusitiské," *Sborník historický*, IX (1962).

Odložilík, O., *The Hussite King* (New Brunswick, 1965).

Palacký, F., *Dějiny národu českého*, II-III (Prague, 1848-1850; 2nd ed., 1870-1871). Rep. 1939.

_____, *Die Geschichte des Hussitenthums und Prof. C. Höfler* (Prague, 1868).

_____, "Pomučky ku poznánj staročeského práwa i řadu saudnjho," *Časopis českého museum*, IX (1835).

Pekař, J., *Žižka a jeho doba*, 4 vols. (Prague, 1927-1933).

Rieger, B., *Zřizení krajské v Čechách*, I (Prague, 1894).

Schlenz, J., *Das Kirchenpatronat in Böhmen* (Prague, 1928).

Schmid, H.F., "Die rechtliche Grundlagen der Pfarrorganisation auf westslavischen Boden," *Zeitschrift der Savigny-Stiftung für Rechtsgeschichte Kanonistische Abteilung*, XIV (1926).

Sedláček, A., *Hrady, zámky a tvrze království českého*, 15 vols. (Prague, 1880-1927; 2nd ed. 1931-1936).

_____, "Úvahy o osobách v stížných listech 1. 1415 psaných," *ČČH*, XXIII (1917).

Sedlák, J., *M. Jan Hus* (Prague, 1915).

Seibt, F., "Die Zeit der Luxembürger und der hussitischen Revolution," *Handbuch der Geschichte der Böhmischen Länder*, ed. Bosl, K., (Stuttgart, 1967).

_____, *Hussitica. Zur Struktur einer Revolution* (Cologne, 1965).

_____, "Land und Herrschaft in Böhmen," *Historische Zeitschrift* CC (1965).

Slavík, J., *Husitská Revoluce* (Prague, 1934).

Šmahel, F., "Le mouvement des etudiants a Prague dans les annees 1409-1412," *Historica*, XIV (1967).

_____, "Pražské universitní studentstvo v předrevolučním období 1399-1419," *RČSAV*, no. 3 (1967).

_____, "The Idea of the 'Nation' in Hussite Bohemia," *Historica*, XVI, (1969). Also in Czech in book form, *Idea Národa v husitských Čechach* (Česke Budějovice, 1971).

Spinka, M., *John Hus' Concept of the Church* (Princeton, 1966).

Švehla, J., "Farní kostel v Ústí Sezimové," *JHS*, III (1930).

Tomek, V.V., *Dějepis města Prahy*, III-V (Prague, 1875-1882; 2nd ed. 1899).

_____, "O církevní správě strany podoboji v Čechách od 1415 až 1622," *Časopis českého museum*, IV-V (1848).

Urbánek, R., *Lipany a konec polních vojsk* (Prague, 1934).

————, *Věk poděbradský*, 4 vols. (Prague, 1915-1962).

Vaněček, V., *Dějiny státu a práva v Československu do roku 1945* (Prague, 1964).

Vyskočil, J., *Arnošt z Pardubice a jeho doba* (Prague-Vyšehrad, 1947).

Weltsch, R.H., *Archbishop John of Jenstein 1348-1400* (The Hague, 1968).

Winter, Z., *Život církevní v Čechách* (Prague, 1895-1896).

INDEX

Ach, Henry of, 171
Alberovice, Naršik of, 122
Albert, Duke of Austria, 138
Albert, Duke of Bavaria, 139
Arc, Joan of, 89
Augustine, St., 63

Benedict XIII, Pope, 95
Bergov, Otto of, 30, 49, 56-58, 70-72, 106, 114, 148, 162, 169
Bernard of Clairveaux, 63, 114
Běstvina, John of, 121
Bethlehem Chapel, 69, 87-88
Bohdáneč, Stibor and Milota, 167
Bohemia (see also Land Government) 130; divisions in, 50, 126-28, 146-147; governing council 1423, 133; powers of the estates, 138-40
Bořejov, Přibek Tluxa, 172
Breži, Aleš of, 69
Březova, Laurence of, 100
Bridget of Sweden, 63
Brod, Andrew of, 40, 117
Budyně, See Nicholas of Hazmburk

Casimir IV of Poland, 141
Časlav, Diet of (1421), 131
Častolovice, Půta of, 57, 120, 133, 140, 162
Cathars, 85
Čejkovice, Strežka of, 166
Červený Hrádek, Herman of, 110-111, 152, 168
Charles IV, King of Bohemia, (1346-1378), 13, 15, 17, 23, 40, 45, 50-51, 54, 64
Chlum, John Kepka, 90, 92-93, 170, See also Lacembok
Chlumec, Peter of (also of Janovice), 169
Chrast, Všebor of, 30
Church Organization, 35-36
Chustník, Beneš of, 147, 164
Coinage devaluation, 15
Conrad Vechta, Archbishop of Prague, 73, 79, 91, 101, 104-106, 116; attack on the Hussites, 106-107, 114-115, 118-119, 129, 171

Council of Basel, 4, 135
Council of Constance, 3-4, 45, 59, 64, 68, 81, 90-100, 103, 107-108, 121
Council of Pisa, 86
Crusade, anti-Hussite, 66
Czech National feeling, 63-65, 72-73, 93

Dětenice, Nicholas of, 110
Doupov, William of, 167
Dradenice, John Hřič of, 168
Dráhov, Buzek and Henry of, 118
Dražice, John of 28
Dubá, Henry of, 69, 78-79
Dubá, John Roháč, 131, 168
Dubá, Wenceslas, of, 90, 92, 147; Andrew of, 147
Dubá, Wenceslas Leštno of, 147
Dubá (Berka), 74, 140, 146-148, 151; Hynek Hlaváč of Lipá, 106, 115, 148, 151, 162, 171; Hynek of Honštejn, 40, 74, 89, 146-148, 160, 163, 165, 171; Henry of Houska, 40, 136, 147, 163; John Berka of Dubá, 136
Dubá (Škopek), Aleš Skopek, 89-90, 147-148, 162, 167; Henry Sr., 55, 57, 72, 88, 146-148, 161; Henry Jr., 58; Zbyněk and Albert, 57-58

Economic conditions, 5; countryside, 6-17; city, 17-26
Elsterberg, Henry of, 115, 118, 150, 151, 171

Feudal tenure in Bohemia, 47-49, 54
Feuds See under nobility
Frederick I, of Hohenzollern, Margrave and Elector of Brandenburg, 134
Frederick III, of Habsburg, Holy Roman Emperor, 139
Frimburk, John of 167

Gall, St., Diet of (1423), 132-133
Gentry, titles, 7; church patronage, 43, 38-40, 105-106; patronage on behalf of Hussitism, 44, 102, 110-112; Hussite pact (1417), 110-111, 152-153

Gerson, Jean, 64
Gregorian reforms, 26
Gregory XII, Pope, 86, 95
Guilds, 18-19
Gutštejn, Burian of, 136

Harbatová, Anna, 20
Hazmburk, Nicholas Zajíc of, 42, 117, 150; Ulrich Zajíc of, 70-72, 89, 147, 164; William Zajíc of, 118, 129, 147, 150, 162, 164, 171; Zbyněk of (Archbishop of Prague), 85, 87-88
Henry V. King of England, 85
Herman, Titular bishop of Nicopolis, 108
Hermanice, William of, 96, 168
Hertvikov, Chval of, 171n 7
Historiography of the nobility and Hussitism, 1-2
Hofart, Keruše, 63
Hospital for retired priests, 156n18
Hradec, (Jindřichův), Henry of, 148; John Sr. of, 77, 89, 146, 162; John Jr. of, 42, 62, 89, 114, 123, 134, 147-148, 169; Menhart of, 123, leadership, 134-137, 138-139, 175; Ulrich Vávák of, 110, 146-148, 162
Hrádek, See Červený Hrádek
Hradiště, Cistercian monastery, 33, 119-120
Hromádka, Peter, 104, 125
Huler, Sigismund, 73
Hugh of St. Victor, 63
Hus, John, 11, 63-65, 68-69, 72-73, 77, 79, 82; his death, 95, 100; cooperates with archbishop, 85; opposition to indulgences, 86; reform of the university, 86; appeal to the nobility, 88-91, 119; in Constance, 91-95
Hussite, priests ordained, 108; seek legitimacy, 88, 108-109, 128-129; ideas, 26, 63-65; radicals, 3-4, 82, 125, 127, 131; negotiations with Catholics, 134-136
Husinec, Nicholas of, 106, 116, 127, 130
Huska, Martin, 67

Janov, Matthew, 20, 45, 63, 65, 87
Janovice, John of (and of Petersburk) 171
Jemniště, Mikeš of, 91
Jenštejn, John of, Archbishop of Prague, 11, 31, 53, 77, 81
Jenštejn, Paul of, 168
Jesenice, John, 91, 123, 170
John Dominici (papal legate) 121
John Kardinál, 103
John, King of Bohemia (1311-1346), 47, 50, 54, 160
John, Duke of Zhořelec (Wenceslas' brother), 52
John, Bishop of Litomyšl, 38, 43-44, 58, 69-70, 72-76, 78, 80, 81, 96, 99, 114, 117, 168
John XIII, Pope, 86, 93
Jošt, Margrave of Moravia, 52, 78

Klenov, Přibek of, 110
Koldice, Albert of, 150, 160, 162, 171; Anna of, 140; Těma of, 55
Kolovraty, lords of, 136, 146, 147
Kolštejn, Hynek of, 174
Korybut, See Sigismund
Kostelec, John Sadlo of, 104, 132, 149
Kozí, Stibor of, 90
Kralovice, John of, 118
Krása, John, merchant of Prague, 129
Kraselov, See Žimutice
Kravaře, Eliška of (Rožmberk), 69; Lacek of, 69, 74, 82-83, 88, 99; Perchta of, 167; Peter of, 88
Kunštát, Erhart of, 79, John Puška of, 174
Kutná Hora, Diet of (1421) 132; Diet of (1431), 134-135

Lacembok-Chlum, lords of, 59, 92
Ladislas Posthumus, Duke of Austria, King of Bohemia and Hungary, 138-139
Ladislas, King of Naples, 86
Land Government of Bohemia, 48-51, 142; land court, 89, 91-92; land records, 41, 50, 52, 115; choosing a king, 138-139

Landštejn, William of, 30, 55, 76, 148; Herman (also of Borotín), 148, 173-174; John of (also of Borotín), 88, 122, 148, 166, 173, 174
Lažan, Henry Lefl of, 90-91
Lemburk, Hašek of, 163
Lestkova, John of 118
Leskovec, John of, 110-111, 152
Lichtenburk, Anežka of, 56; Hynek Krušina, 56, 104, 130, 140, 148, 162, 173, 174; John Krušina Sr., 58-59, 72-74, 130, 147-148: John Krušina Jr., 148
Lipnice, Vitek of, 78, 146
Litomyšl See John, Bishop of,
Lnáře, Wenceslas of, 167
Lobkovice, Nicholas of, 70
Lollards, 85
Lomnice, Beneš Košik of, 174; John Košik of, 148
Lopata, Herman of, 56, 161
Luky, Leonard of, 169
Lunončpas, Peter, 172n26
Lysá, Thomas of, 103, 123

Machlov, Přibek and Hynek, 116
Machovice, Chval of, 168
Majestas Carolina, 51
Martin V, Pope, 68, 120-121
Meissen, Margrave of, 73
Michalovice, John of, 53-55, 73, 88-90, 110, 146-149, 160, 162, 167, 171; Margaret of, 160; Peter of, 160
Mikovec, Oneš of, 167
Milheim, John of, 56, 69, 118; Anna of (also of Hazmburk) 118
Mladonovič, Peter, 167
Mnich, Leon of, 122
Mochov, Anna of 90, 112, 116; Nicholas of, 174
Muta, Maršik of, 116

Náchod, Theodore of, 146-147
Nezero, Nicholas (Prague inquisitor), 91
Nicholas Mnišek, 118
Nobility; Catholic league, 3-4, 61-62, 99, 114-115, 135; Hussite league, 61-62, 99, 104-106, 134; support of

Hussites, 2-3, 43-45, 61, 67, 72, 84, 87-88, 90, 98, 101, 106-113, 130-131; 1415 protest letter, 3, 44, 68, 81, 110-111, 118, 119, 120-123; economic conditions, 6; titles, 6, 36; domination of priests, 30, 31, 119-120; leagues against the king, 2, 51-62, 70-71, 121, 141-142, settlement with the king, 68; compared to the French, 4, 89; motives, 41-42; support for Sigismund, 83, 134; divided loyalties, 83-84, 95-96, 99, 114-115, 136; guardians over church property, 117-119; defectors from Hussitism, 121-124, 129-130; efforts to regain control, 131-137; victory over radicals, 137; gains after revolution, 138-143; women, 87, 90, 111; patronage of university students, 101-104
Nová Rada, 51

Olbram, Archbishop of Prague, 55, 161
Olbramovice, Přech of, 110-111, 152, 168
Oldcastle, John of, 85
Opočno, John Městecký of, 30, 71-72, 132, 149, 167, 169; Jaroslav of, 147
Oreb brotherhood, 131, 134, 137
Orlik, Andrew Huler, 71
Osek, Boreš Sr. and Jr., 57-58, 70, 115, 146, 149
Ostrý, Margaret of, 166
Osvětím, Duchess Anna of, 120

Pacov, Peter Malovec, 78, 169
Pasovary, Ludmila and Catherine, 166
Papal provisions, 32-33
Pardubice, Ernest, Archbishop of Prague, 28-29; Ernest Flaška of (also of Richenburk, 42, 129, 162; Kačna of 76; Smil of, 51-52, 55-56, 76; William, 55-56, 76
Patrons (Church) 27-34; categories of, 36
Patronage ownership; in Prague, 38; class distribution, 38-40
Paul II, Pope, 141

Peasants; free, 7; economic conditions, 8-9, 12, 14, 15; legal status, 9-11; taxes, 13; loss of rights, 141
Pelhřimov, Nicholas, 66-67, 103
Peruce, Margaret of, 103
Pirkštejn, Hynek Ptáček, 139
Plavno, Henry of, 70
Plzeň, city of, 135; Thomas Pabiak of, 118; Procop of, 132
Poděbrady, Boček Sr., 42, 44, 46, 56, 58, 72-74, 79, 89, 92, 130, 146-149, 162, 168, 169, 174; Boček Jr., 99, 104, 110, 162, 168, 149, 173-174; George, King of Bohemia (1458-1471), 1, 138-142; Viktorin, 130, 174; Hynek, 174
Podveky, Hroch of, 88, 166
Poles, relationships to Hussites, 93, 126-129, 131, 132, 138, 141-142, 166-167
Poor classes, 19-21, 24-25
Postupice, Kostkas of, 140
Pozno, Aleš Hříč of, 168
Prachatice, Christian, 132
Prague, economy, 17, 21; housing costs, 23-24; population, 17; social structure, 18-20; monastery of St. Thomas, 13; Four Articles, 66, 82-83, 126-127; University of, 62-65, 75, 86, 93, 101-105, 108-109
Prague, Jerome of, 45, 63-64, 67-68
Prague, Johanka of, 76
Prague, Nicholas the Rich of, 89-90
Prague Castle, 129
Přemysl II, King of Bohemia (1253-1278), 48, 50
Příbram, John, 66, 132, 135
Prices, 22-23, 144
Priests, confirmations, 35-36; dismissals, 29, incomes, 28, installations, 28-29; oath of loyalty, 107; resignations, 32, 104-106
Přimda, lords of, 115
Procop, Margrave of Moravia, 52, 56, 73, 119, 172
Procop the Shaven, 130, 134
Prostitutes, 20, 63-64

Radím, Wenceslas of, 52
Ratiboř, John Medenec, 110
Řepany, Sigismund of, 67
Říčany, Bartos of, 166, 168; Diviš of, 123, 166, 168; Petra of 166
Ronov, Hlaváč of, 167
Royal government, 41, 47-49; feudal powers, 47-48; taxes, 13; loss of power, 138-141
Rožmberk, 40, 44, 51, 105, 108-109, 146; Henry of, 40, 53, 58, 68-69, 72, 74-75, 78, 103, 146, 149, 160, 164; Ulrich of, 40, 117, 122, 123, 129, 131-133, 136, 138, 139, 140, 158
Rožmitál, John and Zdeněk of, 149, 174
Runtinger, German merchant, 21
Rupert, Elector of the Phenish Palatinate, 86
Rural-urban tensions, 16-17
Rvačka, Maurice, 69

Sány, John Čapek of, 130
Sigismund, King of Hungary, 1, 4, 13, 41, 52, 57, 58, 61, 70-74, 80, 82-85, 90-96, 118, 120, 123, 126-128, 131-139, 140, 160, 161, 168, 172, 173, 174; at Constance, 107-108, 111, 113, 114, 117; coronation, 129-130; Czech supporters, 126-128; Negotiations with Hussites, 128-129; death, 138
Sigismund Korybut of Poland-Lithuania, 127, 133-134
Skála, Břeněk of, 58-59, 70-71, 146-147, 149; Půta of, 71
Skuhrov, Vznata of, 55, 172; John of 172
Smiřice, John of, 140
Soběslav, Jacob of, 103
Sophia, Queen of Bohemia, 78, 89, 123-124
Šternberk, Albert of, 147, 149; John of, 69; Peter of, 105, 121, 149, 167; Smil of (and of Holice), 149; Šdeslas (Zdenek) 146-147

Štipoklasy, Hrdibor of, 105
Štitný, Anežka of, 87; Peltra of, 166;
Thomas of, 63, 87, 166
Stojice, Albert of, 122
Stříbro, Jakoubek of, 65, 107, 113
Střimelice, John of, 170
Strygl, Dorothy, 20
Studena, Theodore of, 43
Švamberk, 51, 57, 59, 70-71, 146-
147, 150; Bohuslav, 117-118; Hynek
Krušina, 136
Světec, John of, 171
Švihov, John and William of, 89, 146-
147

Tabor brotherhood, 66-67, 127, 131,
134-135
Těchobuze, Albert of (also of Stojice),
105, 110, 122
Teutonic Knights, Order of, 93, 126-
127
Týnec, Sdeslas (Zdeněk) Medek of,
150, 174

Újezd, John of, 30
Újezdec, John Mladenec of, 110
Ulibice, Mikeš of, 103
University of Prague, See Prague, University of
Ústí, Anna, See Mochov, John Sr.,
150; Ulrich of, 89, 116, 171; William
of, 109; and of Kamenice, John Sr.,
112, 150; John Jr., 112; Procop,
112, 115-116

Valdštejn, Hynek and Hašek, 173, 174
Vaněk (radical priest), 125
Vartemberk, Čeněk Sr. of, 75-76, 163;
Čeněk of, 40, 42, 44, 46, 62, 69,
89, 98, 103, 114, 117, 121-123;
130-132, 143, 147, 150, 158, 163-
165, 167, 170, 173; financial troubles
and success, 75-77; and peasants, 77,
and patronage, 81, 108-109; political
leader, 75-84; religious leader, 99,
104-106, 110-111, 113; indecision, 82,
128-129; moderate policies, 83-84,

90, 92, 104, 108-113, 128-129; his
son Henry, 143
Vartemberk, Henry of, 77-78, 147,
150, 160, 174
Vartemberk, John (also of Děčín),
33, 57, 146, 150, 162; Benes and
Sigismund of (also of Děčín), 150;
Jarek of, (also of Děčín), 33
Vartemberk, John of, (also of Kost),
147
Vartemberk, John of (also of Ralsko),
42, 119-120, 150, 160, 171, 172
Vartemberk, Kunka of, 166
Vartemberk, Marquart of, 56, 161
Vartemberk, Peter of (and of Kost),
56, 150
Vartemberk, Peter of (and of Veliš),
76-78, 167
Vartemberk, Wenceslas of, 77
Veselé, Amcha of, 116, 171
Vimburk, Conrad of, 111
Vitold, Duke of Lithuania, 133
Vlačice, Nicholas and Beneš of, 96
Vladislav II, King of Bohemia (1471-
1516), 139, 141-142
Vladislav II, King of Poland, 129, 133
Vlašim, John of, 169; Henry of, 168
Vlašim, John of (also of Chotěmice),
119, 150
Vlk, Jacob, 134
Vraba, Catherine of, 87
Vřesovice, Jakoubek of, 140
Vřeštov, Aleš Riesenburk of, 137

Wages, 22
Wenceslas IV, King of Bohemia (1378-
1419), 2, 13, 15, 21, 65, 68-75, 80,
89, 104, 106, 107, 117, 125, 151,
161, 167; hostility to reform, 86,
120-121, 130; against noble leagues,
47-60, 62; death, 83, 126, 128
Women, as patrons, 38
Wyclifism, 65, 104, 106, 122
Wyclifites, 85, 88

Žampach, Nicholas (Mikeš) of (and of
Potštejn), 88, 104, 149

Zarov, John of, 120
Zbraslavice, John Podolec of, 105, 122
Zdebuzeves, John of, 122
Zhoř, Jost of, 122
Žehusice, Vitek of, 122
Želivsky, John, 63, 66, 113, 125, 127, 130, 132, 134
Žimutice, Leopold Kraselov of, 116, 172-173
Žirotín, lords of, 76
Žižka, John, 2, 68, 127, 130-132, 173
Zmrzlík, Peter, 168
Zvířetice, Peter of, 167, 174; Sdeslas, of, 88; Wenceslas and Beneš of, 174; William of, 89, 92, 167

EAST EUROPEAN MONOGRAPHS

The *East European Monographs* comprise scholarly books on the history and civilization of Eastern Europe. They are published by the *East European Quarterly* in the belief that these studies contribute substantially to the knowledge of the area and serve to stimulate scholarship and research.

1. *Political Ideas and the Enlightenment in the Romanian Principalities, 1750–1831.* By Vlad Georgescu. 1971.

2. *America, Italy and the Birth of Yugoslavia, 1917–1919.* By Dragan R. Zivojinovic. 1972.

3. *Jewish Nobles and Geniuses in Modern Hungary.* By William O. McCagg, Jr. 1972.

4. *Mixail Soloxov in Yugoslavia: Reception and Literary Impact.* By Robert F. Price. 1973.

5. *The Historical and National Thought of Nicolae Iorga.* By William O. Oldson. 1973.

6. *Guide to Polish Libraries and Archives.* By Richard C. Lewanski. 1974.

7. *Vienna Broadcasts to Slovakia, 1938–1939: A Case Study in Subversion.* By Henry Delfiner. 1974.

8. *The 1917 Revolution in Latvia.* By Andrew Ezergailis. 1974.

9. *The Ukraine in the United Nations Organization: A Study in Soviet Foreign Policy. 1944–1950.* By Konstantin Sawczuk. 1975.

10. *The Bosnian Church: A New Interpretation.* By John V. A. Fine, Jr. 1975.

11. *Intellectual and Social Developments in the Habsburg Empire from Maria Theresa to World War I.* Edited by Stanley B. Winters and Joseph Held. 1975.

12. *Ljudevit Gaj and the Illyrian Movement.* By Elinor Murray Despalatovic. 1975.

13. *Tolerance and Movements of Religious Dissent in Eastern Europe.* Edited by Bela K. Kiraly. 1975.

14. *The Parish Republic: Hlinka's Slovak People's Party, 1939–1945.* By Yeshayahu Jelinek. 1976.

15. *The Russian Annexation of Bessarabia, 1774–1828.* By George F. Jewsbury. 1976.

16. *Modern Hungarian Historiography.* By Steven Bela Vardy. 1976.

17. *Values and Community in Multi-National Yugoslavia.* By Gary K. Bertsch. 1976.

19. *The Radical Left in the Hungarian Revolution of 1848.* By Laszlo Deme. 1976.
20. *Hungary between Wilson and Lenin: The Hungarian Revolution of 1918-1919 and the Big Three.* By Peter Pastor. 1976.
21. *The Crises of France's East-Central European Diplomacy, 1933-1938.* By Anthony J. Komjathy. 1976.
22. *Polish Politics and National Reform, 1775-1788.* By Daniel Stone. 1976.
23. *The Habsburg Empire in World War I.* Robert A. Kann, Bela K. Kiraly, and Paula S. Fichtner, eds. 1977.
24. *The Slovenes and Yugoslavism, 1890-1914.* By Carole Rogel. 1977.
25. *German-Hungarian Relations and the Swabian Problem.* By Thomas Spira. 1977.
26. *The Metamorphosis of a Social Class in Hungary During the Reign of Young Franz Joseph.* By Peter I. Hidas. 1977.
27. *Tax Reform in Eighteenth Century Lombardy.* By Daniel M. Klang. 1977.
28. *Tradition versus Revolution: Russia and the Balkans in 1917.* By Robert H. Johnston. 1977.
29. *Winter into Spring: The Czechoslovak Press and the Reform Movement 1963-1968.* By Frank L. Kaplan. 1977.
30. *The Catholic Church and the Soviet Government, 1939-1949.* By Dennis J. Dunn. 1977.
31. *The Hungarian Labor Service System, 1939-1945.* By Randolph L. Braham. 1977.
32. *Consciousness and History: Nationalist Critics of Greek Society 1897-1914.* By Gerasimos Augustinos. 1977.
33. *Emigration in Polish Social and Political Thought, 1870-1914.* By Benjamin P. Murdzek. 1977.
34. *Serbian Poetry and Milutin Bojic.* By Mihailo Dordevic. 1977.
35. *The Baranya Dispute: Diplomacy in the Vortex of Ideologies, 1918-1921.* By Leslie C. Tihany. 1978.
36. *The United States in Prague, 1945-1948.* By Walter Ullmann. 1978.
37. *Rush to the Alps: The Evolution of Vacationing in Switzerland.* By Paul P. Bernard. 1978.
38. *Transportation in Eastern Europe: Empirical Findings.* By Bogdan Mieczkowski. 1978.
39. *The Polish Underground State: A Guide to the Underground, 1939-1945.* By Stefan Korbonski. 1978.
40. *The Hungarian Revolution of 1956 in Retrospect.* Edited by Bela K. Kiraly and Paul Jonas. 1978.
41. *Boleslaw Limanowski (1835-1935): A Study in Socialism and Nationalism.* By Kazimiera Janina Cottam. 1978.
42. *The Lingering Shadow of Nazism: The Austrian Independent Party Movement Since 1945.* By Max E. Riedlsperger. 1978.

J1